A Life of Character

A Life of Character

previously published as

The Building of Character and *Life's Open Door*

J. R. Miller, D.D.

AMG
PUBLISHERS
Chattanooga, TN 37421

A Life of Character

ISBN 0–89957–239–1

Printed in the United States of America

03 02 01 00 99 98 –R– 6 5 4 3 2 1

Contents

Foreword

James Russell Miller, an American Presbyterian clergyman and author, was born in Harshaville, Pennsylvania, on March 20, 1840, and died in Philadelphia on July 2, 1912. He was educated at Westminster College, New Wilmington, Pennsylvania, and the Allegheny Theological Seminary of the United Presbyterian Church, from which he was graduated in 1867 and was ordained a minister.

He was editorial superintendent of the Presbyterian Board of Publication in Philadelphia from 1887 until the time of his death, and was the author of more than 60 devotional books, notably *Devotional Hours with the Bible,* in 8 volumes, published from 1909 to 1913, which sold more than two million copies.

A Life of Character combines two of J. R. Miller's works, *The Building of Character* and *Life's Open Door.* The books are separated by a title page and have separate chapter numbering. The preface has been combined and placed in the opening pages of the work. The subheads of book one and the poetry in book two are landmarks to help readers find sections in the book, making it easy to pick up and put down without losing their place. This makes *A Life of Character* a great devotional book.

In creating this volume, we at AMG Publishers have made a few minor changes to the original work to help clarify its content for modern readers by updating spelling according to the change of our language over the years, and in some cases, by simplifying unusual forms of punctuation. However, Miller's original meaning has not been changed in any way, and his inspiring devotionals have been preserved for generations to come.

Preface of Combined Work

Life's Open Door

The manuscript of *Life's Open Door* was nearly ready for the press when Dr. Miller was called to his reward, July 2, 1912. He was busy revising some of the chapters not long before his death; the original manuscript is filled with interlineations and corrections in his trembling handwriting; to the last he wished to use his failing strength in perfecting the message that would make his readers better acquainted with the Friend to whom his life was given.

Every chapter gives hints of the ripening for heaven of a life that had always been so like the life of the Master that a friend said of him: "The sweetness of his presence in our home was just like what I think the presence of Jesus must have been in the home of Mary and Martha." Thus the chapter "When We Are Laid Aside" was written when the infirmities of years kept him from many of the activities in which he had always delighted; while "The Christian View of Death" was the expression of his own attitude as he waited for the summons of the King.

It has been a labor of love to complete the preparation for the press of this last annual volume in the series of Dr. Miller's marvelously helpful devotional books.

JOHN T. FARIS
PHILADELPHIA, *August 6, 1912*

The Building of Character

Here is a gem of the past that provides excellent guidelines for the present. It will also prepare you for the future. You and others should not be deprived of the thoughts of a godly man like J. R. Miller.

It has been my honor and privilege to have a part in bringing *The Building of Character* to the public again. Next to the Word of God, it has had the most profound effect upon my life. Although written almost a hundred years ago, it is uniquely relevant to the Christian life of our generation. Very little change was needed to bring it up to date and it comes to scatter its blessings in the same loving and gentle spirit this saintly author must have prayed for many years ago. If others are as inspired by reading this book as I have been in working on it, my efforts will have been well worthwhile.

JOAN ZODHIATES

1975

Book One:

The Building of Character

1

The Building of Character

Finally, brethren, whatsoever things are true, whatsoever things are honest, whatsoever things are just, whatsoever things are pure, whatsoever things are of good report; if there be any virtue, and if there be any praise, think of these things (Phil. 4:8).

The building of character is the most important business of life. It matters little what works a man may leave in the world; his real success is measured by what he has accomplished along the years in his own being.

True Character Built on Divine Patterns

True character must be built on divine patterns. "Every man's life is a plan of God." There is a divine purpose concerning it which it should realize. In the Scriptures we find the patterns for all the parts of the character, not only for its great and prominent elements, but also for its most minute features, the delicate lines and shadings of its ornamentation. The commandments, the beatitudes, all Christ's precepts, the ethical teachings of the apostles, all show us the patterns after which we are to fashion our character. It is a great thing for us to have a high ideal of life, and ever to seek to reach it. Said Michelangelo; "Nothing makes the soul so pure, so religious, as the endeavor to create something perfect; for God is perfection, and whoever strives for it strives for something that is god-like." The seeking itself makes us nobler, holier, purer, stronger, We grow ever toward that for which we long. Then this is a desire which is rewarded.

Every building requires a good foundation. Without this, it never can rise into real strength and grandeur. The most lovely building reared on sand is insecure and must fall. There is only one foundation for Christian character. We must build on the rock—that is, we must have as the basis of our character great, eternal principles.

Principles for Building Character:

A. TRUTH

One of these principles is truth. [Ruskin] tells us that in a famous Italian cathedral there are a number of colossal figures high up among the heavy timbers that support the roof. From the pavement these statues have the appearance of great beauty. Curious to examine them, Ruskin says he climbed to the roof and stood close beside them. He was bitterly disappointed to find that only the parts of the figures which could be seen from the pavement were finished. The hidden side was rough and unfinished. It is not enough to make our lives true only so far as men can see them. We have only scorn for men who profess truth, and then in their secret life reveal falsehood, deception, insincerity. There must be truth through and through in the sure foundation. A little flaw, made by a bubble of air in the casting, had been the cause of the breaking of a great girder years afterward, and the falling of the immense bridge whose weight rested upon it. Truth must be in the character, absolute truth.

B. PURITY

Another of these principles is purity. "Whatsoever things are pure," says the apostle, in the same breath with "whatsoever things are true and just and honorable." It is a canon of art that an artist who lives badly never can paint a good picture. Nor can one who lives badly ever build up a beautiful character. Only he who has a pure heart can see God to know what life's ideal is. Only he whose hands are clean can build after the perfect pattern. Purity is an essential fundamental principle in the perfect character.

C. LOVE

Love is another quality which must be wrought into this foundation. Love is the reverse of selfishness. It is considering one's life as Christ's to be used to bless others. "So long as I have been here," said President Lincoln after his second election, "I have not willingly planted a thorn in any man's bosom." That is one phase of love—never needlessly to give pain or to hurt a fellow-being. The other part is the positive—to live to do the greatest good to every other being, whenever opportunity offers.

Truth, purity, love—these are examples of the immutable principles which must be built into the foundation of the temple of character. We never can have a strong structure without a very strong and secure foundation.

We Must Build Our Own Character

On the foundation the character must be built. No magnificent building ever grew up by miracle. Stone by stone it rose, each block laid in its place by toil and strength. "You cannot dream yourself into character," says Froude; "you must hammer and forge yourself one." Even with the best foundation there must be faithful, patient building unto the end.

Then each one must build his own character. No one can do it for him. No one but yourself can make your life beautiful. No one can be true, pure, honorable, and loving for you. A mother's prayers and teachings cannot give you strength of soul and grandeur of spirit. We are taught to edify one another, and we do, indeed, help to build up each other's life-temple. In every book we read, the author lays something new on the wall of our lives. Every hour's companionship with another gives either a touch of beauty or a stain to our spirit. Every song that is sung in our ears enters into our heart and becomes part of our being. Even the natural scenery amid which we dwell leaves its impressions upon us. Thus others, thus all things about us, do indeed have their place as builders of our character.

But we are ourselves always the real builders. Others may lift the blocks into place, but we must lay them on the wall. Our own hands give the touches of beauty or of marring, even though hands of others hold the brushes or mix the colors for us. If the building is marred or unsightly when it is finished, we cannot say it was someone else's fault. Others may have sinned, and the inheritance of the sin is yours. Others may have sorely wronged you, and the hurt yet stays in your life. You never can be the same in this world as you might have been but for this wounding. You are not responsible for these marrings of your character which were caused by others' hands. Still you are the builder—you and God. Even the broken fragments of what seems a ruin you can take, and with them, through God's grace, you can make a noble life. It is strange how many of earth's most beautiful lives have grown up out of what seemed defeat and failure. Indeed, God seems to love to build spiritual loveliness out of the castaway fragments of lives, even out of sin's debris. In a great cathedral there is said to be a window, made by an apprentice, out of the bits of stained glass that were thrown away as refuse and worthless when the other windows were made, and this is the most beautiful window of all. You can build a noble character for yourself, in spite of all the wrongs and injuries done to you, wittingly or unwittingly, by others, with the fragments of the broken hopes and joys and the lost opportunities that lie scattered about your feet. No others by their worst work of harm or damage can prevent your building a beautiful character for yourself.

We Must Search for Our Building Blocks

When the ancient temple of Solomon was reared, the face of the whole world was searched, and its most costly and beautiful things were gathered and put into the sacred house. We should search everywhere for whatsoever things are pure, to build into our lives. All that we can learn from books, from music, from art, from friends; all that we can gather from the Bible, and receive from the hand of Christ Himself, we should take and build into our character to make it worthy. In order to find all that is lovely we must have the loveliness in our own soul. "Though we travel the world over to find the beautiful," says one, "we must carry it in our own heart or we shall find it not." Only a true, pure, loving heart can find the things that are true, pure, and loving to build in the character. We must have Christ in us, and then we shall find Christlike things everywhere, and can gather them into our own life.

It Is Never Too Late to Beautify Our Character

There are some everywhere who in the discouragement of defeat and failure feel that it is now too late for them to make their character beautiful. They have lost their opportunity. But this is never true in this world in which Christ died. A poet tells of walking in his garden and seeing a birds' nest lying on the ground. The storm had swept through the tree and ruined the nest. While he mused sadly over the wreck of the birds' home, he looked up, and there he saw them building a new one in the branches. The birds teach us immortals a lesson. Though all seems lost, let us not sit down and weep in despair, but let us rise and begin to build again. No one can undo a wrong past. No one can repair the ruins of years that are gone. We cannot live our lives over again. But at our Father's feet we can begin anew, and make all our lives new.

2

Unfinished Life-Building

> *Brethren, I count not myself to have apprehended: but this one thing I do, forgetting those things which are behind, and reaching forth unto those things which are before, I press toward the mark for the prize of the high calling of God in Christ Jesus (Phil. 3:13, 14).*

Building Blocks

We are all builders. We may not erect any house or temple on a city street for human eyes to see, but every one of us builds an edifice which God and angels see. Life is a building. It rises slowly, day by day, through the years. Every new lesson we learn lays another block on the edifice which is rising silently within us. Every experience, every touch of another life on ours, every influence that impresses us, every book we read, every conversation we have, every act of our commonest days, adds something to the invisible building. Sorrow, too, has its place in preparing the stones to lie on the life-wall. All life furnishes the material.

Unfinished Buildings

There are many noble structures reared in this world. But there are also many who build only low, mean huts, without beauty, which will be swept away in the testing fires of judgment. There are many, too, whose

9

life-work presents the spectacle of an unfinished building. There was a beautiful plan to begin with, and the work was promising for a little time, but after a while it was abandoned and left standing, with walls halfway up, a useless fragment, open and exposed, an incomplete inglorious ruin, telling no story of past splendor as do the ruins of some old castle or coliseum, a monument only of folly and failure.

One writes:

> There is nothing sadder than an incomplete ruin, one that has never been of use, that never was what it was meant to be, about which no pure, holy, lofty associations cling, no thoughts of battles fought and victories won, or of defeats as glorious as victories. God sees them where we do not. The highest tower may be more unfinished than the lowest to Him.

We must not forget the truth of this last sentence. There are lives which to our eyes seem only to have been begun and then abandoned, which to God's eyes are still rising into more and more graceful beauty. Here is one who began his life-work with all the ardor of youth and all the enthusiasm of a consecrated spirit. For a time his hand never tired, his energy never slackened. Friends expected great things from him. Then his health gave way. The diligent hand lies folded now on his breast. His enthusiasm no more drives him onward. His work lies unfinished.

"What a pity!" men say. But wait. He has not left an unfinished life-work as God sees it. He is resting in submission at the Master's feet, and is growing meanwhile as a Christian. The spiritual temple in his soul is rising slowly in the silence. Every day is adding something to the beauty of his character as he learns the lessons of patience, confidence, peace, joy, love. His building in the end will be more beautiful than if he had been permitted to toil on through many busy years, carrying out his own plans. He is fulfilling God's plan for his life.

We must not measure spiritual building by earthly standards. Where the heart remains loyal and true to Christ; where the cross of suffering is taken up cheerfully and borne sweetly; where the spirit is obedient though the hands must lie folded and the feet must be still, the temple rises continually toward finished beauty.

Abandoned Life-Buildings

But there are abandoned life-buildings whose story tells only of shame and failure. Many persons begin to follow Christ, and after a little time turn away from their profession, and leave only a pretentious beginning to stand as a ruin, to be laughed at by the world, and to dishonor the Master's name.

Discouragement

Sometimes it is discouragement that leads men to give up the work which they have begun. In one of his poems Wordsworth tells a pathetic story of a straggling heap of unhewn stones and the beginning of a sheepfold which was never finished. With his wife and only son, old Michael, a Highland shepherd, dwelt for many years in peace. But trouble came which made it necessary that the son should go away to do for himself for a while. For a time good reports came from him, and the old shepherd would go when he had leisure and work on the sheepfold which he was building. By and by, however, sad news came from his son Luke. In the great dissolute city he had given himself to evil ways. Shame fell on him, and he sought a hiding place beyond the seas. The sad tidings broke the old father's heart. He went about as before, caring for his sheep. To the hollow valley he would go from time to time, to build at the unfinished fold. But the neighbors in their pity noticed that he did little work in those sad days.

Years after the shepherd was gone, the remains of the unfinished fold were still there, a sad memorial of one who began to build but did not finish. Sorrow broke his heart, and his hand slacked.

Too often noble life-buildings are abandoned in the time of sorrow, and the hands that were quick and skillful before grief came, hang down and do nothing more on the temple-wall. Instead, however, of leading us to give up our work and falter in our diligence, it should inspire us to yet greater earnestness in all duty and greater fidelity in all life.

Lack of Faith

Want of faith is another cause which leads many to abandon their life-temples unfinished. Throngs followed Christ in the earlier days of His ministry, when all seemed bright, who when they saw the shadow of the cross, turned back and walked no more with Him. They lost their faith in Him. It is startling to read how near even the apostles came to leaving their buildings unfinished. Had not their faith come again after Christ arose, they would have left in this world only sad memorials of failure instead of glorious finished temples. In these very days there are many who, through the losing of their faith, are abandoning their work on the wall of the temple of Christian discipleship which they have begun to build. Who doesn't know those who once were earnest and enthusiastic in Christian life while there was but little opposition, but who fainted and failed when it became hard to confess Christ and walk with Him?

Sin

Sin in some form draws many a builder away from his work to leave it unfinished. It may be the world's fascinations that lure him from Christ's side. It may be sinful human companionships that tempt him from loyal friendship to his Savior. It may be riches that enter his heart and blind his eyes to the attractions of heaven. It may be some secret debasing lust that gains power over him and paralyzes his spiritual life. Many are those now amid the world's throngs who once sat at the Lord's Table and were among God's people. Their lives are unfinished buildings, towers begun with great enthusiasm and then left to tell their sad story of failure to all who pass by. They began to build and were not able to finish.

Giving Up

It is sad to think how much of this unfinished work God's angels see as they look down upon our earth. Think of the good beginnings which never came to anything in the end; the excellent resolutions which are never carried out, the noble life-plans entered upon by so many young people with ardent enthusiasm, but soon given up. Think of the beautiful visions and high hopes which might be made splendid realities, but which fade out, with not even one earnest attempt to work them into life.

In all aspects of life we see these abandoned buildings. The business world is full of them. Men began to build, but in a little time they were gone, leaving their work uncompleted. They set out with enthusiasm, but became tired in time with the effort or grew disheartened at the slow coming of success, and abandoned their ideal when it was perhaps just ready to be realized. Many homes present the spectacle of thousands of abandoned dreams of love. For a time the beautiful vision shone, and two hearts tried to make it come true, and they gave it up in despair, either enduring in misery or going their own separate ways.

So life everywhere is full of beginnings never carried on to completion. There is not a soul-wreck on the streets, not a prisoner serving out a sentence behind prison bars, not a debased, fallen one anywhere, in whose soul there were not once visions of beauty, high hopes, holy thoughts and purposes and high resolves—an ideal of something lovely and noble. But alas! the visions, the hopes, and purposes, the resolves never grew into more than beginnings. God's angels bend down and see a great wilderness of unfinished buildings, bright possibilities unfulfilled, noble might-have-beens abandoned, ghastly ruins now, sad memorials only of failure.

Let Us Press On

The lesson from all this is that we should finish our work, that we should allow nothing to draw us away from our duty, that we should never become weary in following Christ, that we should persevere from the beginning of our ideals steadfast unto the end. We should not falter under any burden, in the face of any danger, before any demand of cost or sacrifice. No discouragement, no sorrow, no worldly attraction, no hardship, should weaken for one moment our determination to be faithful unto death. No one who has begun to build for Christ should leave an unfinished, abandoned life-work to grieve the heart of the Master, and to be sneered at as a reproach to the name He bears.

We Only Become Complete in Christ

Yet we must remember, unless we become discouraged, that only in a relative, human sense can any life-building be made altogether complete. Our best work is marred and imperfect. It is only when we are in Christ, and are co-workers with Him, that anything we do can ever be made perfect and beautiful. But the weakest and the humblest who are simply faithful will stand at last complete in Him. Even the merest fragment of life, as it appears in men's eyes, if it be truly in Christ and filled with His love and with His Spirit, will appear finished, when presented before the divine presence. To do God's will, whatever that may be, to fill out His plan, is to be complete in Christ, even though we live but a day, and though the work we have done fills no great human plan and leaves no brilliant record among men.

3

The Making of Character

A good name is rather to be chosen than great riches, and loving favor rather than silver or gold (Prov. 22:1).

No Treasures Will Go with Us Beyond the Grave

We ought to seek to gather in this world treasure that we can carry with us through death's gates into the other world. We should strive to build into our lives qualities that shall endure. Men slave and work to get a little money, or to obtain honor, or power, or to win a crown to wear, but when they pass into the great vast forever, they take nothing of all this with them. A great conqueror who had won empires and hoards of spoil, requested that he be buried with his hands uncovered, that everyone might see that his hands were empty, that he carried away with him nothing of all his vast conquests.

Our Character Survives Us

Yet there are things, qualities, fruits of character, gains, treasures, victories of moral conquests, that men do carry with them out of this world. Someone says: "The only thing that walks back from the tomb with the mourners and refuses to be buried, is character." This is true. What a man is, survives him. It never can be buried. It stays about his home when his

15

footsteps come there no more. It lives in the community where he was known. And that same thing—what a man is—he does carry with him into the other life. Money and rank and circumstances and earthly gains he leaves behind him, but his character he takes with him into eternity.

Character and Reputation Not the Same

This suggests at once the importance of character and character-building. And the two are not always the same. A man may not be as good as his reputation. An honored flag may float over a smuggler on the sea. A good reputation may hide an evil heart and life. Character is not what a man professes to be, but what he really is as God sees him. Definition is important. Reputation is not character. Reputation is what a man's neighbors and friends think of him; character is what the man is.

Every Influence Affects Our Character

The history of the word is interesting. Anciently character was the stamp or make by which a brickmaker, an engraver, or other worker marked the thing he made. Applied to life, character is that which one's experiences impress or print on his soul. A baby has no character. Its life is but a piece of white paper on which something is to be written, some song or story, perhaps a tragedy of sorrow. Character grows as the baby passes into manhood. Every day something is written here, some mark made. The mother writes something; the teacher writes something; every day's experiences write some words; every touch or influence of other lives leaves some mark; temptation and struggle do their part in filling the page; books, education, sorrow, joy, companions, friends—all of life touches and paints some line of beauty or scratches some mark of damage. Final character is the result of all these influences that work and co-work upon the life. It is the page written full, the picture finished.

Christ, Our Ideal

Christ's character is the model, the ideal, for every Christian life. In the end we are to be altogether like Him; therefore all life's aiming and striving should be towards Christ's blessed beauty. His image we find in the Gospels. We can look at it every day. We can study it in its details, as we follow our Lord in His life among men, in all the variations of experience through which He passed. A little Christian girl answered, when asked the question, "What is it for you to be a Christian?" "It is to do as Jesus would do, and behave as He would behave, if He were a little girl and lived at our house." No better answer could have been given. And there is scarcely any experience of life for which we cannot find something in Christ's life to instruct us. We can see how Jesus did behave as a child in the home, as a man amid human needs and duties, as a friend with faulty and imperfect friends, as a comforter among sorrow-stricken ones, as a helper of others in their ills and infirmities. We can find the traits and qualities of His life as they shine out in His contact with temptation, with enmity, with wrong, with pain, with sorrow.

The study of the story of Christ's life is not like the study of a picture or marble statue; we see Christ in all human relations, and can learn just how He acted, how He bore Himself. A child asked the mother, "Is Jesus like anybody I know?" It is possible to find dim reflections of Christ's beauty in His true followers; yet we don't need to turn to human lives, even the most perfect, to learn what Jesus was like, for we can see him in the Gospel story for ourselves. We have no excuse for not knowing what the ideal is for a true human life.

Development of a Beautiful Character Takes Effort

The next thing, when we have the vision of Christ before us, is to get it implanted into our own life. Someone says, "God never yet permitted us to envision theory too beautiful for His power to make practical." This is true, and yet never without toil and struggle can we make an honorable character for ourselves. We cannot merely dream ourselves into worthy manhood or womanhood, we must forge for ourselves, with sweat and anguish, the nobleness that shall shine before God and man.

In the presence of a great painting, a young artist said to Mr. Ruskin, "Ah! if I could put such a dream on canvas." "Dream on canvas?" growled the critic. "It will take ten thousand touches of the brush on the canvas to make your dream come true." It is easier to put on canvas the artist's dreams than to put upon our human lives the beautiful visions of Christlikeness which we find on the Gospel pages. Yet that is the real problem of Christian living. And though hard, it is not impossible. If we but struggled and tried and worked, in our efforts to get our visions of character translated into reality, as artists do to paint their visions on canvas, or carve them in stone, we should all be very noble. Never yet has an ideal been too high to be realized at last, through the help of Christ. The heavenly visions God gives us are prophecies of what we may become, what we are born to become.

The Cost Is High

Yet the cost is always high to carve the beauty God shows us as an ideal for our lives. It costs self-discipline, oftentimes anguish, as we must deny ourselves, and cut off the things we love. Self must be crucified if the noble manhood in us is ever to be set free to shine in its beauty, if the angel within the marble block is to be unimprisoned. Michelangelo used to say, as the chips fell thick and fast from the marble on the floor of his studio, "While the marble wastes the image grows." There must be a wasting of self, a chipping away continually of the things that are dear to our human nature, if the things that are true and pure and just and lovely are to be allowed to come out in us. The marble must waste while the image grows. It is not easy to become a good man, a Christlike man. Yet we must never forget that it is possible. God never yet put into a soul a dream of noble manhood or womanhood which He is not able and ready to help make real.

4

Influence of Companionship

He that walketh with wise men shall be wise: but a companion of fools shall be destroyed (Prov. 13:20).

Every Contact Leaves Its Impression

The power of one person's life over another's is something almost startling. There have been single looks of an eye which have changed a destiny. There have been meetings of only a moment which have left impressions for life, for eternity. No one can understand that mysterious thing we call influence. We read of our blessed Lord that virtue went out of Him and healed the timid woman who came behind Him in the crowd and touched the hem of His garment; again, when the throng surged about Him and sought to touch Him, that virtue went out of Him and healed them all. Of course, there never was another life such as Christ's; yet out of every one of us continually exerts influence, either to heal, to bless, to leave marks of beauty; or to wound, to hurt, to poison, to stain other lives.

Our Imprint on Others

We are forever either adding to the world's health and happiness and good, or to its pain, sorrow, and curse. Every moment of true and honest living, every victory we win over self or sin, and even the smallest fragment of a sweet life we live, make it easier for others to be brave and true and gentle. We are always exerting influence.

Companionship

And so it is that companionship always leaves its impression. One cannot even look another in the eye, in a deep, earnest gaze, but a touch has been left on his soul. A man, well past middle life, said that in his sensitive youth another young man drew him aside and secretly showed him an obscene picture. He looked at it just for one moment and then turned away. But a spot had been burned upon his soul. The memory of that glance he had never been able to wash out. It had come back to him along all the forty years he had lived since, even breaking in upon him in his most sacred moments, and staining his most hallowed thoughts. We do not know what we are letting into our lives when we take into companionship, even for one hour, one who is not good, not pure, not true. Then, who can estimate the debasing influence of such companionship when continued until it becomes intimacy, friendship; when confidences are exchanged, when soul touches soul, when life flows into and blends with life?

Cut Off Evil Companionship

When one awakens to the consciousness of the fact that he has formed or is forming a companionship with one whose influence can hurt him and perhaps destroy him, there is only one proper thing to do—it must instantly be given up.

A rabbit's foot was caught in the hunter's steel trap. The little creature seemed to know that unless it could get free its life would soon be lost. So with a bravery which commands our greatest admiration, it gnawed off its leg with its own teeth, so setting itself free although leaving its foot in the trap. But who will say that it was not wiser to escape death in this manner even with the loss of its foot, than to have kept the foot and died? If anyone discovers that he is being caught in the snare of evil companionship or friendship, no matter what it may cost him, he should tear himself away from it. Better enter into pure, noble, and worthy life, with one hand or one foot, or both hands and feet cut away, than to save these members and be dragged down to eternal death. Young people should be careful not to get caught up in evil companionship. It is like the machinery of a mill, which, when it once seizes even the fringe of one's clothing, quickly winds in the whole garment and whirls the person's body to a swift and terrible death.

Influence of Good Companionship

But a good and honest character has also its influence. Good companionship has only blessing and benediction for a life. There have been mere chance meetings, just for a moment, as when ships pass and signal each other at sea, which nevertheless have left blessings whose influence shall never perish. There is an old legend about the origin of the pearl. It says that a star dropped out of the sky into the sea, and being enclosed in a shell became a pearl.

So it is with the influence of good lives. Words, thoughts, songs, kindly deeds, the power of example, the inspiration of noble things, drop out of the heaven of pure friendship deep into a person's heart, and falling, are enfolded there and become beautiful gems and holy adornments in the life. Even brief moments of worthy companionship leave their mark of blessing. Then, who can tell the power of a close and long-continued friendship, running through many years, sharing the deepest experiences, heart and heart knit together, life and life woven as it were into one web?

Our Friends Are Our Ideals

Our friends are also our ideals. At least in every beautiful friend's life we see some little glimpse of life "as it is in heaven," a little fragment of the beauty of the Lord, which becomes part of the glory into which we should fashion our lives.

There is a wonderful restraining and constraining power over us in the life of one we love. We dare not do wrong in the presence of a pure and gentle friend. Everyone knows how unworthy he feels when he comes, with the consciousness and recollection of some sin or some meanness, into the company of one he honors as a friend. It is a kind of "Jesus-presence" that our friend is to us, in which we dare not do wrong.

George Eliot, in a similar thought says:

> There are natures in which, if they love us, we are conscious of having a sort of baptism and consecration. They bind us over to rectitude and purity by their pure belief about us; and our sins become the worst kind of sacrilege which tears down the invisible altar of trust.

Another says:

> A friend has many functions. He comes as the brightener into our lives, to
> double our joys and halve our griefs. He comes as the counselor to give wis-
> dom to our plans. He comes as the strengthener, to multiply our oppor-
> tunities and be hands and feet for us in our absence. But above all other uses
> like this, he comes as our rebuker, to explain our failures and shame us from
> our lowness; as our purifier, our uplifter, our ideal, whose life to us is a con-
> stant challenge in our heart—"Friend, come up higher, higher along with
> me; that you and I may be those truest true friends who are nearest to God
> when nearest to each other."

The Importance of Companionship

If these things are true—and no one can doubt their truth—this matter
of companionship is one of vital importance. It is especially important
for young people to give watchful thought and careful attention to the
choosing of their associates and friends. Of course, they cannot choose
those with whom they shall mingle in a general way, at school, or in work
or business. One is often compelled to sit or stand day after day beside
those who are not good or worthy. The law of Christian love requires that
in all such cases the utmost courtesy and kindness be shown. But this can
be done and the heart not opened to real companionship. It is companionship that leaves its mark on the life—that is, the entering into
friendships in which the spirits blend. Jesus Himself showed love to all
men, but He took as companions only a few chosen ones. We are to be
like Him, seeking to be a blessing to all, but receiving into personal relationships and confidences only those who are worthy and whose lives
will help in the upbuilding of our own lives.

Getting Help from Criticism

The Lord God hath opened mine ear, and I was not rebellious, neither turned away back (Is. 50:5).

Two Pairs of Eyes See More Than One

We ought to profit from criticism. Two pairs of eyes should see more than one. None of us have all the wisdom there is in the world. However wise one of us may be, there are others who know some things better than we know them, and who can make valuable and helpful suggestions to us concerning at least a few points of our work.

The shoemaker never could have painted the picture, but he could criticize the buckle when he stood before the canvas which the famous artist had covered with his splendid creations, and the artist was wise enough to welcome the criticism and quickly change his picture to make it correct. Of course the shoemaker knows more about shoes, and the tailor or dressmaker more about clothes, and the furniture-maker more about furniture, than the artist does. The criticisms these artisans render on things in their own special lines ought to be of great value to the artist, and he would be a very foolish painter who would sneer at their suggestions and refuse to profit by them.

Accept Advice

The same is true in other things besides art. No one's knowledge is encyclopedic. There are some things somebody else knows better than you do, however wide is your range of intelligence. There are very average people who could give you suggestions well worth taking on certain matters concerning which they have more correct knowledge than you have. If you wish to make your work perfect, you must condescend to take hints and information from anyone and everyone who may be ready to give it to you.

A Self-Made Man Is Poorly Made

It is also true that others can see faults and imperfections in us which we ourselves cannot see. We are too closely identified with our own life and work to be unprejudiced observers or honest critics. We can never make the most and the best of our lives if we refuse to be taught by anyone other than ourselves. A really self-made man is very poorly made, because he is the product of only one man's thought. The strong characteristics in his own individuality are likely to be emphasized to such a degree that they become idiosyncrasies, while he becomes increasingly defective in his weak points. The best-made man is the one who in his formative years has the benefit of wholesome criticism. His life is developed on all sides. Faults are corrected. His nature is restrained at points where the tendency is to overgrowth, while points of weakness are strengthened. We all need, not only as a part of our education, but in all our lives and work, the corrective influence of the opinions and suggestions of others.

Some People Resent All Criticism

But in order to get profit from criticism, we must relate ourselves to it in a receptive way. We must be ready to believe and give hospitable thought to the things that others may say of us and of what we are doing. Some people are only hurt, never helped, by criticism. They regard it always unkindly, and meet it with a bitter feeling. They resent it from whatever source it may come, and in whatever form, as something impertinent. They regard it as unfriendly, as a personal assault against which they must defend themselves. They seem to think of their own lives as something fenced about by such sanctions that no other person can with propriety offer even a suggestion concerning anything that is theirs, unless it be in the way of commendation. They have such opinions of the infallibility of their own judgment and the excellence of their own performance, that it never seems to occur to them as a possibility that the judgment of others might add further wisdom, or point out anything better. So they utterly refuse to accept criticism, however kindly, or any suggestion which may be different from their own ideas.

He Is No Longer Teachable, No Longer a Learner

We all know people of this kind. So long as others will compliment them on their work, they give respectful attention and are pleased, but the moment a criticism is made, however slight, or even the question is asked as to whether something else would not be an improvement they are offended. They regard as an enemy anyone who even intimates disapproval, or who hints, however gently, that this or that might be otherwise. It is hard to maintain a cordial friendship with such persons, for no one wants to be forbidden to express an opinion that is not an echo of another's. Not many people will take the trouble to keep a lock on the door of their lips all the while for fear of offending a self-conceited friend. Then one who rejects and resents all criticisms cuts himself off from one of the best means of growth and improvement. He is no longer teachable, and, therefore, is no longer a learner. He would rather keep his faults than be humbled by being told of them in order to have them corrected. So he pays no attention to what any other person has to say about his work, and gets no benefit whatever from the opinions and judgments of others.

We Should Be Thankful to Learn of Our Imperfections

Such a spirit is very unwise. It is infinitely better that we keep ourselves always ready to receive instruction from every source. We are not making the most of our lives if we are not eager to do our very best in whatever we do, and to make constant progress in our doing. In order to do this, we must continually be made aware of the imperfections of our performances, that we may correct them. No doubt it hurts our pride to be told of our faults, but we would do better to let the pain work amendment than work resentment. Really we ought to be thankful to anyone who shows us a blemish in our lives which we can then correct. No friend is truer and kinder to us than he who does this, for he helps us to grow into nobler and more beautiful character.

Different Ways of Pointing Out a Fault

Of course there are different ways of pointing out a fault. One person does it bluntly and harshly, almost rudely. Another will find a way to make us aware of our faults without causing us any feeling of humiliation. Doubtless it is more pleasant to have our correction come in this gentle way. It seems also the more Christian way.

Wisdom Is Needed

Great wisdom is required in those who would point out faults to others. They need deep love in their hearts, that they may truly seek the good of those in whom they detect flaws or errors, and not criticize in a spirit of superiority. Too many take delight in discovering faults in other people and in pointing them out. Others do it only when they are angry, blurting out their sharp criticisms in fits of bad temper. We should all seek to possess the spirit of Christ, who was most patient and gentle in telling His friends wherein they failed.

We Must Not Speak in Anger, Only in Love

Harm is often done by the lack of this spirit in those whose duty it is to teach others. Paul enjoins fathers not to provoke their children to wrath, lest they be discouraged. There are parents who almost never correct their children save in anger. They are continually telling them of their faults, as if their whole existence were a dreary and impertinent mistake, as if everything they say or do were wrong, and as if parents can fulfill their duty to their children only by continually nagging at them and scolding them. Those who are called to train and teach the young have a tremendous responsibility for the wise and loving exercise of the power that is theirs. We should never criticize or correct, save in love. If we find ourselves angry, or nourishing any bitter, unkind, or resentful feeling, as we are about to point out an error or a mistake in another person or in the other's work, we would do better to be silent and not speak until we can speak in love. Only when our heart is full of love are we fit to speak to another of his faults.

Criticism Gives Us Opportunity To Rise to a More Noble Life

But while this is the Christian way for all who would offer criticism to others, it is true also that, in whatever manner we may learn of our faults, we would do better to accept the correction in a humble, loving way and profit by it. Perhaps few of us hear the honest truth about ourselves until someone grows angry with us and blurts it out in bitter words. It may be an enemy who says the ugly thing about us, or it may be someone who is degraded and unworthy of respect, but whoever it may be, we had better ask whether there may not be some truth in the criticism, and if there is, then set ourselves to get rid of it. In whatever way we are made aware of a fault, we ought to be grateful for the fact, for the discovery gives us an opportunity to rise to a better, nobler life or to a higher and finer achievement.

Do Not Resent Criticism

This then is the lesson—that we should not resent criticism, whether it is made in a kindly or in an unkindly way; that we should be willing and eager to learn from anyone, since the humblest and most ignorant man knows something better than we do, and is able to be our teacher at some point; that truth should be welcomed—especially the truth about our-selves, which affects our own life and work—however it may wound our pride and humble us, or however much its manner of coming to us may hurt; that the moment we learn of anything that is not beautiful in us we should seek its correction. Thus only can we ever reach the best things in character or do the best things in achievement.

"Good listeners believe
they can learn something
from everyone."

6

Our Undiscovered Faults

Who can understand his errors? Cleanse Thou me
from secret faults (Ps. 19:12).

Sins of Ignorance

The Bible speaks of sins of ignorance. So there are sins which we commit of which we are not conscious. In one of the Psalms there is a prayer to be cleansed of secret or hidden faults. So we have faults which are not seen by ourselves.

No One Can Really Know Our Hidden Motives

We all have in us many things, both good and bad, which our fellow men cannot see, but of which we ourselves are aware. We cannot reveal ourselves perfectly even to our most intimate companions. With no intention to hide anything, even desiring to live a perfectly open life, there will yet be many things in the inner depths of our being which our nearest friends cannot discover. No one knows the motives that actuate us but ourselves. Sometimes neighbors praise our good deed when we know well that the good was blurred by a self-seeking intent. Or others may criticize something we do, charging us with a wrong spirit, when we know in our heart that it was love that prompted it.

The Beauty in Each of Us

We are both better and worse than others think us to be. The best things
in good lives do not flash their beauty before human eyes. None of us can
ever show to others all that is worthy in us. There are countless stars in
the depths of the sky which no human eye ever sees; so in the depths even
of the most commonplace soul there are splendors unrevealed to human
gaze.

Who is there who ever says all the truth he tries to say when he at-
tempts to speak for his Master? What singer ever gets into his song all
the music that is in his soul? What painter ever transfers to his canvas
all the loveliness of the vision which fills his heart? What Christian ever
lives out all the loyalty to Christ, all the purity and holiness, all the gentleness and sweetness, all the unselfishness and helpfulness, all the grace
and beauty he longs to show in his life? Even in those who fail and fall
in defeat, and whose lives are little but shame and sin, there are yet gleams
of beauty, like shattered fragments of a once very high ideal. We do not
know what struggles, what penitences, what efforts to do better, what
tears of sorrow, what hungerings after God and home there are in the
heart even of the depraved, in whom the world, even nearest friends, see
nothing beautiful. No doubt in every life there is good which human eyes
cannot see.

The Ugliness in Each of Us

But there is evil also which our friends cannot detect, things no one sus-
pects, but of which we are painfully aware. Many a man goes out in the
morning to be loved and welcomed by his friends, and praised and honored by the world, yet carrying in his own breast the memory of some
deed of sin or shame committed in secret the night before. "If people only
knew me," he says, "as I know myself today, they would despise me instead of trusting me and honoring me." All of us are conscious of miserable things hidden within us—secret habits, the entertainment of
unholy thoughts and feelings, the rising up of ugly passions and tempers,
the movements of pride, vanity, self-conceit, envy, jealousy, doubt,
which do not reveal themselves to any eye without. There are evils in
everyone, of which the person knows but which others do not suspect.

But there are also faults, unlovely things, and sins in our hearts of
which even we ourselves are unaware. In one place Paul says, "I know

nothing against myself; yet am I not hereby justified: but He that judgeth me is the Lord" (1 Cor. 4:4). It is not enough to be innocent of conscious transgression; there are sins of ignorance. Only God sees us through and through.

The Self We Do Not See

We cannot see our faults even as our neighbor sees them. The Pharisee in his prayer, which really was not a prayer at all, spoke much of other people's sins, but saw none in himself. We are all much like him. We are prejudiced in our own favor. We are very charitable toward our own short-comings. We make all manner of allowance for our own faults, and are wonderfully patient with our own infirmities. We see our good things magnified, and our blemishes in a light that makes them seem almost virtues. So true is this, that if we met ourselves someday on the street, the self God sees, even the self our neighbor sees, we probably should not rec-ognize it as really ourselves. Our own judgment of our lives is not con-clusive. There is a self we do not see.

Subtle Sins May Eventually Control Us

Then we cannot see into the future to know where the subtle tendencies of our lives are leading us. We do many things which to our own eyes ap-pear innocent and harmless, but which have in them a hidden evil we can-not see. We indulge ourselves in many things which to us do not appear sinful, but which leave on our souls a touch of blight, a soiling of purity of which we do not dream. We permit ourselves many little habits in which we see no danger, but which are silently twining their invisible threads into a cable which someday shall bind us hand and foot. We spare ourselves self-denials and sacrifices, thinking there is no reason why we should make them, unaware that we are lowering our standard of living and permitting the subtle beginnings of self-indulgence to creep into our heart.

Sin Will Deceive Us

There is another class of hidden faults. Sin is deceitful. No doubt there are many things in most of us—ways of living, traits of character, quali-ties of disposition—which we consider, perhaps, among our strong points, or at least fair and commendable things in us, which in God's eye are not only flaws and blemishes, but sins. Good and evil in certain qualities do not lie very far apart. It is quite easy for devotion to principle to shade off into obstinacy. It is quite easy for self-respect and consciousness of ability to pass over into miserable self-conceit. It is easy for a man to make himself believe that he is cherishing justifiable anger, when in truth he is only giving way to very bad temper. It is easy to let gentleness become weakness, and tolerance toward sinners grow into tolerance toward sin. It is easy for us to become very careful in many phases of our conduct, while in general we are really quite careless. For example, a man may be giving his life to the good of his fellowmen in the larger sense, while in his own home he has utter disregard for the comfort and convenience of those nearest to him. Without, he is polite, thoughtful, kind; within, he doesn't care how much trouble he causes, exacting and demanding attention and service, and playing the petty tyrant instead of the large-hearted, generous Christian.

Who of us does not have little or greater secret blemishes lying alongside his most shining virtues? We do not see them. We see the faults cropping out in our neighbor and we say, "What a pity so fine a character is so marred!" and our neighbor looks at us and says, "What a pity that with so much that is good, he has so many damaging faults!" Sin is deceitful.

Only God Knows All Our Faults

The substance of it all is that besides the faults our neighbors see in us, besides those our closest friends see, besides those of which we ourselves are aware, all of us have undiscovered errors in our lives, hidden faults, of which only God knows.

Pray That Flaws May Be Revealed

If we are living God-pleasing lives, we want to find every flaw or blemish of whatever kind there is in us. He is a coward who shrinks from the discovery of his own faults. We should always be glad to learn of any hidden unloveliness in ourselves. Someone says:

> Count yourself richer that day you discover a new fault in yourself—not richer because it is there, but richer because it is no longer a hidden fault; and if you have not yet found all your faults, pray to have them revealed to you, even if the revelation must come in a way that hurts your pride.

7

What Is Consecration?

I beseech you therefore, brethren, by the mercies of God, that ye present your bodies a living sacrifice, holy, acceptable unto God, which is your reasonable service (Rom. 12:1).

First Condition of Consecration

The first condition of consecration must always be entire readiness to accept God's will for our lives. It is not enough to be willing to do Christian work. There are many people who are quite ready to do certain things in the service, of Christ, but who are not ready to do everything He might want them to do. Many of us have our little pet projects in Christian work, our pleasant pastimes of service for our Master and things we like to do. Into these we enter with enthusiasm, and we suppose we are thoroughly consecrated to Christ's work because we are so willing to do these things.

Devotion to the Divine Will

But the heart of consecration is not devotion to this or that kind of service for Christ; it is devotion to the divine will. It is readiness to do, not what we want to do in Christ's service, but what He gives us to do. When we reach this state of spirit, we shall not need to wait long to find our work.

Second Condition of Consecration

The next condition of consecration, resulting from this, is the holding of our lives directly and always at the disposal of Christ. Not only must we be willing to do His will, whatever it is, but we must do it. This is the practical part. The moment Christ wants us for any service, we must drop everything and respond to His call. Our little plans must be made always under His eye, as fitting into, and as parts of His perfect plan for our lives. We must make our arrangements and engagements with the consciousness that the Master may have other use or work for us, and at His bidding we must give up our plans for His.

Interruptions

We are apt to chafe at interruptions which break in upon our favorite work. We anticipate an unbroken day in some occupation which we have very much at heart, or perhaps a day in relaxation which we have sought in order to obtain needed rest. We hope that nothing will spoil our dream for that day. But the first hour is scarcely passed before the quiet is broken. Someone calls and the call is not one that gives personal pleasure. Perhaps it is to ask some service which we do not see how we can render. Or it may seem even more needless and purposeless—a neighbor just drops in to sit awhile; someone without occupation comes to pass away an hour of time that hangs heavily. Or you are seeking rest, and there breaks in upon you a call for thought, sympathy, and help which can be given only at much cost to yourself.

The Old Nature Protests

In all such cases, the old nature rises up to protest. We do not want to be interrupted. We want to have this whole day for the piece of work we are doing, or for the delightful book we are reading, or for the little pet plan we had made for it. Or we are really very tired and need the rest for which we have planned, and it does not seem our duty to let anything interrupt our quiet. But you gave yourself to Christ this morning, and gave Him your day. You asked Him to prosper your plans if they were His plans; if not, to let you know what He had for you to do. It seems clear that the calls which have so disturbed you have some connection with your consecration and with your morning prayer. The people who called, Christ sent to you. Perhaps they need you. There may be in one a discouragement which you should change to cheer, possibly a despair which you should change to hope. With another it may be an hour of strong temptation, a crisis hour, and the destiny of an immortal soul may be decided in a little talk with you.

Interruptions Are God's Training

Or if there is no such need in any of those who come in and spoil your hour of quiet, perhaps the person may bring a blessing to you in the very discipline which comes in the interruption. God wants to train us to that condition of readiness for His will, that nothing He sends, no call that He makes for service, shall ever disturb us or cause one moment's chafing or murmuring. Often it takes a long while, with many lessons, to bring us to this state of preparedness for His will.

Christ Our Example

Once our Lord Himself took His disciples apart to rest awhile, since there were so many coming and going that they scarcely had time to eat. But no sooner had they reached their place of resting than the eager people, hurrying around the shore of the lake, began to gather about them, with their needs, their sorrows, and their sicknesses. Christ did not murmur when His little plan for rest was thus broken in upon. He did not resent the coming of the throngs nor refuse to receive them. He did not say to them that He had come to this place for needed rest, and they must excuse Him. He forgot His weariness, and gave Himself at once, without the slightest reluctance or withholding, with all His heart's loving warmth and earnestness, to the serving and helping of the people who had followed Him, even in the most inconsiderate fashion to His place of retirement.

Our Calls for Service May Come at an Inopportune Time

From the example of our Master we get our lesson. He may follow us to our vacation resorts with fragments of His will. He may call us out into the darkness and the storm on errands of mercy after we have worked all day, and have put on our slippers and prepared ourselves for a cozy evening of relaxation with our loved ones. He may wake us up out of our sleep by the loud ringing of the bell or phone, and call us out at midnight on some ministry of kindness. It seems we would have an excuse for not listening to these calls. It would not appear too unreasonable if we should say that we are exhausted and cannot go on these errands. There are limits to human strength and endurance. Perhaps, too, these people who want us to have no just claim on us. Besides, why didn't they send for us at an earlier hour, instead of waiting till this unreasonable hour? Or why won't tomorrow do? Then we shall be fresh and strong, and the storm will be over.

Refusal to Answer May Be to Neglect Christ Himself

But, ordinarily, none of these answers will quite satisfy the spirit of our consecration. It is the will of God that rings our bell and calls us out. Somewhere there is a soul that needs us, and we dare not shut our ears. When the least of His little ones comes to us for any ministry—hungry to be fed, thirsty to receive a cup of cold water, in trouble to be helped—to refuse to answer the call is to neglect Christ Himself. Thus true consecration becomes very practical. There is no place in it for beautiful theories which will not work, for splendid visions which will not become hands and feet in service. "Dedication meetings," with their roll-call and their Scripture verses, their pledges and their hymns, are very pleasing to God, if—if we go out to prove our sincerity in the doing of His will.

Third Condition of Consecration

Another condition of consecration is humility. It does not usually mean great things, conspicuous services, but little lowly things, for which we shall get neither praise nor thanks. Most of us must be content to live commonplace lives. Ninety-nine-hundredths of the work which blesses the world, and which most advances the kingdom of Christ, must always be inconspicuous, along the lines of common duties, in home relationships, in personal associations, in neighborhood helpfulness. Consecration must first be a spirit in us, a spirit of love, a life in our hearts which shall flow out to everyone, in a desire to bless and help and make better. Thackeray tells of one who kept his pocket full of acorns, and whenever he saw a vacant place in his estate, he took out one and planted it. In like manner he exhorts his readers to speak with kind words as they go through life, never losing a chance of saying one. "An acorn costs nothing, but it may sprout into a prodigious bit of timber." True consecration prompts and inspires us to such a life of service, and it takes lowliness of mind in many of us to accept such service.

We shall never lack guidance in finding the duties of our consecration; if only we will follow. One day's work leads to another. One duty opens the way to another. We are never shown maps of continents with all the course of our lives projected on them, but we shall be shown always the next duty, and then the next. If only we are obedient, there shall never come a time when we cannot know what our next duty is. Those who follow Christ never walk in darkness.

8

Making Life a Song

Let the saints be joyful in glory: let them sing aloud upon their beds (Ps. 149:5).

We Cannot All Write Songs

It is a great thing to write a song that lives. To have composed such a hymn as "Rock of Ages, Cleft for Me," or "Jesus, Lover of My Soul," is a greater achievement than to have built a pyramid. But we cannot all write songs. We are not all poets, able to weave sweet thoughts into rhythmic verse that will charm men's souls. We cannot all make hymns which shall come as angels of peace, comfort, joy, or inspiration to weary lives. Only to a few men and women in a generation is the poet's tongue given.

We May Make Our Life a Song

But there is a way in which we may all make songs; we can make our own life a song if we will. It does not need the poet's gift and art to do this, nor does it require that we shall be taught and trained in colleges and universities. The most uneducated man may live so that gentle music shall breathe forth from his life through all his days. He needs only to be kind and loving. Every beautiful life is a song.

A Sweet Song Amid Hardship

There are many people who live in circumstances and conditions of hardness and hardship, and who seem to make no music in the world. Their lives are of that utterly prosaic kind which is devoid of all sentiment, which has no place for sentiment amid its severe toils and under its heavy burdens. Even home tendernesses seem to find no opportunity for growth in the long leisureless days. Yet even such lives as these, doomed to hardest, dreariest toil, may and often do become songs which minister blessing to many others. The other day a laborer presented himself for admission to the church. He was asked what sermon or what appeal led him to take this step. No sermon, no one's word, he answered, but a fellow-workman for years at the bench beside him had been so true, so faithful, so Christlike in his character and conduct, that his influence had brought his companion to Christ. This man's life, amid all its hardness, was a sweet song of love.

Bell Towers

A visitor to an old European city desired to hear the wonderful chimes which were part of the city's fame. Finding the church, he climbed up into the tower—supposing that to be the way to hear the sweet music of the chimes. There he found a man who wore heavy wooden gloves on his hands. Soon this man went to a rude keyboard and began to pound on the keys. There was a terrible clatter as the wood struck the keys, and close over head there was a deafening crash and clangor among the bells as they were pounded upon by the heavy hammers. But there was no sweet music. The tourist soon fled away from the place, wondering why men came so far to listen to this noisy hammering and this harsh clanging. Meanwhile, however, there floated out over the city from the bells in the tower the most exquisite music. Men working in the fields far off heard it and paused to listen to it. People in their homes, and at their work, and on the streets were charmed by the marvelous sweetness of the rich bell-tones that dropped upon their ears.

Hard Toil and Lovely Lives

There are many people whose lives have their best illustration in the work of the old chime-ringer. They are shut up in narrow spheres. They must give all their strength to hard toil. They dwell continually amid the noise and clatter of the most common work. They seem to their friends to be doing nothing with their lives but striking heavy hammers on noisy keys. They make no music—only a deafening clatter at the best. They do not dream themselves that they are making any music for the world. Yet all the while, as they live true, patient, honest, unselfish and helpful lives, they are putting cheer and strength and joy in other hearts. A little home is blessed by their love, its wants provided for by their hard work. Future generations may be better and happier because of some influence or ministry of theirs. From such families many of the world's greatest and best men have sprung. Thus, as with the chimes, the clatter and clangor that the life makes for those who stand close beside become gentle songs and quiet music to those who listen farther away.

We Arrange the Music of Our Lives

God wants all our lives to be songs. He gives us the words in the duties and the experiences of our lives which come to us day by day, and it is our part to set them to music through our obedience and submission. It makes a great deal of difference in music how the notes are arranged on the staff. To scatter them along the lines and spaces without order would make only bars of sad discord. They must be put upon the staff according to the rules and principles of harmony, and then they make beautiful music. It is easy to set the notes of life on the staff so that they shall yield only enervating discord. Many people do this, and the result is discontent, unhappiness, distrust and worry, for themselves; and in their relations to others, bitterness, strife, wrangling. It is our duty, whatever the notes may be that God gives to us, whatever the words He writes for us to sing, to make harmonious music. Jesus said, "My peace I give unto you" (John 14:27). An inspired promise reads: "The peace of God shall keep your heart and mind through Christ Jesus" (Phil. 4:7). A heavenly counsel is: "Let the peace of God rule in your heart" (Col. 3:15). Whatever the notes or the words, therefore, the song which we sing should be peace.

Someday the Music Will Be Perfect

A perfectly holy life would be a perfect song. At the best on the earth our lives are imperfect in their harmonies, but if we are Christ's disciples, we are learning to sing while here, and someday the music will be perfect. It grows in beauty and sweetness here just as we learn to do God's will on earth as it is done in heaven.

The Master's Hand Can Bring Music from Our Souls

Only the Master's hand can bring out of our souls the music that slumbers in them. A violin lies on the table silent and without beauty. One picks it up and draws the bow across the strings, but it yields only wailing discords. Then a master comes and takes it up, and he brings from the little instrument the most marvelous music. Other men touch our lives and draw from them only jangled notes; Christ takes them, and when He has put the chords in tune, He brings from them the music of love and joy and peace.

Mendelssohn Refused Permission to Play Freiburg Organ

It is said that once Mendelssohn came to see the great Freiburg organ. The old custodian refused him permission to play upon the instrument, not knowing who he was. After much persuasion, however, he granted him permission to play a few notes. Mendelssohn took his seat, and soon the most wonderful music was breaking forth from the organ. The custodian was spellbound. At length he came up beside the great musician and asked his name. Learning it, he stood humiliated, self-condemned, saying, "And I refused you permission to play upon my organ." There comes One to us who desires to take our lives and play upon them. But we withhold ourselves from Him, and refuse Him permission, when if we would only yield ourselves to Him, He would bring from our souls heavenly music.

We Must Not Add Discord to the World's Music

Come what may, we should make our lives songs. We have no right to add to the world's discords or to sing anything but sweet strains in the ears of others. We should play no note of sadness in this world which is already so full of sadness. We should add something every day to the stock of the world's happiness. If we are really Christ's, and walk with Him, we cannot but sing.

9

Making Life Music in Chorus

Fulfill ye my joy, that ye be like-minded, having the same love, being of one accord, of one mind (Phil. 2:2).

Making Life a Song

There is more to be said about making life a song. Each one of us should live so as to make music in this world. This we can do by simple, cheerful obedience. He who does God's will faithfully each day makes his life a song. The music is peace. It has no jarring dissonance, no anxieties or worries, no rebellions or doubts.

Blending in Harmony

But we must make music also in relation to others. We do not live alone; we live with others, in families, in friendship's circles, in communities. It is one thing for a singer to sing solos, and to sing sweetly, sincerely in perfect time, in harmonious proportion; and quite another thing for several persons to sing together, in choir or chorus, and their voices all to blend in harmony. It is necessary in this latter case that they should all have the same key and that they should sing carefully, each listening to the others and controlling or repressing or restraining his own voice for

43

the sake of the effect of the whole full music. If one sings independently, out of tune, or out of time, he mars the harmony of the chorus. If one sings without regard to the other voices, only for the display of his own, his part is out of proportion and the effect is discord.

Independent Living

It is necessary not only that we make sweet music in our individual lives, but also that in choirs or choruses we produce pleasing harmony. Some people are very good alone, where no other life comes in contact with theirs, where they are entirely their own master and have to think only of themselves, but make a wretched business of living when they come into relationships with others. There they are selfish, tyrannical, despotic, willful. They will not tolerate suggestion, request, or authority. They will not make any compromise, will not yield their own opinions, preferences, or prejudices and will not submit to any inconvenience, any sacrifice.

The Blending of Two Lives

But we are not good Christians until we have learned to live harmoniously with others, for example, in the family. A true marriage means the ultimate bringing of two lives into such perfect oneness that there shall not be any discord in the blended music. To attain this, each must give up much. There must be on the part of both self-repression and self-renunciation. The aim of each must be—what always is true love's aim— to serve the other. Only in perfect love, which is utterly self-forgetful, can there be perfect blending.

Family Harmony

Then, as a family grows up in the home, it is harder still to keep the music without dissonance, with the varying individual tastes and preferences which are disposed to assert themselves often in aggressive ways. It can be done only by keeping love always the ruling motive. But there are families that never do learn to live together lovingly. Oftentimes the harmony is spoiled by one member of the household who will not yield to the sway of unselfishness or repress and deny self for the good of all. On the other hand, in homes that do grow into the closeness of love, there is frequently one life that by its calm, patient, serene peace that nothing can disturb, at length draws all the discordant elements of the household life into accord with itself, and so perfects the music of the home.

"In Honor Preferring One Another"

In all relations, the same lesson must somehow be learned. We must learn to live with people and live with them sweetly. And people are not all good and gentle. Not many of them are willing to do all the yielding, all the giving up or sacrificing. We must each do our share if we are to live congenially with others. Some people's idea of giving up is that the other person must do it all. That is what some despotic husbands think their wives ought to do. In all associated life there is this same tendency to let the yielding be by the other person. "We get along splendidly," a man says, referring to his business, or to some associated work. "So-and-so is very easy to live with. He is gentle and yielding, and always gives up. So I have things my own way, and we get along together beautifully." Certainly, but that is not the Christian way. The self-repression and self-renunciation should be mutual. "In honor preferring one another," is Paul's rule. When each person in any association of lives does this, seeking the honor and promotion of the other, not thinking of himself, the music is full of harmony. The essential thing in love is not receiving, but giving; not the desire to be helped or humored, but to help or humor.

The Music May Change and Mellow

Then not in our relationships only, but in circumstances also, must we learn to make our lives a song. This is not hard when all things are to our liking, when we are in prosperity, when friends surround us, when the family circle is unbroken, when health is good, when there are no crosses, and when no self-denials are required. But it is not so easy when the flow of pleasant circumstances is rudely broken, when sorrow comes, when bitter disappointment dashes away the hopes of years. Yet Christian faith can keep the music unbroken even through such experiences as these. The music is changed. It grows more tender. Its tones become deeper, tremulous sometimes, as the tears creep into them. But it is really enriched and made more mellow and beautiful.

There is a story of a German baron who stretched wires from tower to tower of his castle to make a great Aeolian harp. Then he waited and listened for the music. For a time the air was still, no sound was heard. The wires hung silent in the air. After a while there came gentle breezes, and then soft strains of music were heard. At length the cold wintry winds blew storm-like in their wild fury; then the wires gave forth majestic music.

Our Lives Are Harps of God

Our lives are harps of God, but many of them do not give out their sweetest music in the calm of quiet, prosperous days. It is only in the heavy storm of trial, in adversity, in grievous pain or loss, that the richest, most majestic music comes from our souls. Most of us have to learn our best and most valuable lessons in the stress of trial.

Self-Discipline

We should seek to have our lives so trained, so disciplined, that no sudden change of circumstances shall ever stop its music; that if we are carried out of our summer of joy today into a winter of grief tomorrow, the song shall still go on, the song of faith, love, peace. Paul had learned this when he could say, "I have learned, in whatever state I am, therein to be content. I know how to be abased, and I know also how to abound" (Phil. 4:12). Circumstances did not affect him, for the source of his peace and joy was in Christ.

Only the Lord Jesus Christ Can Bring Our Lives into Tune

How can we get these lessons? There is an old legend of an instrument that hung on a castle wall. Its strings were broken. It was covered with dust. No one understood it, and none could put it in order. But one day a stranger came to the castle. He saw the instrument on the wall. Taking it down, he quickly brushed the webs and dust from it, tenderly reset the broken strings, then played upon it. The chords long silent woke beneath his touch, and the castle was filled with rich music.

Every human life in its unrenewed state is such a harp, with broken strings, tarnished by sin. It is capable of giving forth music marvelously rich and majestic, but first it must be restored, and the only one who can do this is the Maker of the harp, the Lord Jesus Christ. Only He can bring the jangled chords of our lives into tune, so that when played upon they shall give forth sweet music. We must, therefore, surrender our hearts to Him, that He may repair and restore them. Then we shall be able to make music, not in our individual lives only, but in whatsoever relations or circumstances our lot may be cast.

10

The Beauty of the Lord

And let the beauty of the Lord our God be upon us;
and establish thou the work of our hands upon us; yea,
the work of our hands establish thou it (Ps. 90:17).

The Surpassing Loveliness of God

When Charles Kingsley was dying, he seemed to have a glimpse of the heavenly splendor into which he was going, and of God in His brightness and loveliness, and he exclaimed, "How beautiful God is!"

Every revelation of God that is made to us is a revelation of beauty. Everywhere in nature, in the flower that blooms, in the bird that sings, in the dewdrop that sparkles, in the star that shines, in the sunset that burns with splendor, we see reflections of God's beauty. "He hath made everything beautiful in its time" (Eccl. 3:11). In the holy Scriptures every revelation of the divine character presents God to us in surpassing loveliness. Christ was "God manifest in the flesh" (1 Tim. 3:16), the beauty of the invisible God made visible to human eyes, and such enrapturing beauty has never been seen, save in that one blessed life.

The Beauty of God Referred to in Scripture

The beauty of God is frequently referred to in the Scriptures. In one of his Psalms David declared that the supreme desire of his heart was to dwell in the house of the Lord all the days of his life, to behold the beauty of the Lord. Then, in the prayer of Moses, we have the petition, "Let the beauty of the Lord our God be upon us." This was a prayer that the charm of God's excellence might be given to His people, that the divine beauty might shine in them, in their lives, in their faces, in their souls. We think of the face of Moses himself, when he came down from the mountain after his forty days' communing with God. He had been so long wrapped in the divine glory that his very body was as it were, saturated with its brightness. Or we think of Stephen, before his martyrdom, when a window of heaven was opened and a ray of the glory from the holy place fell on him, so irradiating his features that even to his enemies they appeared like the features of an angel.

The Beauty of the Lord Our God upon Us

There is a spiritual light which makes the plainest face radiant and the homeliest features lovely. There is a beauty of soul which shines like a star in this world of sin. It is for this beauty that we are taught to pray, "Let the beauty of the Lord our God be upon us." It is not the beauty which fades when sickness smites the body, or which is lost in the withering touch of years, or which blanches when death's pallor overspreads the features, but the beauty which grows lovelier in pain or suffering, which shines out in sorrow like a star in the night, which transfigures the wrinkled and faded features of old age, and which bursts out in death into the full likeness of Christ.

Christian Life Beautiful in Representation of Christ

Every Christian life is beautiful so far as it fairly and truly represents Christ. Anything in religion that is not beautiful is not a just or adequate expression of the divine thought. Holiness of character is simply the reproduction in human life of the likeness of Christ, and any feature that is not lovely and winning is not truly Christlike, and hence misrepresents Christ. It is not the Christian religion itself that is unlovely in any case, but the human interpretation of it in disposition and conduct.

Spiritual Aspirations

There are certain qualities that belong to the beauty of the Lord whenever it appears in any life. One of these is spiritual thirst. The eyes look upward and beyond the things of earth. The heart is fixed on things above.

The aspiration is for more holiness, and finds expression in such yearnings as "Nearer, my God, to Thee," and "More love, O Christ, to Thee," and in the prayer, "Let the beauty of the Lord our God be upon us." A faith that is satisfied with any ordinary attainments, or that is ever satisfied at all, is not a living faith. The Master's benediction is upon those that hunger and thirst after righteousness. The longing soul is the healthy soul. Spiritual longing is the heart's cry which God hears always and answers with more and more of His fullness. Such longing is the ascending angel that climbs the starry ladder, to return on the same radiant stairway, with ever new blessings from God. It is nothing less than the very life of God in the human soul, struggling to grow up into the fullness of the stature of Christ. It is the transfiguring spirit in us, which cleanses these dull earthly lives of ours and changes them little by little into the divine image.

The Beauty of the Lord Is Practical

But the beauty of the Lord in a human life is not merely a heavenly yearning. It is intensely practical. It is more than religious sentimentality, more than devout feeling, more than holy aspiration. True spiritual longing draws the whole life upward with it. Joan of Arc said that her white standard was so victorious because she said to it, "Go boldly among the English," and then *followed it herself.* We must have our spiritual aspirations, but we must follow them ourselves if we would make our lives beautiful. True holiness does not make people unsuitable for living well in this world. It has its visions of Christ, but it brings them down to brighten its daily path and to become inspirations to beautiful living. It has its joyful emotions, but they become impulses to self-denial and patient work for the Master.

Results of Grace in the Heart

One of the first results of grace in the heart is sweeter, kindlier, truer, more helpful living, in all life's common relations. It makes a man a kinder neighbor, a more thoughtful husband, a gentler father. A Christian girl, whose religion does not make her a better daughter and a more loving, patient sister, does not have the right concept of Christ. A wife and mother shows the beauty of holiness not only in her earnestness in prayer and church work, but in her devotion to the interests of her home. Mrs. Prentiss said: "A mother can pray with a sick child on her lap more acceptably than if she left it alone in order to go and pray by herself."

Legend of St. Francesca

In the old monastic legends it is said of St. Francesca that though un-wearied in her devotions, yet if, during her prayers she was called away by her husband or by any domestic duty, she would close the book cheer-fully, saying that a wife and a mother, when called upon, must cease to serve God at the altar to serve Him in her domestic duties.

Serving God in Daily Duties

Heavenly contemplation must not draw us away from earthly duty. When we get to heaven we shall find heavenly work to do, but for the present our duty is here, and he is the best Christian who does it best. We do not want a religion that will lift us up into a seventh heaven of rapture, making us forget our duties to those about us, but a religion that will bring God down to walk with us on all the hard paths of toil and struggle, and that will lead us out into a gentle and patient ministry of love. It is the fashion to praise Mary and censure Martha. Jesus blamed Martha's worry, but not her service. It is good to sit at the Master's feet.

The piety which best pleases Christ is that which waits most lovingly at His feet to receive blessing and strength, and then goes forth, diligent in all love's duties and fidelities.

Purity

One other feature of the beauty of the Lord, as worn by His children on the earth, is moral purity. Christ's benediction is for the pure in heart. Bodily health is beautiful, mental ability is beautiful, but heart purity is the charm of all. All spiritual loveliness begins within. That the beauty of the Lord our God may be on us, that the winning charm of God's love-liness may shine in the features of our lives which men can see, we must first have the divine beauty in us. A holy heart will in time transfigure all the life. And the only way to have a holy heart is to have Christ within.

11

Getting Christ's Touch

Then said Jesus to them again, peace be unto you: as My Father hath sent me, even so send I you (John 20:21).

Christ with Each of His People

There was wonderful power in the touch of Christ when He was on the earth. Wherever He laid His hand He left a blessing. Virtue went out of Him each time He touched the sick, sad, and weary ones, always giving health, comfort, and peace. That hand, glorified, now holds in its clasp the seven stars. Yet there is a sense in which the blessed touch of Christ is felt yet on the earth. He is as truly in this world today as He was when He walked through Judea and Galilee in human form. He is with each one of His people. His parting promise was: "I am with you all the days" (Matt. 28:20).

The Touch of Christ

The hand of Christ is still laid on the weary, the suffering, the sorrowing, and though its pressure is unfelt, its power to bless is the same as in the ancient days. It is laid on the sick, when precious heavenly words of cheer and encouragement from the Scriptures are read at their bedside, giving them sweet patience and quieting their fears. It is laid on the sorrowing, when the consolations of divine love come to their hearts with blessed comfort, giving them strength to submit to God's will and rejoice in the midst of trial. It is laid on the faint and weary, when the grace of Christ comes to them with its holy peace, hushing the wild tumult and giving calm rest of soul.

Christ's Disciples Represent Him

There is another way in which the hand of Christ is laid on human lives. He sends His disciples into the world to represent Him. "As the Father hath sent Me, even so send I you" (John 20:21), is His own word. Of course the best and holiest Christian life can be only the dimmest, faintest reproduction of the rich, full, blessed life of Christ. Yet it is in this way, through these earthen vessels, that He has ordained to save the world, and to heal, help, comfort, lift up and build up men.

God's Human Instruments

Perhaps in thinking of what God does for the world, we are too apt to overlook the human instruments and think of Him touching lives directly and immediately. A friend of ours is in sorrow, and going to our knees we pray God to send comfort. But couldn't it be that He would send the comfort through our own hearts and lips? One we love is not doing well, is drifting away from the Christian life, is in danger of being lost. In anguish of heart we cry out to God, beseeching Him to lay His hand on the imperiled life and rescue it. But could it not be that ours is the hand that must be stretched out in love, and laid in Christ's name on the life that is in danger?

Christ Loves Others through Us

It is certain, at least, that each one of us who knows the love of Christ is ordained to be as Christ to others; that is, to show to them the spirit of Christ, the patience, gentleness, thoughtfulness, love, and yearning of Christ. We are taught to say "Christ liveth in me." If this is true, Christ loves others through us, and our touch must be to others as the very touch of Christ Himself. Every Christian ought to be, in a human measure, a new incarnation of the Christ, so that people shall say: "He interprets Christ to me. He comforts me in my sorrow as Christ Himself would do if He were to come and sit down beside me, and is helpful and patient as Christ would be if He were to return and take me as His disciple."

We Must First Be Filled with the Spirit of Christ

But before we can be in the place of Christ to sorrowing, suffering, and struggling ones, we must have the mind in us which was in Him. When Paul said, "The love of Christ constraineth me" (2 Cor. 5:14), he meant that he had the very love of Christ in him—the love that loved even the most unlovely, that helped even the most unworthy, that was gentle and affectionate even to the most loathsome. We are never ready to do good in the world, in a real sense, or in any large measure, until we have become thus filled with the very spirit of Christ.

We Must First Love Others Before We Serve Them

We may help people in a certain way without loving them. We may render them services of a certain kind, benefiting them externally or temporally. We may put gifts into their hands, build them houses, purchase clothing for them, carry them food, or improve their circumstances and condition. In such a manner we do many things for them without having any sincere love in our hearts for them, anything better than common philanthropy. But the highest and most real help we can give them is only through loving them. "When I have attempted," says Emerson, "to give myself to others, by services, it proved an intellectual trick—no more. They eat your service like apples, and leave you out. But love them, and they feel you, and delight in you, all the time."

A Loathsome Child Transformed through Love

There is a touching and very illustrative story of a good woman in Sweden who opened a home for crippled and diseased children—children for whom no one else was ready to care. Eventually she received into her home about twenty of these unfortunate little ones. Among them was a boy of three years, who was a most frightful and disagreeable object. He resembled a skeleton. His skin was covered with hideous blotches and sores. He was always whining and crying. This poor little fellow gave the good lady more care and trouble than all the others together. She did her best for him, nursed him. But the child was so repulsive in his looks and ways, that, try as she would, she could not bring herself to like him, and often her disgust would show itself in her face, in spite of her effort to hide it. She could not really love the child.

One day she was sitting on the verandah steps with this child in her arms. The sun was shining brightly and the perfume of the autumn honeysuckles, the chirping of the birds, and the buzzing of the insects, lulled her into a sort of sleep. Then in a half-waking, half-dreaming state, she thought of herself as having changed places with the child, and as lying there, only more foul, more repulsive than he was.

Over her she saw the Lord Jesus bending, looking lovingly into her face, yet with an expression of gentle rebuke in His eye, as if He meant to say, "If I can bear with you, who are so full of sin, surely you ought, for My sake, to love that innocent child who suffers for the sin of his parents."

She woke up with a sudden start, and looked into the boy's face. He had awakened too, and he looked earnestly into her face. Sorry for her past repulsion, and feeling in her heart a new compassion for him, a new love springing up into her bosom for him, she bent her face to his and kissed him as tenderly as ever she had kissed a baby of her own. With a startled look in his eyes, and a flush on his cheeks, the boy gave her back a smile so sweet that she had never seen one like it before. From that moment a wonderful change came over the child. He understood the new love that had come, instead of dislike and loathing, in the woman's heart. That touch of human love transformed his peevish, fretful nature into gentle quiet and beauty. The woman had seen a vision of herself in that blotched, repulsive child, and of Christ's wonderful love for her in spite of her sinfulness. Under the inspiration of this vision she had become, indeed, Christ to the child. The love of Christ had come into her heart.

Christ Loves the Unlovely

Christ loves the unlovely, the loathsome, the deformed, the leprous. We have only to think of ourselves as we are in His sight, and then remember that, in spite of all the moral and spiritual loathsomeness in us. He yet loves us, does not shrink from us, lays His hand upon us to heal us. This Christian woman had seen a vision of herself, and of Christ loving her by condescending to bless her and save her; and now she was ready to be Christ, to show the spirit of Christ, to be the love of Christ, to this poor loathsome child lying on her knee.

We Get the "Touch of Christ" By Having the Love of Christ

She had gotten the "touch of Christ" by getting the love of Christ in her heart. And we can get it in no other way. We must see ourselves as Christ's servants, to be to others what He is to us. Then shall we be enabled to bless every life which our lives touch. Our words shall throb with love, and will find their way to the hearts of the weary and sorrowing. There will be a sympathetic thrill in our lives, which will give a strange power of helpfulness to whatever we do. Says a thoughtful writer, speaking of influence: "Let a man press nearer to Christ, and open his nature more widely to admit the energy of Christ, and, whether he knows it or not—it is better, perhaps, if he does not know it—he will certainly be growing in power for God with men, and for men with God."

Souls All about Us May Be Changed by Our Influence

Everywhere about us there are lives which, by the touch of our hand, in loving warmth, in Christ's name, would be wondrously blessed. Someone tells of going into a jeweler's store to look at certain gems. Among other stones he was shown an opal. As it lay there, however, it appeared dull and altogether lusterless. Then the jeweler took it in his hand and held it for some moments, and again showed it to his customer. Now it gleamed and flashed with all the glories of the rainbow. It needed the touch and the warmth of a human hand to bring out its iridescence. There are human lives everywhere about us that are rich in their possibilities of beauty and glory. No gems or jewels are so precious. But as we see them they are dull and lusterless, without brightness. Perhaps they are even covered with stain, and defiled by sin. Yet they need only the touch of the hand of Christ to bring out the radiance, the loveliness, the beauty, of the divine image in them. And you and I must be the hand of Christ to these lusterless or stained lives.

12

The Responsibility of Greatness

And the children of Joseph spake unto Joshua, saying, why hast thou given me but one lot and one portion to inherit, seeing I am a great people, forasmuch as the Lord Hath blessed me hitherto? And Joshua answered them, if thou be a great people, then get thee up to the wood country, and cut down for thyself there in the land of the Perizzites and of the giants, if Mount Ephraim be too narrow for thee (Josh. 17:14, 15).

Joshua's Response to a Complaint

It is related in an ancient Bible record that the people of Joseph came once to Joshua with a complaint concerning their allotment in the promised land. They said, "Why hast thou given me but one lot and one part for an inheritance, seeing I am a great people?" Joshua's answer was, "If thou be a great people, get thee up to the forest, and cut down for thyself there." The incident is full of suggestion. It gives us an example of a premise with two different conclusions. The people said, "We are a great tribe; therefore, give us a larger portion," Joshua said, "Yes, you are a great people; therefore, clear the forests from the mountain, drive out the enemy and take possession." To his mind their greatness was a reason why they should take care of themselves and win their own larger portion.

Many Men Would Rise on Others' Efforts

One teaching from the incident is that it is not a courageous and wholesome thing to be too eager for favors and for help from others. These people wished to be recognized as the most important tribe, but they wanted this prominence and wealth to be bestowed upon them without exertion of their own. There are men of this class in every community. They want to rise in the world, but they try to rise on the exertions and sacrifices of others—not their own. They want larger farms, but they would rather have some other hand than their own clear away the forests and cultivate the soil.

Seeking Spiritual Attainments without Effort

We find the same in spiritual life. There are those who sigh for holiness and beauty of character, but they are not willing to pay the price. They sing "More holiness give me," and dream of some great spiritual attainment, some transfiguration, but they are not willing to endure the toils, fight the battles, and make the self-sacrifices necessary to win these celestial heights. They would rather make prayer a substitute for effort, for struggle, for the crucifying of self. They want a larger spiritual inheritance, but they have no thought of taking it in primeval forests which their own hands must cut down.

Each One Must Win His Own Spiritual Inheritance

The truth is, however, that God gives us our inheritance just as He gave Joseph's lot to him. Our promised land has to be won, every inch of it. And each one must win his own personal portion. No one can win the inheritance for any other. You must conquer your own temptations—your dearest friend by your side cannot overcome them for you. You must nurture your own faith. You must cultivate your own spiritual life. You must learn patience, gentleness, and all the lessons of love for yourself. No one can give you any Christian grace.

Grace Is Not Transferable

There is a deep truth in that touch in the parable, when the wise virgins refused to give of their oil to those whose lamps were going out. Perhaps you have thought they were selfish, when you heard them say, "Go to them that sell, and buy for yourselves. We have not enough for us and you" (Matt. 25:9). But the teaching is that grace is not transferable, cannot be passed from heart to heart. The wise could not give of their oil to the foolish. No one can live for another at any point. Even God cannot give us holiness, peace, and all the results of victorious living, without struggle, battle, or self-denial on our own part. Surely it is here that God worketh in us both to will and to do, but the text begins, "Work out your own salvation" (Phil. 2:12).

Man Must Do for Himself What He Can

Another lesson here is that true friendship often declines to do for men what they can do for themselves. Joshua may have seemed a little unkind to his own tribe, but really he was not. The best kindness to them was to send them out to do the things they could do. It was far better to command them to go into the forest and cut down the timber and clear off the land for themselves, than it would have been to give them a large acreage of new land all cleared and under cultivation. It was far better to send them to drive out the enemies with the iron chariots, conquering the valley for themselves, than it would have been to send any army to make the conquest for them.

Damage Can Be Done by Too Much Help

Our best friends are not those who make life easy for us; our best friends are those who put courage, energy, and resolution into our hearts. There are thousands of lives dwarfed and hurt irreparably by pampering. Parents frequently in the very warmth and eagerness of their love, harm their children's lives by over-protecting and helping them; by doing things for them which it were better to teach them to do for themselves; by sparing them struggles, self-denials, and hardships, which it were far better for the children to meet. Friendship is in constant danger of over-helping. When one we love comes to us with a difficulty, it is love's first impulse to solve the problem for him, whereas it would be a thousand times better to guide him into solving it for himself.

Blessing in Winning as Much as in Possessing

If you can wake up a young man, and arouse his sleeping or undiscovered powers, so that he will make a fortune with his own hands and brain, it is an infinitely better thing to do for him than if you were to give him a fortune as a present. In the former case in making his fortune, he has also developed powers, energy, strength, self-reliance, disciplined character and all the elements that belong to a mature manhood. In the latter case he has nothing but the money.

This was precisely the way Joshua showed his friendship for these children of Joseph. He would not do them the unkindness of freeing them from the hardships of conquest and subjugation. He told them to win the land for themselves, because the blessing lay as much in the winning as in the possessing.

God's Way with Us

That is God's way with us. He does not make life easy for us. He does not promise to lift the burden off our shoulder even when we cast it upon Him. It is God's gift to us, this burden of ours, and to lay it down would be to lay down a blessing. It is something our lives need, and it would not be right to take it away. Surely it is a wiser love that puts new strength into your heart and arm, so that you can go on with your hard duty—your heavy responsibility, your weight of care—without fainting, than would be the love which would take all the load away and leave you free from any burden.

Exercise Makes Us Stronger

You may think you would prefer the latter way, which would be easier, but you would miss the blessing, and your life would be weaker and poorer in the end. God's purpose always is to make something out of us, to bring out the best that is in us. Therefore He does not clear the forest for us, but puts the ax into our own hands and urges us to cut it down for ourselves. And while we prepare the ground for cultivation we grow healthy and strong ourselves through the exercise. He does not drive out the enemies for us; He puts the sword into our own hands and sends us to drive them out. The battle does us good. The wrestling makes us strong.

The Place of Honor is Always the Hardest

Still another lesson from this incident is that real greatness should show itself, not in demanding favors or privileges, but in achieving great things. The people of Joseph thought that their prominence entitled them to a portion larger than others. "No," said Joshua, "your prominence en-

titles you only to the privilege of the finest heroism and the hardest labor."
So he gave them the hardest task. The way a commander honors the best
regiment on the field of battle is not by assigning it to some easy post, to
some duty away from danger. He honors it by giving it the most perilous
post, the duty requiring the most outstanding courage. So it is in all of
life—the place of honor is always the hardest place, where the most stren-
uous and difficult duty must be done, where the heaviest burden of responsibility must be carried. It is never a real honor to be given an easy
place. Instead of demanding a place of honor as a favor of friendship,
which sets no crown of real greatness upon our head, we should win our
place of honor by worthy deeds and services.

The Lord's Place of Honor Not Given, but Won

Our Lord taught this lesson when the disciples were looking for the highest positions. They wished that He would merely *appoint* them to seats
on His right and left hand. His answer is very important. Men are not
appointed to the high places in spiritual life. He said, "It is not Mine to
give." Even Christ cannot *give* any disciple rank or place in His kingdom.
It must be won by the disciple himself. In human governments, rulers
may put their favorites in places of honor. Appointments are often ar-
bitrary, and unworthy men are set in exalted seats. But places are never
given to men in Christ's kingdom; they must be won.

Rank in Christ's Kingdom According to Service

Then our Lord went further and explained the principle on which places
are assigned to His disciples. "Whosoever would become great among you
shall be your minister; and whosoever would be first among you shall be
your servant" (Matt. 20:26, 27). That is, rank in Christ's kingdom is in
proportion to service. He who serves his fellow men the most sacrificially,
in Christ's name, is the highest among men. Or, to put it in another form,
instead of claiming rank by appointment or favor, you must win it by serving your fellow men, by using your strength, your abilities, your greatness,
in doing good to others. The only privilege your superiority over others
gives you is the privilege of doing good to others in superior ways.

Aggrandizement Is Not the Law of Love

This truth is far-reaching in its applications. It should sweep out of our
thought forever all feeling that others owe us favors, all that superiority

complex which shows itself in self-seeking, in claims for place or precedence over others. It should make us despise all the miserable attitudes of self-importance and aggrandizement in which so many people play such farces. What are you doing with your life? is the only question that is asked, when rank is to be measured. The law of love is that with whatsoever we have we must serve our fellow men. Selfishness debases a life. The least talented man in the world, who uses his little powers to serve and help others, is higher in rank in God's sight than the most highly gifted man who uses his great power only to advance his own interests.

The most highly endowed life that this world ever saw was that of Jesus Christ. Yet He demanded no recognition of men. He claimed no rank. He never said His lowly place was too small, too narrow, for the exercise of His great abilities. He used His greatness in doing good, in blessing the world. He washed men's feet with those hands which angels would have kissed. He took the place of a servant. He gave His very life itself to save the lost. He was the greatest among men, and He was the servant of all. That is the true mission of greatness. There is no better or more worthy way of using whatever gifts God has bestowed upon us. Instead of claiming place, distinction, rank, position, and attention, because of our gifts, abilities, wisdom, or name, we must use all we have to bless the world and to honor God.

13

The Blessing of Weakness

> *Therefore, I take pleasure in infirmities, in re-*
> *proaches, in necessities, in persecutions, in distresses for*
> *Christ's sake; for when I am weak, then am I strong*
> *(2 Cor. 12:10).*

Weakness as a Beatitude

We are not accustomed to think of weakness as a condition of blessing. We would say, "Blessed is strength. Blessed are the strong." But Bible beatitudes are usually the reverse of what nature would say. "Blessed are they that mourn." "Blessed are the meek" (Matt. 5:4, 5). "Blessed are ye when men shall reproach you" (Luke 6:22). The law of the cross lies deep in spiritual life. It is by the crucifying of the flesh that the spirit grows into beauty. So, "Blessed are the weak, for they shall have God's strength," is a true scriptural beatitude, although its very words are not found in the Bible.

Weakness Ensures Us More of the Sympathy and Help of Christ

Weakness is blessed because it ensures to us more of the sympathy and help of Christ. Weakness always appeals to a gentle heart. We see illustrations of this truth in our common human life. What can be more weak and helpless than blindness? Here is a blind child in a home. Her condition seems pitiable. She gropes about in darkness. She is unaware of dangers around her, and cannot shield herself from any harm that threatens her. The windows through which others see the world are closed to her, and she is shut up in darkness. She is almost utterly helpless. Yet her very weakness is her strength. It draws to itself the best love and help of the whole household. The mother's heart carries no such tender emotion for any of the other children as for the blind girl. The father enfolds her continually in his affection, and is ever doing gentle things for her. Brothers and sisters strive in all ways to supply her lack. The result is that no other member of the family is sheltered so safely as she is, and that none is half so strong. Her very helplessness is her strength. Her closed eyes and outstretched hands and tottering feet appeal resistlessly to all who love her, inspiring them to loving care and help, as do the strength and winning grace of no other one in the household.

This illustrates also the special divine thought and care for the weak. All the best things in human life are but hints and gleams of the divine life. The heart of Christ goes out in special interest toward the weak. Paul could well afford to keep his "thorn" with its burdening weakness, because it made him far more the object of divine sympathy and help. So always weakness makes strong appeal to the divine compassion. We think of suffering or feebleness as a misfortune. It is not necessarily so, however, if it makes us dearer and brings us nearer to the heart of the Christ. Blessed is weakness, for it draws to itself the strength of God.

Paul's "Thorn" Kept Him Humble

Weakness is blessed, also, because it saves from spiritual peril. Paul tells us that his "thorn" was given to him to keep him humble. Without it he would have been overly exalted, and would have lost his spirituality. We do not know how much of his deep insight into the things of God and his power in service for his Master Paul owed to this torturing "thorn." It seemed to hinder him and it caused him incessant suffering, but it detained him in the low valley of humility, made him ever conscious of his own weakness and insufficiency, and thus kept him near to Christ whose home is with the humble.

Adversity Brings Spiritual Enrichment

Spiritual history is full of similar cases. Many of God's noblest servants have carried "thorns" in their flesh all their days, but meanwhile they have had spiritual blessings and enrichment which they never would have had if their cries for relief had been granted. We do not know what we owe to the suffering of those who have gone before us. Prosperity has not en-riched the world as adversity has done. The best thoughts, the richest lessons of life, the sweetest songs that have come down to us from the past, have not come from lives that have known no privation, no adversity, but are the fruit of pain, of weakness, of trial. Men have cried out for eman-cipation from the bondage of hardship, of sickness, of infirmity, of self-denying necessity, and knowing that the thing which seemed to be hindering them in their career was the very making of whatever was noble, beautiful, and blessed in their lives.

Most People Have a "Thorn"

There are few people who do not have some "thorn" rankling in their flesh. In one it is an infirmity of speech, in another an infirmity of sight, in an-other an infirmity of hearing. Or it may be lameness, or a disease, slow but incurable, or constitutional timidity, or excessive nervousness, or a dis-figuring bodily deformity. Or it may be in one's home, which is cold, unlov-ing, and uncongenial; or it may be in the life of a loved one—sorrow or moral failure, or it may be a bitter personal disappointment through a de-ceitful friendship or love unrequited. Who has not his "thorn"?

Our "Thorn" Can Harm or Help Us

We should never forget that in one sense our "thorn" is a "messenger of Satan," who desires by it to hurt our lives, to mar our peace, to spoil the divine beauty in us, to break our communion with Christ. On the other hand, however, Christ Himself has a loving design in our " thorn." He wants it to be a blessing to us. He would have it keep us humble, save us from becoming vain; or He may mean it to soften our heart and make us more gentle. He would have the uncongenial things in our environment discipline us into heavenly-mindedness, give us greater self-control, help us to keep our hearts loving and sweet amid harsh and unloving sur-roundings. He would have our pain teach us endurance and patience, and our sorrow and loss teach us faith.

The Effect of Our "Thorn" Depends upon Ourselves

That is, our "thorn" may either be a blessing to us, or it may do us ir-reparable harm, which depends upon ourselves. If we allow it to irritate us; if we chafe, resist, and complain; if we lose faith and lose heart, it will spoil our lives. But if we accept it in the faith that in its ugly burden it has a blessing for us; if we endure it patiently, submissively, unmurmuring; if we seek grace to keep our heart gentle and unembittered amid all the trial, temptation, and suffering it causes; it will work good, and out of it bitterness will come sweet fruit. The responsibility is ours, and we should so relate ourselves to our "thorn" and to Christ, that growth and good—not harm and marring—shall come to us from it. Such weakness is blessed only if we get the victory over it through faith in Christ.

Weakness Nourishes Dependence on God

There is a blessing in weakness, also, because it nourishes dependence on God. When we are strong, or think we are strong, we are really weak, since then we trust in ourselves and do not seek divine help. But when we are consciously weak, knowing ourselves unequal to our duties and responsibilities, we are strong, because then we turn to God and get His strength. Too many people think their weakness is a barrier to their usefulness, or make it an excuse for doing little with their lives. Instead of this, however, if we give it to Christ He will transform it into strength. He says His strength is made perfect in weakness; that is, what is wanting in human strength He fills and makes up with divine strength. Paul had learned this when he said he gloried now in his weaknesses, because on account of them the strength of Christ rested upon him, so that when he was weak then he was strong.

Christ Transforms Our Weakness into Strength

We only need to make sure of one thing: that we do indeed bring our weakness to Christ, and lean on Him in simple faith. This is the vital link in getting the blessing. Weakness itself is a burden; it is like chains on our limbs. If we try to carry it alone we shall only fail. But if we lay it on the strong Son of God, and let Him carry us and our burden, going on quietly and firmly in the way of duty; He will transform our very weakness into strength. He will not take the weakness from us—that is not His promise—but He will so fill it with His own power that we shall be strong, more than conquerors, able to do all things through Christ who strengtheneth us.

It is a blessed secret—this secret of having our burdening weakness transformed into strength. It can be learned only in Christ, but in Him it can be learned by every lowly, trusting disciple.

14

The Strength of Quietness

> *Whose adorning . . . let it be the hidden man of the heart, in that which is not corruptible, even the ornament of a meek and quiet spirit, which is in the sight of God of great price* (1 Pet. 3:3, 4).

The Bible Speaks Much of Quietness

The Bible says a great deal about being quiet. The effect of righteousness is quietness. The Shepherd leads His sheep by the waters of quietness. We are told to study to be quiet, or to be ambitious to be quiet, as a marginal reading gives it. A quiet spirit in a woman is, in God's sight, an ornament of great price. Then we are told that a secret of strength lies in quietness.

So when we look into the matter we learn that few things are so greatly praised or are so repeatedly encouraged in the Bible as quietness. Quietness is a result rather than a factor. It indicates an attainment in the Christian life which can be reached only through certain spiritual experiences.

Noise Not Necessarily Strength

A deep truth lies here. Many people suppose that noise indicates strength, that the loud bombastic man is the strong one, that we are doing the most when we make the most bluster and show. But this is not true.

The Quiet Forces Accomplish Most

In all of life it is the quiet forces that have the greatest effect. The sunbeams fall silently all the day, yet what immeasurable energy there is in them, and what power for blessing and good! Gravitation is a silent force, with no rattle of machinery, no noise of engines, and yet it holds all the stars and worlds in perfect orbit with its invisible chains. The dew falls silently at night when men sleep, and yet it touches every plant and leaf and flower with new life and beauty.

Strength in Quietness

So it is in the calm, quiet life that the greatest strength is found. The power that is blessing the world these days comes from the purity and sweetness of gentle mother-love, from the quiet influence of example in faithful fathers, from the patience and unselfishness of devoted sisters, from the tender beauty of innocent child-life in homes, above all, from the silent cross and the divine Spirit's breathings of gentle stillness. The noiseless agencies are doing the most to bless the world. There is strength in quietness.

Quietness, a Mark of Self-Mastery

If therefore we want to be strong, we must learn to be quiet. A noisy talker is always weak. Quietness in speech is a mark of self-mastery. The tendency of the grace of Christ in the heart is to soften and refine the whole nature. It makes the very tones of the voice more gentle. It curbs boisterousness into quietness. It represses angry feelings and softens them into the gentleness of love. It restrains resentments, teaching us to return kindness for unkindness, gentleness for rudeness, blessing for cursing, prayer for scorn and defiance. "Love suffereth long and is kind; love envieth not; love vaunteth not itself, is not puffed up, doth not behave itself unseemly, seeketh not its own, is not provoked; beareth all things, believeth all things, hopeth all things, endureth all things" (1 Cor. 13:4–7). The love of Christ in the heart makes one like Christ, and He was quiet. He was never flustered, never fumed or fussed, was never tense or worried. He never spoke impatiently. His voice was never heard on the street. There was a calmness in His soul that showed itself in every word He spoke, in all His bearing.

Quietness Will Keep Us from Compounding Our Troubles

We will do well to learn this lesson of quietness. It will keep us from outbursts of temper, and from saying the rash and hasty words which an hour later we are sorry for saying, and which often make so much bitterness and trouble for us. It will enable us to be cheerful and patient amid all the cares and vexations of life.

Quietness for Wives and Mothers

Quietness is a blessed secret for wives and mothers in a home. It is impossible for any woman, even though her household life be ideally Christian and happy, to avoid having experiences that try her sensitive spirit. Probably the most perfect marriage has its harsh incidents and its rude contacts, which tend to disturb a wife and give her heartache. It is hard for a man to learn to be so gentle that no word or touch or act or habit or disposition of his shall ever hurt the heart of the woman he loves. Nothing but the love that is not provoked, that doth not behave itself unseemly, that can be silent and sweet—not silent and sullen—in any circumstances, can make even holiest wedded life what it should be. Blessed is the wife who has learned this lesson!

Every Home Presents Problems

Every home, with its parents and children, presents problems which only quietness can solve. Tastes differ. Individuality is often strong. There are almost sure to be self-assertive spirits in even the smallest family, those that want their own way, that are not disposed to do even their fair share of yielding. In some homes there are despotic spirits. In the best there are diversities of spirit, and the process of self-discipline and training requires years before all the household can dwell together in ideal sweetness.

One Voice, in Tune, Can Influence Others

A German musician, with an ear exquisitely sensitive to harmony, soon after arriving in our country, was drawn into a church by the sound of singing. But the singing was badly out of tune, jarring his nerves painfully. He could not courteously go out, and so resolved to endure the torture as patiently as possible. Soon he distinguished amid the discord one voice, the soft clear voice of a woman, singing calmly, steadily, and in perfect tune. She was not disturbed by the noisy voices of her companions, but sang on patiently and sweetly. And as he listened one voice after another was drawn by her gentle influence into harmony, until before the hymn was finished the whole congregation was singing in perfect tune.

So it often is in the making of a home. At first the individual lives are self-assertive, and there is discord in the household. It takes time and patient love to bring all into harmony. But if the wife and mother, the real homemaker, has learned this blessed lesson of quietness, her life is the one calm, clear, true song, which never falters, and which brings all the other lives, little by little, up to its own sweet key, until at last the life of the home is indeed a song of love.

A Daughter or Sister in the Home May Be the Peacemaker

Sometimes it is a daughter and sister in the home, whose quiet sweetness blesses the whole household. She has learned the lesson of patience and gentleness. She has smiles for everyone. She has the happy tact to dissipate little quarrels by her kind words. She softens the father's ill-temper when he comes in weary from the day's cares. She is a peacemaker in the home, a happiness-maker, through the influence of her own lovingness of spirit, and draws all into her own quietness and peacefulness.

Quietness Can Be Learned

These are familiar illustrations of the blessing of quietness. Wherever we find it in any life, it has a wonder-working influence. It surely is a lesson worth learning, better than the winning of a crown. But can it be learned? Can the blustering, quick-tempered, rash-speaking man or woman learn to be quiet and self-mastered? Yes; Moses learned it, until he became the meekest of men. John learned it, until he became the beloved disciple, lying on Jesus' bosom. It can be learned by anyone who will enter Christ's school, for He says, "Come unto Me. Take My yoke upon you and learn of Me; and ye shall find rest unto your souls" (Matt. 11:28, 29).

But quietness never can come through the smoothing of circumstances, so that there shall be nothing to trouble or irritate the spirit. We cannot find or make a quiet place to live in, and thus get quiet in our own soul. We cannot make the people about us so loving and sweet that we shall never have anything to irritate or annoy us. The quietness must be within us. Nothing but the peace of God in the heart can give it. Yet we can have this peace if we will simply and always do God's will and then trust Him. A quiet heart will give a quiet life.

15

The Benediction of Patience

The Lord direct your hearts into the love of God,
and into the patience of Christ (2 Thess. 3:5).

All People Would Like to Have Patience

In one of Paul's epistles is a benediction which in the Revised Version reads: "The Lord direct your hearts . . . into the patience of Christ" (2 Thess. 3:5). This is a benediction which all of us would like to bow our heads to receive. "Patience among the virtues," says one, "is like the pearl among the gems. By its quiet radiance it brightens every human grace and adorns every Christian excellence."

Patience Had Its Perfection in Christ

In Christ, patience, like all virtues, had its perfection. And His was not a sheltered life, without such trials of patience as we must endure, but one exposed to all that makes it hard for us to live patiently. Besides, His nature was one that was sensitive to all rudeness and pain, so that He suffered in His contacts with life far more than we do.

Yet His patience was perfect. "He came unto His own, and His own received Him not." He pressed upon them the gifts of love, but they rejected them. Yet He never failed in His loving, never grew impatient, never wearied in His offers of blessings, never withdrew His gracious gifts. He stood with His hands outstretched toward them until they nailed those hands on the cross, and even then He let drop out of them the gifts of redemption for the world.

Christ's Patience with His Disciples

His patience appears also in His dealings with His own disciples. They were very ignorant and learned slowly. They tried Him at every point by their want of faith, their lack of spirituality, and their weak, faltering friendship. But He never wearied in His love nor in His teaching.

Christ's Patience with the People about Him

His patience is seen in His treatment of the people who pressed about Him wherever He went, with their begging for healing. We have only to think what an Oriental crowd is, and then remember that it was the very wreckage of misery and wretchedness that came to Him, to get a thought of the wearisomeness of moving day after day amid the clamors and cries of these poor sufferers. Yet He never showed the slightest impatience, but gave out freely and lovingly of the richest and best of His own precious life to heal and comfort them.

Christ's Patience with His Enemies

His patience with His enemies is also wonderful. It was not the patience of weakness, for any moment He might have summoned legions of angels from heaven to strike down His opponents. Nor was it the patience of stoicism that did not care for the stings of hate and persecution; for never was there another life on earth that felt so keenly the hurts of enmity. Nor was it the patience of sullenness, such as is sometimes seen in savages, who bear torture in grim, haughty silence. Never did the world see any other patience so loving. He prayed for His murderers. He gave back the most gentle answers to the most cruel words. His response to the world's enmity was the gift of salvation. From the cruel wounds made by nail and spear came the blood of human redemption.

Christ's Patience in His Work

We see His patience also in His work. He saw very few results from His preaching. He was a sower, not a reaper. Multitudes flocked after Him and heard His words, but went away unimpressed.

Sublime Patience is Seen in Christ

Thus to whatever phase of Christ's wonderful life we turn, we see sublime patience. He was patient in accepting His Father's will, patient toward the world's sin and sorrow, patient with men's unreasonableness, uncharity, unkindness, patient with ignorance and prejudice, patient in suffering wrong. Marvelous, indeed, is this quality in our Lord's life. Who is not ready to turn the benediction into a prayer? "Lord, direct my heart . . . into the patience of Christ."

Patience in the Family

We all need patience. Without it we never really can make anything of our lives. We need it in our homes. The very closeness and familiarity of the family members within our own doors make it hard at times for us to preserve perfect sweetness of spirit. There is much lack of discipline in most earthly families. We throw off our reserve and our carefulness, and are apt to speak or act disagreeably. It is easy in the friction that too often is felt in our homes, to lose our patience and speak unadvisedly and unkindly. Such impatient words hurt gentle hearts, sometimes irreparably. But wherever else we may fail in patience, it should not be in our own homes. Only the sweetest life should be lived there. We have not long to stay together, and we should be patient and gentle while we may.

Patience in Relationships That Are Not Congenial

We need the patience of Christ also in our mingling with others, in our business associations and contacts, in our social relations, and in all our dealings with our neighbors. Not all people are congenial to us in spirit. Some want their own way. Some are unreasonable. Some fail to treat us right. Possibly in some cases the fault may be ours, at least in part. Others may sometimes think of us as we do of them. However this may be, the patience of Christ may teach us to bear sweetly and lovingly with even the most unreasonable people. He was patient with everyone, and we are to be like Him. If we are impatient with anyone, we fail to be true to the interest of our Master, whom we are always to represent.

Patience in Meeting the Trials of Life

We need the patience of Christ in meeting the trials of life. We need only remember how sweetly He endured all wrongs, all pain and suffering, to get a vision of a very beautiful ideal of life to follow. The lesson is hard to learn, but the Lord can direct our hearts even into this gentleness of spirit. He can help us to be silent in the time of distress. He can turn our cry of pain into a song of submission and joy. He can give us His steadfast peace, so that even in the wildest strife our heart shall be quiet.

Patience to Prepare for Christ's Service

We need the patience of Christ to prepare us for His service. The moment we enter the company of His disciples, He gives us work to do for Him. We are sent to find other souls, to bind up broken hearts, to comfort sorrow, to help lost ones find home through the gloom. All this work is delicate and important, and for it we need the patience as well as the gentleness of Christ. It must be done lovingly, in faith, unhurriedly, under the Spirit's guidance. Mothers need the lesson that they may wisely teach and train their children, and not hurt their lives by impatience. All who are dealing with the ignorant need it. Those who would put their hands in any way on other lives need a large measure of the patience of Christ. These are Christ's little ones, and we must seek to do His work for them as He would do it with those gentle hands of His if He were here. We need His patience also in waiting, as we work for God. We are in danger continually, in our very interest in others, of speaking inopportunely. Even eager, loving words must wait for the perfect time for speaking them, or else they may do harm. Even in our hunger we must not pluck the fruit while it is yet unripe.

16

"As It Is in Heaven"

Thy will be done in earth, as it is in heaven (Matt. 6:10).

Heaven in Our Hearts

"As it is in heaven" is the standard which the Lord's Prayer sets for us in doing God's will on earth. It is a high ideal, and yet there can be no lower. The petition is a prayer that heaven may begin in our hearts here on the earth. When a child was looking thoughtfully up into the depths of an evening sky and wondering how one could get to heaven, as it seemed so far away and he could see no ladder, he was told by his wise mother, "Heaven must first come down to you; heaven must first come into your heart." We must not forget this. We can never enter heaven until heaven has entered into us. We must have the life of God in us before we are ready to dwell in blessedness with God.

Heaven Must Begin in Our Everyday Lives

An author with much understanding recently said:

> We are too much in the habit of looking forward to heaven as something that *will be*—an easier, pleasanter story for us to read when we have finished this tiresome earth narrative; a luxurious palace chamber to rest in after this life's drudgery is ended; a remote celestial mountain-retreat, where the sound

of the restless waves of humanity forever beating these shores will vex our ear no longer.

We forget that heaven is not far off yonder, but begins right here in our everyday lives, if it is ever to begin at all for us. Isn't that what the prayer means—"Thy will be done on earth as it is in heaven"? "On earth"—in our shops, and our drudgery and care; in our times of temptation and sorrow. It is not a prayer to be taken away out of this world into heaven, to begin there the doing of God's will; it is a prayer that right here and now on earth we may learn to live as they do in heaven.

Bringing Our Wills into Accord with God's

How do they live in heaven? There all wills are in perfect accord with the divine will. We begin our Christian lives on earth with hearts and wills much attune to our old nature. Naturally we want our own way, not God's. The beginning of the new life is the acceptance of Christ as our King. But not at once does the kingdom in us become fully His. It has to be subdued. Christian growth is simply the bringing of our wills into perfect accord with God's. It is learning to do always the things that please God.

Our Wills Are Ours

"Our wills are ours." This is the profound truth of human sovereignty. God made us in His own image, made us free to do as we will. Even God Himself cannot compel our will. "Our wills are ours." But this is only half the truth.

They are ours to give to God, to yield to His will. This is the whole work of Christian growth, of spiritual culture. We begin making our wills God's when we first begin to follow Christ. But it takes all life to make the surrender complete. But taught of God and helped by the divine Spirit, we come every day a little nearer doing God's will on earth as it is done in heaven if we are faithful.

Obedience, Full and Complete

"Thy will be done." That means obedience, not partial, but full and complete. It is taking the word of God into our heart and conforming our whole lives to it. It is accepting God's way always, sweetly, quietly, with love and faith.

Love

The divine law is summed up in one word—love. "Thou shalt love." God is love. "As it is in heaven" means love shining out in a pure, beautiful, holy life. "Thy will be done on earth" means, therefore, love. All the lessons may be gathered into one—learning to love. Loving God is first. Then loving God begets in us love to all men.

Loving Means Giving

Do we understand what love is? Don't we usually think only of its earthly side? We like to be loved, that is, to have other people love us and live for us, and do things for us. We like the gratifications of love. But that is only miserable selfishness, if it goes no further. It is a desecration of the sacred name of love to think that, at its heart, it means only getting, receiving. No, love gives. Getting is earthly; "as it is in heaven" is giving. That is what God's love does—it finds its blessedness in giving. "God so loved the world that He gave His only begotten Son" (John 3:16). That is what Christ's love does—it pours out its very life-blood, to the last drop. The essential meaning of love must always be giving, not receiving.

The Blessing of Giving in Heaven

Perhaps our thought of the blessings of heaven is often a selfish one, that it will be all enjoyment, all receiving. But even heaven will not be an eternity of self-gratification, or the bliss of receiving. Even there, especially there, where all imperfections will be left behind, love must find its supreme blessedness in giving, in serving others, in pouring out into other lives. There it will forever be more blessed to give than to receive, to minister rather than to be ministered unto.

Longing for Love May Become Unwholesome

"On earth as it is in heaven" means therefore not merely the gratification of being loved, but the blessedness of loving others and giving out the richest and best of one's life for others. Sometimes we hear people sighing to have friends, to be loved. This is natural. We all hunger for love. But this craving may become unwholesome, even miserably morbid. As one writer puts it: "It may be only a covetous outreach after a blessing which belongs to another, and without which that other life must be left wholly without sunshine." A great deal more wholesome is the desire to give love, to be a blessing to others, to pour out the heart in refreshing other weary hearts.

God's Will May Be To Give and Not Receive Love

It is God's will that we should love; it may not always be God's will that we should be loved. It seems to be the mission of some in this world to give and not receive. They are to shine in the darkness, burning up their own lives as the lamp's oil burns, to be light to other souls. They are called to serve, to minister, to wear out their lives in giving light, comfort, and help to others, while none come to minister to them, to pour love's sweetness into their hearts, and to give them the daily bread of affection, cheer, and help. In many homes we find such lives—a patient wife and mother, or a gentle, unselfish sister—blessing, caring for, serving, giving perpetually love's richest gifts; themselves meanwhile unloved, unserved, unrecognized, and unhelped. We are apt to pity such persons, but couldn't it be that they are nearer the heavenly ideal of doing God's will than are some of those who sit in the sunshine of love, receiving, ministered unto, but not giving or serving?

Few Expressed Love to Christ

Was it not so with our Lord Himself: He loved and gave and blessed many, at last giving His very life, but few came to give Him blessing and the encouragement of love in His own soul. It is more divine to love than to be loved. At least, God's will for us is that we should love, pouring out our hearts' richest treasures upon others, not asking meanwhile for any return. Loving is its own best return and reward.

The Ideal of Our Earthly Lives

Thus "as it is in heaven" always shines before us as the ideal of our earthly lives. It is not a vague, shadowy ideal, for it is simply the complete doing of God's will. Perfect obedience is heaven. Sometimes it is serving others; sometimes it is quiet, patient suffering, or passive waiting. The one great lesson to be learned is perfect accord with the will of God for us every moment, whatever that will may be.

"As it is in heaven" may seem far above us today. The song is too melodious for our unmusical voices to sing. The life is too ideal for us, with Christian faith; if only we strive always to do our imperfect, inharmonious natures, to live. But if only we are true to our Father's will; if only we keep our hearts always open to the love of Christ and to the help and sanctifying influence of the Holy Spirit, we shall rise day by day toward heaven's perfection, until at last we shall enter the gates of peace and be with Christ and be like Him. For the present our effort and our prayer should continually be: "Thy will be done on earth, in us, as it is done in heaven."

17

The Shadows We Cast

For none of us liveth to himself, and no man dieth to himself (Rom. 14:7).

Personal Influence

Every one of us casts a shadow. There hangs about us a sort of penumbra—a strange, indefinable something we call personal influence—that has its effect on every other life on which it falls. It goes with us wherever we go. It is not something we can have when we want to have it, and then lay aside when we will, as we lay aside a garment. It is something that always pours out from our lives, as light from a lamp, as heat from flame, as perfume from a flower.

Our Influence on Others

The ministry of personal influence is something very wonderful. Without being conscious of it we are always impressing others by this strange power that goes out from us. Others watch us, and their actions are modified by ours. Many a life has been started on a career of beauty and blessing by the influence of a noble act. The disciples saw their Master praying, and were so impressed by His earnestness or by the radiance they saw on His face as He communed with His Father, that when He joined them again they asked Him to teach them how to pray. Every sincere person is impressed continually by the glimpses he has of loveliness, of holiness, or of nobleness in others. One kind deed often inspires others to act in a kinder way.

One Kind Act Begets Others

Here is a story from a newspaper which illustrates this. A little newsboy entered a subway train, and dropping into a seat was soon asleep. At the next stop two young ladies came in and took seats opposite to him. The child's feet were bare, his clothes were ragged, and his face was pinched and drawn, showing marks of hunger and suffering. The young ladies noticed him, and seeing that his cheek rested against the hard window-sill, one of them arose and quietly raising his head slipped her folded scarf under it for a pillow.

The kind act was observed, and now mark its influence. An old gentleman in the next seat, without a word, held out a quarter to the young lady, nodding toward the boy. After a moment's hesitation she took it, and as she did so another man handed her a dime, a woman across the aisle held out some pennies and almost before the young woman realized what she was doing, she was taking a collection, everyone in the car passing her something for the poor boy. Thus from the young woman's one gentle little act there had gone out a wave of influence touching the hearts of almost forty people, and leading each of them to do something.

Our Influences Are Twofold

Common life is full of just such illustrations of the influence of kind deeds. Every good life leaves in this world a twofold ministry: that of the things it does directly to bless others, and that of the silent influence it exerts, through which others are made better, or inspired to do like good things.

Influence Continues after Death

Influence is something, too, which even death does not end. When earthly life closes, a good man's work ceases. He is missed in the places where his familiar presence has brought benedictions. No more are his words heard by those who have many times been cheered or comforted by them. No more do his benefactions find their way to homes of need where so often they have brought relief. No more does his loving friendship minister strength or hope or courage to hearts that have learned to love him. The death of a good man in the midst of his usefulness cuts off a blessed ministry of helpfulness in the circle in which he has lived. But his influence continues.

Death May Enhance One's Influence

The influence which our dead have over us is frequently very great. We think we have lost them when we see their faces no more, nor hear their voices, nor receive the accustomed kindness at their hands. But in many cases there is no doubt that what our loved ones do for us after they are gone is quite as important as what they could have done for us had they stayed with us. The memory of beautiful lives is a benediction, softened and made more rich and impressive by the sorrow which their departure caused. The influence of such sacred memories is in a certain sense more tender than that of life itself. Death transfigures our loved one, as it were, sweeping away the faults and blemishes of the mortal life, and leaving us an abiding vision in which all that was beautiful and pure and gentle and true in him remains to us.

We often lose friends in the competitions and strife of earthly life, whom we would have kept forever had death taken them away in the earlier days when love was strong. Often is it true, as Cardinal Newman writes: "He lives to us who dies; he is but lost who lives." Thus even death does not quench the influence of a good life. It continues to bless others long after the life has passed from earth.

Men Must Account to God for Their Evil Deeds

Therefore, we need to guard our influence with most conscientious care. It is a crime to throw into the street an infected garment which may carry contagion to men's homes. It is a worse crime to send out a printed page bearing words infected with the virus of moral death. The men who prepare and publish the vile literature which today goes everywhere polluting and defiling innocent lives, will have a dreadful account to render when they stand at God's bar to meet their influence. If we would make our lives worthy of God and a blessing to the world, we must see to it that nothing we do shall influence others to do evil in the slightest degree.

An Artist's Concern over the Influence of His Paintings

In the early days of American art there went from the States to London a young artist of genius and of a pure heart. He was poor, but had an inspiration for a holy life as well as fine painting. Among his pictures was one that in itself was pure but that by a sensuous mind might possibly be interpreted in an evil way. A lover of art saw this picture and purchased it. But when it was gone the young artist began to think of its possible damaging influence over the weak, and his conscience troubled him. He went to the buyer and said: "I have come to buy back my picture." The purchaser could not understand him. "Didn't I pay you enough for it? Do you want more money?" he asked. "I am poor," replied the artist, "but my art is my life. Its mission must be good. The influence of that picture may possibly be harmful. I cannot be happy with it before the eyes of the world. It must be withdrawn."

Guard Your Influence with Care

We should keep watch over our words and deeds not only in their intent and purpose, but also in their possible influence over others. There may be liberties which in us lead to no danger, but which to others with a less stable character and less helpful environments would be full of peril. It is part of our duty to think of these weaker ones and of the influence of our example upon them. We may not do anything in our strength and security which might possibly harm others. We must be willing to sacrifice our liberty if by its exercise we endanger another's soul. This is the teaching of Paul in the words: "It is good not to eat flesh, nor to drink wine nor to do anything whereby thy brother stumbleth" (Romans 14:21); and "If meat maketh my brother to offend, I will eat no flesh while the world standeth, lest I make my brother to offend" (1 Cor. 8:13).

How can we make sure influence shall be only a benediction? There is no way but by making our lives pure and good. Just in the measure that we are filled with the Spirit of God and have the love of Christ in us, shall our influence be holy and a blessing to the world.

18

On the Bearing of Our Burden

Come unto Me, all ye that labor and are heavy laden, and I will give you rest. Take My yoke upon you, and learn of Me, for I am meek and lowly in heart: and ye shall find rest unto your souls. For My yoke is easy, and My burden is light (Matt. 11:28–30).

Everybody Has Burdens

We all have our burdens. Of course, they are not the same in all. Some are more apparent than others. There are people whose burdens we all see. These get our sympathy; we come up to them with love's warmth and help. There are others, however, whose burdens are not visible. It seems to us they have no trouble, no struggle, no loads to carry. We envy their lot. Probably, however, if we knew all that the angels know about their lot, our envy would change to sympathy. The burdens that the world cannot see are often the heaviest. The sorrows that are not announced in the obituaries and endure no viewing are often the hardest to bear.

If We Could Choose We Would Rather Have Our Own Burden

It is not wise for us to think that our load is greater than our neighbor's; perhaps his is really greater than ours. We sometimes wish that we might change places with some other person. We imagine that our lives would be a great deal easier if we could do this, and that we could live more amiably and beautifully than we do, or more usefully and helpfully. If we could change places with anyone, the one who, of all we know, seems to us to have the most favored lot; if we could take this person's place, with all its conditions, its circumstances, its responsibilities, its cares, its duties, its inheritance, there is little doubt that we would quickly cry out to God to give us back our own old place and our own burden. It is because we do not know everything that we think our neighbor's load lighter and more easily borne than our own.

"Every Man Shall Bear His Own Burden"

There are three Bible words about the bearing of burdens. One tells us that "Every man shall bear his own burden" (Gal. 6:5). There are burdens that no one can carry for us—not even Christ; burdens that no one can even share. This is true in a very real sense of life itself, of duty, of one's relation to God, of one's personal responsibility. No one can live your life for you. Friends may help you by encouragement, by sympathy, by counsel, by guidance, but, after all, in the innermost meaning of your life, you must live it yourself. No one can make your decisions for you. No one can have faith in God for you. No one can obey the commandments for you. No one can get your sins forgiven for you. No one can do your duties or meet your responsibilities for you. No one can take your place in any of the great experiences of life. A friend might be willing to do it, but it is simply impossible. David would have died for Absalom—he loved his son well enough to do this—but he could not do it. Many a mother would take her child's burden of pain as she sees it in anguish and bear it for the child, but she can only sit beside it and watch it suffer; she cannot take its place. Everyone must live his own life.

"Bear One Another's Burdens"

There is another Bible word which tells us that we should "bear one another's burdens" (Gal. 6:2). So there are burdens which others can help us carry. No one can do our duty for us, or take our load of suffering, but human friendship can put strength into our heart to make us better able to do or to endure. It is a great thing to have brotherly help in life. We all need each other. Not one of us could carry on without others to share his burdens. And we begin to be like Christ only when we begin to help others, to be of use to them, to make life a little easier for them, to give them some of our strength in their weakness, some of our joy in their sorrow. When we have learned this lesson we have begun to live worthily.

"Cast Our Burden upon the Lord"

There is another inspired word which tells us to "cast our burden upon the Lord" (Ps. 55:22). The word "burden" in this passage, in the margin of the King James Version, is rendered "gift"—"Cast thy gift upon the Lord." In the Revised Version the marginal reading is, "Cast that He hath given thee upon the Lord." This is very suggestive. Our burden is that which God has given to us. It may be duty; it may be struggle and conflict; it may be sorrow; it may be our environment. But whatever it is, it is that which He hath given us, and we may cast it upon the Lord.

There is Blessing in Bearing Our Burden

The form of the promise is also suggestive. We are not told that the Lord will carry our burden for us, or that He will remove it from us. Many people infer that this is the meaning, but it is not. Since it is that which God has given to us it is in some way needful for us. It is something under which we will best grow into strength and beauty. Our burden has a blessing in it for us. This is true of duty, of trials and temptations of the things which to us seem hindrances, of our disappointments and sorrows; these are all ordained of God as the best means for the development of our lives. Hence it would not be a true kindness to us for God to take away our burden, even at our most earnest pleading It is part of our lives. There is a blessing in the bearing of it.

Christ Strengthens Us to Bear Our Load

The promise is, therefore, not that the Lord will remove the load we cast upon Him, nor that He will carry it for us, but that He will sustain us so that we may carry it. He does not free us from duty, but He strengthens us for it. He does not deliver us from conflict, but He enables us to overcome. He does not withhold or withdraw trial from us, but He helps us in trial to be submissive and victorious, and makes it a blessing to us. He does not mitigate the hardness or severity of our circumstances, taking away the uncongenial elements, removing the thorns, making life easy for us, but He puts into our hearts divine grace, so that we can live serenely in all the hard, adverse circumstances.

The Law of Spiritual Life

This is the law of all spiritual life—not the lifting away of the burden, but the giving of help to enable us to carry it with joy. Much human love, in its shortsightedness, errs in always trying to remove the burden. Parents think they are showing true and wise affections to their children when they make their tasks and duties easy for them, but really they may be doing them irreparable harm, dwarfing their lives and marring their future. So all tender friendship is apt to over-help and over-protect. It ministers relief, lifts away loads, gathers hindrances out of the way, when it would help far more wisely by seeking rather to impart hope, energy, courage.

God Trains Us To Be Strong

But God never makes this mistake with His children. He never fails us in need, but He loves us too much to relive us of weights which we need to carry to make our growth healthful and vigorous. He never over-helps. He wants us to grow strong, and therefore He trains us to strain, to struggle, to endure, to overcome, not heeding our requests for the lightening of the burdens, but, instead, putting into us more grace as the load grows heavier, that we may always live courageously and victoriously.

"Thy Will Be Done"

This is the secret of the peace of many a sickroom, where one sees always a smile on the face of the weary sufferer. The pain is not taken away, but the power of Christ is given, and the suffering is endured with patience. It is the secret of the deep, quiet joy we frequently see in the Christian home of sorrow. The grief is crushing, but God's blessed comfort comes in gentle whispers, and the mourner rejoices. The grief is not taken away. The dead are not restored. But the divine love comes into the heart, making it strong to accept the sorrow and say, "Thy will be done" (Matt. 6:10).

19

On Judging Others

Judge not, that ye be not judged (Matt. 7:1).

We Cannot Help Judging Others

Our Lord said, "Judge not, that ye be not judged." Just what do the words mean? We cannot help judging others. We ought to be able to read character, and to know whether men are good or bad. As we watch men's acts we cannot help forming opinions about them. The holier we grow and the more like Christ, the keener will be our moral judgments. We are not told to shut our eyes and to be blind to people's faults and sins.

We Are Warned Against Uncharitable Judgments

What then do our Lord's words mean? It is "uncharitable judging" against which He warns us. We are not to look for the evil things in others. We are not to see others through the warped glasses of prejudice and unkindness. We are not to arrogate to ourselves the function of judging, as if men were answerable to us. We are to avoid a critical or censorious spirit. Nothing is said against speaking of the good in those we see and know; it is uncharitable judging and censure that is condemned.

We Put Ourselves in God's Place When Judging

One reason why this is wrong is it is putting one's self in God's place. He is the one Judge with whom every human soul has to deal. Judgment is not ours but God's. "One only is the Lawgiver and the Judge, even He who is able to save and to destroy; but who art thou that judgest thy neighbor?" (James 4:12). In condemning and censuring others we are thrusting ourselves into God's seat, taking His scepter into our hands and presuming to exercise one of His prerogatives.

We Cannot Judge Others Fairly and Justly

Another reason for this command is that we cannot judge others justly and fairly. We do not have sufficient knowledge of them. Paul says: "Judge nothing before the time, until the Lord come, who will both bring to light hidden things of darkness, and make manifest the counsels of the hearts" (1 Cor. 4:5). Men's judgments cannot be anything but partial and superficial.

We Do Not Know What May Cause Others' Faults

We do not know what may be the causes of the faults we would condemn in others. Some people's flaws are an inheritance they have received from their parents. They were born with the weaknesses that now impair their manhood. Or their faults come through errors in their training and education. The nurse fell with the baby, and all down through the years the man goes about with a lameness or a deformity which mars his beauty of form. But he is not responsible for the marring, and criticism of him is cruel and unjust. There are shortcomings in character, woundings of the soul, which it is quite as unjust to condemn with anything but pity, for they are the inheritance of other men's wrong-doings.

If We Knew Another's Burdens, We Would Pity, Not Censure

Then we do not know the things in a person's circumstances or experiences which are the real cause of the faults or peculiarities we are disposed to censure. We do not know what troubles people have, what secret sorrows, that so weight upon their hearts as to affect their disposition, temper, or conduct. "If we could read the secret history of our enemies," says a writer, "we should find in each man's life sorrow and suffering enough to disarm all hostility." We wonder at a man's lack of cheerfulness. He seems antisocial, sour, cynical, cold. But all the while he is carrying a burden which almost crushes the life out of him. If we knew all that God knows of his life, we would not speak a word of blame, Our censure would turn to pity.

A great deal of our judging of others is misjudging or unjust judging, because we do not know all the facts in their personal lives. Many times it would grieve us and make us sorely ashamed of ourselves, if, when we have judged another severely, we should be shown a glimpse of his inner life, revealing hidden sorrows and struggles, which are the cause of the things in him we have blamed so much.

Judgment Made on Fragments of a Life Are Unfair

We see but fragments of the lives of others, and no judgment formed on a fragment can be just. We see only one side of an act, when there may be another that altogether changes its quality. Whittier tells us of his pressed gentian, one side of which was but a blurred mass of crushed leaves, while the other showed all the exquisite beauty of the flower. Life is full of similar two-sided views of people and of acts. We see a man out in the world, and he appears harsh and stern. We see him someday at home where his invalid child lies and suffers, and there he is another man, kind, thoughtful, almost motherly. It would have been most unfair to this man if we had judged him from the outside view alone, without seeing him in his child's sickroom.

A young man was severely criticized by his companions for being stingy and mercenary. He received a good salary, but lived in a frugal way, without even the plain comforts that his friends thought he could easily have afforded, and without any generous social expenditures in which other young men of his class indulged. Many strictures were made on his stinginess. That was one side of his life, but there was another. That young man had an only sister—they were orphans—who was a great sufferer, shut in her room, kept on her bed continually. This only brother provided for her. That was the reason he lived so economically, saving every penny he could save, and doing without many things other young men thought necessary; that she in her loneliness and pain might be cared for as comfortably as possible. That was the other side of his character, the one side of which appeared so unattractive to his companions. We see how unfair was their judgment, based on knowledge only of the one side of his conduct. Seen in connection with its motive, the quality so severely censured became a mark of noble, manly beauty. To judge from a fragment only is to judge ignorantly and unjustly.

Our Imperfections Disqualify Us From Judging Fairly

Our own imperfections also disqualify us from judging fairly. With beams in our eyes we cannot see clearly to pick motes out of our brother's eye. One of the qualities which make us incapable of impartial judgment of others is envy. There are few of us who can see our neighbor's life, work, and disposition without some warping and distortion of the picture. Envy has a strange effect on our moral vision. It shows the beautiful things in others with the beauty dimmed. It shows the blemishes and faults in them exaggerated. In other forms, too, the miserable selfishness of our hearts obtrudes itself and may make our judgments of others really unkind and uncharitable. The lack of experience in struggle and hardship makes many people incapable of sympathy with sorely tempted ones. Those who have never known a care nor felt the pinching of want cannot understand the experiences of the poor. Thus in many ways we are unfit in ourselves to be judges of others.

Our Duty is to Help, Not Judge Others

Another reason why we should not judge others is that our business with them is to help them to rise out of their faults. We are brought together in life to make each other better. And the way to do this is not by harping continually about the faults we see in others. Nagging and scolding never yet made anybody saintly. Constant pointing out of blemishes never cured anyone of his shortcomings. Perhaps there is a duty of telling others of their faults, but if so, it exists only in certain rare relations, and must be exercised only in a spirit of rare love. We are often told that one of the finest qualities in a true friend is that he can and will faithfully tell our faults. Perhaps that is true, but not many of us have grace enough to welcome and accept profitably such a function in a friend. A mother may tell her own children their faults, if she does it wisely and affectionately, never in anger or impatience. A teacher may tell his pupils of their improvement. But in ordinary friendship one can accept the office of critic, even when asked to do so, only with the strongest probability that the result will be the loss of the friendship as the price paid for the curing of the friend's fault.

Nagging is Not a Means of Grace

Nagging is not a means of grace. There is a "more excellent way," the way of love. It is better when we wish to correct faults in others to be careful to let them see in us, in strong relief, the virtue, the excellence, opposite to the defect we see in them. It is the habit of a certain good man, if one of his family or friends mispronounces a word in his hearing, never pedantically to correct the error, but at some early opportunity to find occasion to use the same word, giving it the correct pronunciation. Something like this is wise in helping others out of their faults of character or conduct.

Christ Patiently Taught His Disciples Over and Over

That was our Lord's way with His disciples. He never scolded them. He bore patiently with their dullness and slowness as scholars. He never wearied of repeating the same lesson over and over. But He was never censorious. Even He did not judge them. He did not keep telling them of all the defects He saw in them. That was not His way of helping them to grow into a better, richer life. His heart was full of love. He saw back of all their infirmities and failures the sincerity and the desire to do right, and with infinite patience and gentleness He helped them over toward the larger, better, more godly life.

Only Love Can Change Another Person

We need to relate ourselves to others as did Christ to His disciples, if we would help others to grow into spiritual beauty. Censoriousness accomplishes nothing in making people better. You can never make anyone sweet by scolding him. Only gentleness will produce gentleness. Only love will cure defects in disposition. As a rule, fault-finding is exercised in anything but a loving spirit. People are not truly grieved by the sins in others which they complacently expose and condemn. Too often they seem to delight in having discovered some shortcoming in a neighbor, and they swoop down upon the wrong thing like a bird of prey on carrion. If ever criticism is indulged in, it should be with deep grief for the friend, that the fault exists in him, and with sincere desire that for his sake it should be removed; and then the criticism should be made, not for the world to hear, but "between him and thee alone."

Train Ourselves to See the Good in Others

We should train ourselves, therefore, to see the good, not the evil, in others. We should speak approving words of what is beautiful in them, not bitter, condemning words of what may be imperfect or unlovely. We should look at others through eyes of love, not eyes of envy or of selfishness, and should seek to heal with true affection's gentleness the things that are not as they should be.

20

Other People

Therefore all things whatsoever ye would that men should do to you, do ye even so to them: for this is the law and the prophets (Matt. 7:12).

The Other People Are Our Brothers

There are other people. We are not the only ones. Some of the others live close to us and some farther away. We have a certain relationship to these other people. They have claims upon us. We owe them duties, services, love. We cannot cut ourselves off from them, from any of them, and say they are nothing to us. We cannot rid ourselves of obligations to them, and say we owe them nothing. So inexorable is this relationship to others that in all the broad earth there is not an individual who has no right to come to us with his needs, claiming at our hand the ministry of love. The other people are our brothers, and there is not one of them that we have a right to despise or neglect or thrust away from our door.

Other People Have Unalienable Rights

We ought to train ourselves to think of the other people. We may not leave them out of any of the plans we make. They have rights as well as we do and we must consider these in asserting our own. No man may set his fence a hairsbreadth over the line on his neighbor's ground. No man may gather even a head of his neighbor's wheat. No man may enter his neighbor's door unbidden. No man may do anything which will harm his neighbor. Other people have inalienable rights which we may not invade.

Our Debt to Others is Love

We owe other people more than their rights; we owe them love. To some of them it is not hard to pay this debt. They are lovable and winsome. They are thoroughly respectable. They are congenial spirits, giving us in return quite as much as we can give them. It is natural to love them, and be very kind and gentle to them. But we have no liberty of selection in this broad duty of loving other people. We may not choose whom we will love if we claim to be Christians. The Master's teaching is inexorable.

> If ye love them which love you, what thank have ye? for sinners also love those that love them. And if ye do good to them which do good to you, what thank have ye? for sinners also do even the same. And if ye lend to them of whom ye hope to receive, what thank have ye? for sinners also lend to sinners, to receive as much again. But love ye your enemies, and do good, and lend, hoping for nothing again: and your reward shall be great, and ye shall be the children of the Highest; for He is kind unto the unthankful and to the evil (Luke 6:32–35).

The Good Samaritan is our Lord's answer to the question, "Who is my neighbor?" and the Good Samaritan's neighbor was a bitter enemy, who, in other circumstances, would have spurned him from his presence. Other people may not be beautiful in their character, nor congenial in their habits, manners, modes of life, or disposition; they may even be unkind to us, unjust, unreasonable, in strict justice altogether undeserving of our favor; yet if we persist in being called Christians ourselves, we owe them the love that thinketh no evil, that seeketh not its own, that beareth all things, endureth all things, and never faileth.

Loving is Giving

That is, we owe other people service. Serving goes with loving. We cannot love sincerely and not serve. Love without serving is but an empty sentiment, a poor mockery. God so loved the world that He gave. Love always gives. If it will not give, it is not love. It is measured always by what it will give. The needs of other people are, therefore, divine commands to us which we dare not disregard or disobey. To refuse to bless a brother who stands before us in any kind of want is as great a sin as to break one of the commandments of the Decalogue. We like to think there is no sin in merely not doing. But Jesus, in His wonderful picture of the Last Judgment, makes men's condemnation turn on not doing the things they ought to have done. They have simply not fed the hungry, nor clothed the naked, nor visited the sick, nor blessed the prisoner. To make these sins of neglect appear still more grievous, our Lord makes a personal matter of each case, puts Himself in the place of the sufferer who needs it and is not cared for, and tells us that all neglect in giving needed kindness to any is shown to Him. This divine word gives a tremendous interest to other people who are brought providentially into the sphere of our lives, so that their wants of any kind must appeal to our sympathy and kindness. To neglect them is to neglect Christ.

Serving Comes in Many Forms

This matter of serving has multitudinous forms. Sometimes it is poverty that stands at our gate, and financial help is wanted. But a thousand times more frequently it is not money, but something else more precious that we must give. It may be loving sympathy. Sorrow is before us. Another's heart is breaking. Money would be of no use; it would be only a bitter mockery. But we can hold to the sufferer's lips a cup filled out of our own heart, which will give new strength. Or it is the anguish of a life struggle, a human Gethsemane, beside which we are called to watch. We can give no actual aid—the soul must fight its battles alone, but we can be as the angel in our Lord's Gethsemane, imparting strength and helping the weary struggler to win the victory.

Selfishness Must Die

The world is very full of sorrow and trial, and we cannot live among our fellow men and be true to Christ without sharing their loads. Selfishness must die, or our own heart's life must be frozen within us. We begin to felicitate ourselves on some special prosperity, and the next moment some human need knocks at our door, and we must share our good things with a suffering brother. We may build up our fine theories of taking care of ourselves, of living for the future, of laying up in the summer of prosperity for the winter of adversity, of providing for old age or for our children, but often all these frugal and economic plans have to yield to the exigencies of human need. The love that seeketh not its own plays havoc with life's hard logic. We cannot say that anything is our own when our brother is suffering for what we can give.

Every Contact with Others Calls for Service

Not a day passes in the commonest experiences of life, in which other people do not stand before us with their needs, appealing to us for some service which we may render. It may be only ordinary courtesy, the gentle kindness of the home circle, the patient treatment of neighbors or customers in business relations, the thoughtful showing of interest in old people or in children. On all sides the lives of other people touch ours and we cannot do just as we please, thinking only of ourselves and our own comfort and good, unless we choose to be false to all the instincts of humanity and all the requirements of the law of Christian love. We must think continually of other people. We may not seek our own pleasure in any way without asking whether it will harm or impair the comfort of some other.

The Golden Rule Would Cure Us of Much Carelessness

For example, we must think of other people's convenience in the exercise of our own liberty and in the indulgence of our own tastes and desires. It may be pleasant for us to lie late in bed in the morning, and we may be inclined to regard the habit as only a little amiable self-indulgence. But there is a more serious side to the practice. It breaks the harmonious flow of the household life. It causes confusion in the family plans for the day. It makes extra work for the wife or mother. It sorely tries the patience of love. The other day an important committee of fifteen was kept waiting for ten minutes for one tardy member whose presence was necessary before anything could he done. At last he came sauntering in without even an apology for having caused fourteen busy men a loss of time that to them was very valuable, besides having put a strain on their patience and good nature. We have no right to forget or disregard the convenience of others. A conscientious application of the Golden Rule would cure us of all such carelessness.

Every Word and Action Affects Others

These are but illustrations of the way other people impinge upon our lives. They are so close to us that we cannot move without touching them. We cannot speak without having our words affect others. We cannot act in the simplest thing without first thinking whether what we are about to do will help or hurt others. We are but one of a great family, and we dare not live for ourselves. We must never forget that there are other people.

21

Thou Shalt Love Thy Neighbor

Thou shalt love thy neighbor as thyself (Mark 12:31).

We Cannot Define Scripture To Suit Our Convenience

Definitions are important. Who is my neighbor? What is it to love my neighbor? If we can make "neighbor" mean just a little set of people, our own set, and if we can define love to suit our own selfish notions, it will be comparatively easy to pray, "Lord, incline our hearts to keep this law." But Scripture does not yield itself to our interpretation in this way. We cannot take its words, as the potter takes the clay, and mold them to suit our pleasure. Both neighbor and love are clearly defined in the Bible.

We Cannot Choose Our Neighbors

It happened that a certain man once asked Jesus who his neighbor was, and we have the answer in the parable of the Good Samaritan. A neighbor is anyone who chances to be near us and is in any need, distress, or danger. He may be the worst man in the land, outlawed by his own sins; still if he is near to us and needs our help, he is our neighbor, the man the commandment bids us to love. We would be willing enough to love our neighbors if we could choose them, but this we cannot do. We must let God choose the particular neighbor He wants us to love.

Even the Unlovely Require Our Love

What is it to love our neighbor? It is the loving that is hard. We could do almost anything else short of loving unpleasant neighbors.

But love is the word, and no revised version changes it. No matter how disagreeable, unlovely, unworthy, our neighbors for the time may be, still the commandment persistently and relentlessly says to us, "Thou shalt love him."

True Love Is Thoughtful

Our neighbors are about us all the time, needing our love. Indeed, they touch our lives so continually that we must guard our every look, word, and act, lest we hurt some sensitive spirit. Some people seem to forget that other people have feelings. They are constantly saying words and doing things which give pain. True love is thoughtful. We ought to train our hearts to the most delicate sense of kindness, that we may never ever jokingly give pain to any other human being. Our neighbors have hearts, and we owe to every one of them—the beggar we meet on the street, the poor wretch we find crawling in the mire of sin's debasement, the enemy who flings his insults in our face—to everyone we owe the love that is thoughtful, gentle, and gives no hurt.

Never Destroy Anyone's Self-Respect

Here is some good advice by Charles Kingsley:

> Never hurt anyone's self-respect. Never trample on any soul, though it may be lying in the veriest mire; for that spark of self-respect is its only hope, its only chance, the last seed of a better life, the voice of God which still whispers to it, "You are not what you ought to be, but you are still God's child, still an immortal soul; you may rise yet, and conquer yet, and be a man yet, after the likeness of God who made you, and of Christ who died for you." Oh, why crush that voice in any heart? If you do, the poor creature is lost, and lies where he or she falls, and never tries to rise again!

We should train ourselves to such reverence, to such regard for human life, that we shall never injure the heart of one of God's creatures, even by a disdainful look.

Bear with One Another's Shortcomings

Our love ought also to be patient. Our neighbor may have his faults. But we are taught to bear with one another's infirmities. If we knew the story of men's lives, the hidden loads they are often carrying for others, the unhealed wound in their heart, we would have most gentle patience with them. Life is hard for most people, certainly hard enough without our adding to its burdens by our criticisms, our jeering and contempt, and our lack of love.

The Neglect of Love's Duty

The things love does *not* do, must also be considered. Many of us fail in our neglect of love's duty quite as much as in the wounds we give to others. We walk in cold silence beside one whose heart is aching or breaking, not saying the warm, rich word of love we might say, and which would give so much comfort. All about us are hungry ones, and the Master is saying to us, "Give ye them to eat" (Mark 6:37), but we are withholding from them what we might give, and they are starving when they might be filled. We do not mean to be neglectful. The fact is, we have no idea that we could be of such blessing to others as we might be. We do not dream that with our poor, coarse barley loaves we might feed thousands. We are too frugal with our heart gifts. God has given us love, that with it we may make life sweeter, better, easier, more victorious and joyful for others. We do a grievous wrong to those about us when we are stingy with the measure of love we give them; when we withhold the words of cheer, appreciation, encouragement, affection, and comfort which are in our hearts to speak, or when we fail to do the gentle, kind things we could so easily do to make life happier and more pleasant for them.

Love Has a Wide Application

The lesson is of wide—the very widest—application. It touches our relationships with all men. It touches the pushing of our business interests; in our ambition to get, we must not forget our neighbor. It touches our influence; we must not do that which will hurt our neighbor or cause him to stumble. It has its important bearing on missions; we owe love to the perishing ones far or near to whom we may carry or send the gospel of salvation.

Love's Duty to Fellow-Christians

Then there is an inner circle. "Thy neighbor" is any man, woman, or child, of whatever character, condition, nation, or religion, whom God may place near you in need. But there is a brotherhood in Christ that is closer still. We are to do good to all men, especially to those who are of the household of faith. That does not mean merely one's own particular church. One who went up in a balloon said that as he arose, the fences that divided the country into fields and farms faded out, until soon he saw only one great, wide, beautiful landscape of meadow and field and forest, with winding stream and river, shining in rich loveliness beneath the pure skies. So it is as we rise nearer to God in love and faith and Christian experience. The fences that divide God's great church into ecclesiastical farms and pasture fields grow smaller and smaller, until at last they vanish altogether, and we see only one wide, holy, Christlike church. We are all one. The accidents of denominationalism are but of minor importance in comparison with the love of Christ, the cross, the Bible, the ordinances, and heaven, which we all have in common. We should learn to love one another as Christians; love soon breaks down the fences. We should comfort one another and help one another on the way home.

22

Helping by Prayer

*Epaphras, who is one of you, a servant of Christ,
saluteth you, always laboring fervently for you in prayers,
that ye may stand perfect and complete in all the will
of God (Col. 4:12).*

The Best Way To Serve Others Is by Intercession

God has put it in our power to help each other in many ways; sometimes by deeds that lift away burdens, sometimes by words that inspire courage and strength, sometimes by sympathy that halves the sorrow. But there is no other way in which we can serve others so wisely, so effectively, so divinely, as by intercession for them.

We Err in Our Help; God Never Does

Our hands are clumsy and awkward, and sometimes hurt the life we would heal with our touch, or strengthen or uphold with our strength, but in prayer we can reach our friend through God, and His hand is infinitely gentle and never hurts a life. We lack wisdom, and sometimes the help we give is untimely or unwise. We lift away burdens that God wants our friend to carry. We make the way easy for him when God has made it hard for his own good, for the development of his powers. We save our friend from hardship or self-denial, or service, when these are the very paths in which God would lead him—the paths to honor, to larger use-fulness, to nobler life. Often our love is short-sighted. We think we are helping our friend, when really we are hindering him in the things that most deeply concern his life. But we can pray and ask God to help him, not in our way, but in His own way, and His help is never unwise nor untimely. He never lifts away a load which our friend will be the better for carrying. He never does things for him which would be better for him to do for himself, nor spares him hardness or suffering which will make him more a man.

Prayer May Be Our Only Means of Helping Others

There are cases, too, which we can help with our love in no other way but by prayer. The friend is beyond our reach, or his experiences of need are such that we can do nothing for him. Human capacity for helpful-ness is very small. We can give a piece of bread when one is hungry, or a cup of cold water when one is thirsty, or raiment when one is naked, or medicine when one is sick. But in the deeper needs of life we can do nothing, Our words are only mockeries. Yet we can pray, and God can send His own help to the heart in any experience.

Love's Best Help

Thus we get hints of the truth that the noblest, divinest way of helping our friends is by prayer. It follows, therefore, that we sin against them when we do not help them in this best and most effective of all ways—by praying for them. The parent who does not pray for his child, what-ever else he may do for him, sins against the child. Whosoever fails to pray for one he loves fails in the most sacred duty of love, because he withholds love's best help. A prayerless love may be very tender, and may speak mur-muring words of sweetest sound, but it lacks real and deep meaning. We never help our dear ones so well as when we pray for them.

A Praying Man Is Never a Useless Man

It is wonderful to think that we can render this best of all service for oth-ers even when we are unable to do any active work on their behalf. A "shut in" who can run no errands and lift away no burdens and speak no words of cheer to weary workers and foot-sore pilgrims in the great world can yet pray for them, and God will send encouragement and help. Said Austin Phelps, when laid aside from active service:

One thought has assumed a new reality in my mind of late as an offshoot of my useless life. When a man can do nothing else, he can add his little rivulet to the great river of intercessory prayer which is always rolling up to the throne of God. The river is made up of such rivulets as the ocean is of drops. A praying man can never be a useless man.

Again he says: "You do not know how my soul longs to get into closer friendship with Christ, and to pray—which is about the only mode of usefulness left to me—as He prayed—to touch the springs of the universe as He touched them. One can almost feel the electric thrill of it." We cannot tell what intercessory prayer does for the world or for our own lives.

Consider Prayer Requests for Friends Carefully

It is well, also, that we think carefully of the things we ask for our friends. There is the same danger that exists in prayer for ourselves—that we press only our own will for them, and request for them only things of an earthly kind. There is a good model for all intercession in the way Epaphras prayed for his friends in Colossae, "Always laboring fervently for you in prayers, that ye may stand perfect and complete in all the will of God." It is not merely health and prosperity and success in life that we are to ask for those we love, but that God's will may be done in them, and that they may fulfill His plan and purpose for them.

A Mother's First Prayer for Her Children Must Be for God's Will

The mother's prayer for her children should not be, first, that they may win worldly honor, but that they may be complete in all God's will, may be what God made them to be. The best place they can reach in this world is that for which God designed them when He gave them their being.

How We Should Pray for Our Friend Who Is Sick

Often we are led to pray for our friends when they are in some trouble. For example, one we love is sick. We are touched with sympathy, and go to God with our heart's burden. What shall our prayer be? That our friend may recover? Yes, that is love's right and natural prayer, and we may ask this very earnestly. Jesus prayed three times that His cup of sorrow might pass. But that must not be all of our prayer. It would be sad if our friend were to get well, and not take some blessing out of the sickroom with him when he leaves it. Therefore we are to pray that he may be enriched in spiritual experience; that he may be made a better man through his illness; that he may be brought into a closer relation with Christ; that his life may be purified; that he may be made more thoughtful, gentle, unselfish, unworldly, more like Christ; in a word, that he may be made perfect and complete in all the will of God.

"Not My Will, But Thine, Be Done"

It may become needful to qualify the prayer that our friend may recover. It may be God's will that he should now go home. We may still give full vent to love's yearning that he may get well, but at the close of our intense supplication we must submit it all to God's wisdom with the refrain, "Nevertheless, not as I will, but as Thou wilt" (Matt. 26:39). If our love is true, it is always better that we ask God's best for our dear ones when we pray for them, and the best for them may not be a longer life in this world, but heaven, the crowning of their lives in immortal glory and blessedness.

Think First of the Highest Spiritual Good

Our friend may be in some trouble. He may be staggering under a heavy load, and it may seem to us that the best blessing which could come to him would be the lifting away of the load. But as we begin to pray we remember that the most sincere and loving prayer for him must be that he may stand perfect and complete in all God's will. Possibly his load is part of God's will to bring out the best that is in him.

In all our praying for our friends we are to think first of their highest spiritual good. We are to seek for them above all things that they may grow into all the beauty of perfected Christian character. It is a shallow, thoughtless friendship which desires chiefly your present ease and mere earthly good. It is asking for you a stone instead of bread, or perhaps a scorpion instead of an egg, a serpent instead of a fish.

Says Archdeacon Farrar:

> There are two things to remember about prayers for earthly things: one, that to ask mainly for earthly blessings is a dreadful dwarfing and vulgarization of the grandeur of prayer, as though you asked for a handful of emeralds; the other, that you must always ask for earthly desires with absolute submission of your own will to God's.

These things are as true of prayers for our friends as of prayers for ourselves. We sin against our loved ones when we seek for them merely the things our own frail, shortsighted judgment may desire for them. Love is true only when it rises into heavenly heights and craves for those who are dear to us the things of God's own blessed, perfect will. This is not always easy. It is hard for us to say, "Thy will be done" (Matt. 6:10), when it means that the one we love must endure unmitigating pain, or walk in deep shadows, or be humbled under God's mighty hand. But whether for ourselves or for our friends, we dare not in prayers press our own wishes against God's. "Even though it be a cross that raiseth" must be our cry for our dearest as well as for ourselves. The standard of pleading must be the same. And someday we shall see and know that our love was purest when it asked even pain and loss for one who was dear, because it was God's will.

23

The Cost of Being a Friend

> *So being affectionately desirous of you, we were willing to have imparted unto you, not the gospel of God only, but also our own souls, because ye were dear unto us* (1 Thess. 2:8).

We Use the Word "Friend" Lightly

We use the word "friend" very lightly. We talk of our dozens of friends, meaning all with whom we have common friendly relations, or even pleasant acquaintance. We say a person is our friend when we know him only in business, or socially, when his heart and ours have never touched in any real communion. There may be nothing amiss in this wide application of the word, but we ought to understand that used in this sense its full sacred meaning is not even touched.

Genuine Friendship

To become another's friend in the true sense is to make the other into such close, living fellowship that his life and ours are knit together as one. It is far more than a pleasant companionship in bright, sunny hours. It is more than an association for mutual interest or profit or enjoyment. A genuine friendship is entirely unselfish. It seeks no benefit or good of its own. It does not love for what it may receive, but for what it may give. Its aim is "Not to be ministered unto, but to minister" (Mark 10:45).

Responsibilities of Friendship

It costs to be a friend. "For better, for worse, for richer, for poorer, in sickness and in health," runs all true friendships. When we take a person into our lives as a friend we do not know what it may cost us to be faithful to our trust. Misfortune may befall our friend, and he may need our help in ways that will lay a heavy burden on us. It may be in his business or in his secular affairs that he may suffer. Timely aid may enable him to overcome his difficulties, and attain to prosperous circumstances. It may be in our power to render him the assistance he needs, without which he must succumb to failure. It will cost us personal inconvenience and trouble to do this. But he is our friend. We have taken him into our lives, thus becoming partner in all his affairs. Can we withhold from him the help which he needs and which we can give, without breaking the holy compact of friendship and failing in our sacred obligations to him?

When Friendships Become Burdensome

It may be the misfortune of sickness and broken health that falls upon our friend. He is no longer able to be helpful to us as he was in the days when the friendship was first formed. Then he could contribute his part in the mutual ministering, giving as well as receiving. Then friendship for him brought us no care, no anxiety; exacted from us no self-denial, no sacrifice; laid on us no load, no burden. On the other hand, it was full of helpfulness. It brought strength to our heart by its loving cheer. It was a benediction to our lives, in its warm inspirations, in its sweet comfort, in its satisfying affection. It stood beside us in all our times of trial, with full sympathy, putting its shoulder under our burdens, aiding us by its counsel, its encouragement. It brought its countless benefits and gains. But now in its feeble and broken state, it can no longer give us this strong help and uplift. Instead, it has become a burden. We must carry the loads alone which his friendship so generously shared. He needs our help now, and can give in return only a weight of care.

Responsibilities of Friendship Compared to Marriage

For example, a wife becomes an invalid. In the early days of her wedded life she was her husband's true helpmeet, his loyal partner in all duty, care, work, and burden-bearing. Her friendship brought back far more than it cost. But now she can only lie still amid the cares and see him meet them alone. Instead of sharing his burdens, she herself has become an added burden which he must carry. But his love doesn't falter for a moment. He loved her not for the help she was to him, but for her own dear sake. Hence his love doesn't change when she is no longer a strong helpmeet, but a burden instead. His heart only grows more tender, his hand more gentle, his spirit braver. He finds even deeper, sweeter joy now in serving her than he found before in being served by her.

Friendship Makes No Calculations

That is the meaning of true friendship wherever it exists. It is not based on any helpfulness or service which it must receive as its condition. Its source is in the heart itself. Its essential desire is to help and serve. It makes no nice calculation of so much to be given and so much to be received. It stops at no cost which faithfulness may entail. It hesitates at no self-denial which may be necessary in the fulfillment of its duties. It does not complain when everything has to be given up. It only grows stronger and more faithful and loyal as the demands for giving and serving become larger.

A Friend's Character is Gradually Revealed

There is another phase of the cost of friendship which must not be overlooked—that which comes with the revealing of faults and flaws and sins. We see persons at first only on the surface of their lives, and we begin to admire them. We are attracted to them by qualities that win our attention. As we become associated with them, we become interested in them. At length our affection goes out to them, and we call them our friends. We walk with them in pleasant companionship that makes no demands on our unselfishness and that discloses but little of their inner life. We know them as yet only on the surface of their character, having no real acquaintance with the self that is hidden behind life's conventionalities. Nothing has occurred in the progress of our friendship to bring out the things in their disposition which are not altogether lovely.

At length closer intimacy or ruder contacts reveal faults. We learn that under the attractive exterior which so pleased us there are blemishes, spots, flaws, shortcomings, which sadly disfigure the beauty of the life. We discover in them elements of selfishness, untruthfulness, deceitfulness, or meanness, which pain us. We find that they have secret habits which are repulsive. There are things in their disposition, never suspected in the days of common social conversation, which show offensively in the closer relations of friendship's intimacy. This is often so in wedded life; the longest and freest acquaintance previous to marriage reveals only the better side of the life of both. But the same is true in a greater or lesser degree in all close friendships.

The Test of Love

Many times this is a severe test of love. It is only as we rise into something of the spirit of Christ that we are able to meet this test of friendship. He takes us as we are and does not weary of us, whatever faults and sins display themselves in us. There is infinite comfort in this for us. We are conscious of our unworthiness and of the unloveliness that is in our souls. There are things in our lives which we would not reveal to the world. Many of us have pages in our biography which we would not dare to spread out before the eyes of men. There are in our inner being feelings, desires, longings, cravings, jealousies, motives, which we would not feel secure in laying bare to our nearest, dearest, and most gentle and patient friend. Yet Christ knows them all. Nothing is hidden, nothing can be hidden from His eyes. To Him there is a perfect revealing of the innermost resources of our heart. Yet we need not be afraid that His friendship for us will change or grow less, or withdraw itself, when He discovers in us repulsive things. This is the ideal human friendship. It is not repelled by the revealing of faults. Even if the friend has fallen into sin the love yet clings, forgiving and seeking his restoration.

We Should Love Our Friends According to Christ's Example

We are apt to complain if our friends do not return as deep, rich, and constant a love as we give them. We feel hurt at any evidence of the ebbing of love in them, when they fail us in some way, when we think they have not been altogether faithful and unselfish, or when they have been thoughtless or indifferent toward us. But Christ saw in "His own" a very feeble return for all His deep love for them, a most inadequate requital for all His wondrous goodness and grace. They were unreliable, weak, unfaithful, sometimes inconsiderate and thoughtless. Yet He continued to love them in spite of all that He found unlovely and unworthy in them. This is the friendship He would teach His disciples. As He loves us He would have us love others. We say men are not worthy of such friendships. True, they are not. Neither are we worthy of Christ's wondrous love for us. But Christ loves us not according to our worthiness, but according to the riches of His own heart. So should it be with our giving of friendship—not as the person deserves, but after the measure of our own character.

The Cost of Friendship

These are illustrations enough to show what it may cost to be a friend. When we receive another into this sacred relationship, we do not know what responsibility we are taking upon ourselves, what burdens it may be ours to carry in being faithful, what sorrows our love may cost us. It is a sacred thing, therefore, to take a new friend into our lives. We accept a solemn responsibility when we do so. We do not know what burdens we may be assuming, what sacrifices we may unconsciously be pledging ourselves to make, what sorrows may come to us through the one to whom we are opening our heart. We should choose our friends, therefore, thoughtfully, wisely, prayerfully, but when we have pledged our love, we should be faithful, whatever the cost may be.

24

Making Friendship Hard

It is more blessed to give than to receive (Acts 20:35).

The Demands of Some People May Be Too Great

There are some people who make it very hard for others to be their friends. They put friendship to unreasonable tests. They make demands upon it to which only the greatest patience and the most generous charity will submit.

There are some persons who complain that they have no friends, and many times the complaint may be almost true. There are none with whom they have a close, personal friendship. No one enters with perfect sympathy into all the experiences of their lives. They have no friend who is ready to share in all their lives, rejoicing with them in their joys, and bearing beside them and with them their load of care, sorrow, or anxiety. They seem to be without real companionship, although all about them throng other lives with the very things of love for which their hearts are crying out. These unbefriended ones think the fault is with the other people, whom they regard as cold, uncongenial, selfish. But really the fault is with themselves. They make it all but impossible for anyone to be their close personal friend. Nothing less holy and less divine than mother-love can endure the requirements and demands they put upon those who would be glad, if they could, to include them in their circle of friends.

Friendships Must Be Mutually Unselfish

A close friendship can be formed and can continue to exist only where there is mutual unselfishness. It cannot all be on one side. We cannot expect our friend to give all while we give nothing. We cannot ask that he be generous, patient, confiding, self-denying, and thoughtful toward us while we in our behavior toward him lack all these qualities. Christ bears with us in all our sad faultiness, is patient toward all our weakness and infirmity and sin, and is our faithful, unfailing Friend; though we give Him but little love, mingled with doubts, complaints, murmurings, and ingratitude. Many of us make it hard for Christ to be our Friend, yet He loves unto the end, unto the uttermost. Mothers come next to Christ in their friendship without return. Many a child makes it difficult for his mother to be his friend, putting her love to severe tests. Yet she loves on, in the face of all ingratitude, unkindness, unworthiness.

Few Maintain Friendship with Ungrateful People

But there are few others who will be such friends to us as Christ and our mothers, who will be so patient with us, who will love us and continue loving us when we do not accept our fair share of the friendship, or when we give only injury or ingratitude in return for love and tenderness. There are few outside our own family who will trouble themselves to maintain a close relationship with us when we make it as hard as we can for them to do so. There may be one or two persons among those who know us, with a love disinterested enough to cling to us in spite of all our wounding of their affection and all the needless burden we put upon their faithfulness. But such friends are rare, and the man is fortunate who had even one who will be such a friend to him while he puts the friendship to such unreasonable proof.

Friendship Made Difficult by Doubt

There are many ways in which friendship is made hard. One way is by doubting and questioning. There are those who demand repeated assertion and assurance in word, every time they meet their friend, that he is still their friend. If he fails to put his abiding, loyal interest into some fervent formula of constancy they begin to wonder if he had not changed in his feeling toward them, and they tell him of their anxiety. A little thought will show anyone how hard friendship is made by such a course. This spirit indicates a lack of full trust, and nothing more effectually stunts and deadens the heart's gentle affections than being doubted. It indicates also a morbid sentimentality which is unwholesome. Such demand for reiterated avowal may be pardoned in very young lovers who have not yet attained to manly or womanly maturity, but in the realm of common friendship it should never be made. The moment a true-hearted man, eager to be helpful to another, finds the sentiment spirit creeping in, he is embarrassed and hindered in his effort to do a friend's part, and if he is not a man of great patience and unwearying kindness, he will find his helpfulness hindered. In any case friendship is made difficult for him.

Friendship Strained by Selfishness

Another way in which friendship is made hard is by an exacting spirit. There are those who seem to think of a friend only as one who shall help them. They value him in proportion to the measure of his usefulness to them. Hence they expect him to show them favors at every point, and to do many things for them. They do not seem to have any conception of the lofty truth that the heart of friendship is not the desire to receive, but the desire to give. We cannot claim to be another's friend if all we want is to be served by him. We are only declaring our unmitigated selfishness when we act on this principle.

Yet there are those who would exact all and give nothing. Their friend may show them kindnesses in unbroken continuity for years, perhaps many times doing large things for them, but the moment he declines or omits to grant some new favor they have sought, all past acts are instantly forgotten.

There are few generous people who do not repeatedly have just this experience. Of course no return in favors is desired by a true friend. There are many cases indeed in which, in one sense, the helpfulness of the friendship must be all on one side. It may be so when one is an invalid, unable to do anything, compelled to be a burden continually upon a friend. But in such a case there is a return possible a thousand times better than if it could be made in kind—a return of gratitude, of affection, of trust. Such a requital makes friendship easy, though the calls upon it for service may be constant and very heavy. But the spirit already referred to makes it very hard for a friend to go on carrying the load year after year.

Possessive Friendship

Another example is that in which one claims a friend exclusively for his own. There are such people. They want their friend to show interest in no other, to be kind to no other. This also might be excused in a certain kind of silly young lovers, but it is not confined to such. It exists in many cases toward others of the same sex, and is not confined to the young. Persons have been known to demand that the one who is their friend shall be theirs so exclusively as scarcely to treat others decently. Any pleasant courtesy to another has been taken as a personal slight and hurt to the chosen "friend." Unless both persons are alike weak and foolish, such a spirit cannot but make friendship hard. No man or woman who has the true conception of life is willing to be bound in such chains. We cannot fulfill our mission in God's great world of human beings by permitting ourselves to be tied up in this sentimental way to any one person. No worthy friendship ever makes such demands.

Jealousy is always ignoble and dishonoring. The mature and sensible wife and husband, bound in one, in the most sacred of ties, make no such weak and selfish demand upon each other. Each desires the other to be the largest possible blessing to the world, knowing that their mutual love is not made less, but richer, by the exercise of unselfishness toward all who need help. The same spirit should be manifested in all friendships, and will be just so far as they are noble and exalted in character. A man need be no less a friend, no less true, no less helpful to me, because he is the friend of hundreds more who turn to him with their cravings and needs and find strength and inspiration in him. "The heart grows rich in loving," and my friend becomes more to me through being the friend of others. But if I demand that he be my friend only, I make it very hard for him to be my friend at all.

We Gain the Most By Demanding the Least from Our Friends

Only a few suggestions have been given of the way in which many people make it hard for others to be their friends. Not only do they make it hard for their friends to continue their faithfulness and helpfulness to them, but they rob themselves of the full, rich blessings which they might receive, lessen the value to them of the friendship they would make of greater value. We can get the most and the best from our friends by being large-hearted and trustful ourselves, by putting no restraints on them, by making no demands or requirements, by seeking to be worthy of whatever they may wish to do for us, by accepting what their love prompts in our behalf, proving our gratitude by a friendship as sincere, as hearty, as disinterested, and as helpful as it is in our power to give. Thus we shall make it easy for others to be our friends, and shall never have occasion to say that nobody cares for us.

25

The Sin of Being a Discourager

But I determined this with myself, that I would not come again to you in heaviness (2 Cor. 2:1).

The Pessimist Makes Life Difficult for Others

There are some people who always look at the dark side. They find all the shadows in life, and persist in walking in them. They make darkness for others wherever they may go—never brightness. These people do a great deal of harm in the world. They make all of life harder for those they influence. They make sorrow harder to bear, because they exaggerate it, and because they blot out all the stars of hope and comfort which God has set to shine in this world's night. They make burdens appear heavier because, by their discouraging philosophy, they leave the heart beneath the burden less strong and brave to endure. They make life's battles harder because by their ominous forebodings, they paralyze the arm that wields the sword. The whole effect of the life of these people is to discourage others; to find unpleasant things and point them out; to discover dangers and tell about them; to look for difficulties and obstacles and proclaim them.

A thoughtful man was asked to contribute to the erection of a monument to one of these discouragers, and replied: "Not a penny. I am ready to contribute toward building monuments to those who make us hope, but I will not give a penny to those who live to make us despair." He was right. Men who make life harder for us cannot be called benefactors. The true benefactors are those who show us light in our darkness, comfort in our sorrows, hope in our despair.

Our Duty Is to Encourage Others

We all need to be strengthened and inspired for life's experiences; never weakened and disheartened. If we meet others cast down and discouraged, it is our duty as their friends not to make their trials and cares seem as large as we can, but rather to point out to them the silver lining in their clouds, and to put new hope and courage in their hearts. If we find others in sorrow, it is our duty not to tell them merely how sorry we are for them, how we pity them, but coming close to them in love, to whisper in their ears the strong comforts of divine grace, to make them stronger to endure their sorrow. If we find others in the midst of difficulties and conflicts, faint and ready almost to yield, it is our duty not merely to bemoan with them the severity and hardness of their battles, and then to leave them to go on to sure defeat, but to inspire them to bravery and victory.

It is of vital importance that we learn this lesson if we want to be true helpers of others in their lives. If we have only sadness to give to men and women, we have no right to go among them. It is only when we have something that will bless them and lift up their hearts and give them glimpses of bright and beautiful things to live for, that we are truly commissioned to go forth as evangels into the world.

The World Has Enough Sorrow without Our Adding to It

It is better that we should not sing of sadness if our song ends there. There are enough sad notes already floating in the world's air, moaning in men's ears. We should sing only and always of hope, joy, and cheer. Jeremiah had a right to weep, for he sat amid the crumbling ruins of his country's prosperity, looking upon the swift and resistless approach of woes which might have been averted. Jesus had a right to weep on the Mount of Olives, for His eye saw the terrible doom coming upon the people He loved, after doing all in His power to avert the doom which sin and unbelief were dragging down upon them. But not many of us are called to live amid grief like that which broke the heart of Jeremiah. And as of

Jesus, we know what a Preacher of hope He was wherever He went. Our mission must be to carry to men not tidings of grief and doom, but joy and good news. "Give me your beliefs," said Goethe; "I have doubts enough of my own." So people are saying to us: "Give us your hopes, your joys, your sunshine, your life, your uplifting truths; we have sorrows, tears, clouds, ills, chains, doubts enough of our own."

The Christian Life Is a Victorious Life

This is the mission of Christianity in the world—to help men to be victorious, to whisper hope wherever there is despair, to give cheer wherever there is discouragement. It goes forth to open prisons, to loosen chains, and to bring out captives. Its symbol is not only a cross—that is one of its symbols, telling of the price of our redemption, telling of love that died, but its final symbol is an open grave, open and empty. We know what that means. It tells of life, not of death; of life victorious over death. We must not suppose that its promise is only for the final resurrection; it is for resurrection every day, every hour, over all death. It means unconquerable, unquenchable, indestructible, immortal life at every point where death seems to have won a victory. Defeat anywhere is simply impossible, if we are in Christ and if Christ is in us. It is just as true of the Christ in us as it was of the Christ who went down into Joseph's tomb, that He cannot be held by death.

Every Burden Has Its Blessing

It follows that there never can be a loss in a Christian's life out of which a gain may not come, as a plant from a buried seed. There can never be a sorrow out of which a blessing may not be born. There can never be a discouragement which may not be made to yield some fruit of strength.

We Must Be Heralds of Hope

If, therefore, we are true and loyal messengers of Christ, we can never be prophets of gloom, disheartenment, and despair. We must ever be heralds of hope. We must always have good news to tell. There is a gospel which we have a right to proclaim to everyone, whatever his sorrow may be. In Christ there is always hope, a secret of victory, a power to transmute loss into gain, to change defeat to victory, to bring life from death. We are living worthily only when we are living victoriously ourselves at every point, when we are inspiring and helping others to live victoriously, and when our lives are songs of hope and gladness, even though we sing out of tears and pain.

26

Summer Gathering for Winter's Needs

He that gathereth in summer is a wise son (Prov. 10:5).

An inspired proverb tells us, "He that gathereth in summer is a wise son." In its simplest form the reference is to the gathering and laying up of food in the summer days. There is a season when the harvest is waving in the fields, when the fruits hang heavy on trees and vines, when earth's good things wait to be gathered. That is the time when men must be diligent if they would lay in store for their winter's needs. Not long does the opportunity wait. No sooner are the fruits ripe than they begin to decay and fall off. No sooner is the harvest golden than it begins to perish. Winter follows summer. Then there are no fruits on the trees or vines, no harvests waving on the fields. The hungry man cannot go out then to gather food, and if he has not gathered in summer he must suffer hunger.

Youth is a Summer

But the principle has wide application. Life has its summers and its winters, its times of health, plenty, opportunity, then its times of sickness or want; and these seasons of need must exist from the stores laid up in the days of abundance. Youth is a summer. It is a time for the forming of habits, for the knitting of the muscles and sinews of character, for the making of friendships. Later on comes "real life," with its duties, its responsibilities, its struggles, its sorrows, its losses. But he who has gathered in life's summer shall not lack in life's winter. A youth-time diligently spent in improvement prepares one for whatever comes in the sterner years, while every opportunity wasted in youth is a chance for misfortune or failure in later life.

The Christian Home Is a Sheltered Home

The same law applies in spiritual life. In our time of quietness and security we may store in our hearts the resources we shall need to draw upon for meeting temptation. Childhood and early youth in a true Christian home are sheltered in a large measure from stern assaults and bitter conflicts. The atmosphere is kindly and genial. The influences are helpful. There is a mother's shoulder to cry on and a father's hand to lead and protect. The family altar holds all the household close to God's feet. The sin of the world outside washes against the very threshold, the spray of its tides dashing against the windows; yet within the sacred walls there is a holy life, unperturbed, unstained, loving, gentle, and sincere. The child that grows up amid influences is sheltered from the temptations that make the world outside so perilous a place in which to live. This is life's summer.

Sooner or Later the Child Must Face Temptation

But the winter comes. No young person can live always in such a shelter. The time comes, sooner or later, when the children must go out to face the temptations of the world. It is possible, however, in the days of quiet in the home, to so gather spiritual resources in the heart that in the conflicts of later days the life shall be safe. When men build a great ship to go upon the sea, they pile away in its keel tremendous strength, staunch ribs, immense beams and stays, and heavy steel plates. They are building the vessel for the ocean, and they make it strong enough to endure the wildest tempests. So human lives should be built in the home in the days of youth—not merely for the sweet experiences of the home itself, but to meet the sternest buffetings and the severest testings that any possible future may bring. Principles should be fixed in the heart so firmly that nothing can ever swerve the life from them. Habits should be so wrought into the conduct that nothing can change them. Conscience should be so trained that it shall do its duty in the greatest stress without wavering.

The lesson is for the young. In the bright sunny days they should gather into their lives stores of moral and spiritual strength from which to draw when they go forth to encounter the world's fierce temptations. Memory should be filled with the words of God. The great essential principles of Christianity should be so fixed in their minds that no assaults of skepticism can make them doubt. The fundamental laws of morality should be settled in their very soul as the laws of their own life. Their spiritual habits should be so firmly fixed that they will carry their faith with them out into the world as they carry their faces or their throbbing hearts. Into the ship of their lives, their characters, they should pile massive strength which nothing can possibly overcome.

Memorizing Scripture in Childhood

The same is true of preparation for sorrow. We are not to forecast trouble, and yet we are to live so that when trouble comes we shall be prepared for it. The wise virgins were not left in darkness as were their foolish sisters when their own lamps went out because they had a reserve of oil in their vessels. If we have a store of divine promises and comforts hidden in our hearts, gathered and laid away there during the bright days, we shall never be left in darkness however suddenly the shadow may fall upon us. Here we see the benefit of memorizing Scripture in childhood. People often ask, "What is the use of teaching children long Bible texts which they cannot understand?" The use will appear by and by.

In a new building the workmen were observed putting gas-pipes and electric wires into the walls. There seemed to be no use in this. It would be months before there could be any need of light or heat. Yes, but the time to put them in is now, when the house is in the process of construction. They will be covered up and hidden behind the plastering and the woodwork. But when the house is occupied it will be necessary only to push a button and the electric lights will fill the rooms with light or to turn a knob and the flame would be there for heat or cooking.

There may seem to be no use in putting into a child's memory words it cannot understand. They make no impression at present. They give out no light. But they are fixed in the life, and someday there will come sorrow. It will grow dark. Then from these words will flash out the sweet light of divine love, pouring the soft radiance of heavenly comfort upon the night of grief.

Prepare for the Future

A touching story is told of a young man who was rapidly and surely losing his eyesight. The physicians told him that he would be able to see but for a few months. At once, accompanied by a sister, he set out to travel over Europe, taking a last look at the beautiful things of this world, before his eyes would be closed forever. He wished to have his memory stored with lovely pictures of mountains, lakes, and waterfalls, of fine buildings and works of art, so that when he should no longer be able to see, he might have these beautiful visions in his soul, to lighten his gloom.

We should walk in the light while we have the light. We should train ourselves to see all the beauty we can find in God's works and word. We should gather into our souls all the love, joy, and gladness that we can store there, while we may. Then when the night settles about us, we shall have light within.

Advice to the Young

In Rose Porter's little book, *Summer Driftwood for the Winter Fire*, the grandfather's counsel to the child is "Annie, the flowers will fade, the sunshine will be hidden when the winter storm-clouds come, and the song birds will fly away. Find something lasting. Begin to gather wood now that will warm the heart when the winter of life comes." No wiser counsel could be given to the young. Let the sunshine into your hearts in the bright days, God's sunshine of love and truth. Read good, wholesome, helpful books that will leave great and honorable thoughts in your memory. Especially read the Bible, and store its words in your mind. Do beautiful things, things of love, of unselfishness, of helpfulness, things that are true, honorable, just, pure, and lovely. Nothing darkens life's winter days as do memories of sinful things. Nothing makes life so sweet in old age as does the memory of right and good things done through the years.

Gather about you, too, in the sunny days, gentle and worthy friends. Be sure they are worthy, for unworthy friends often make bitterness and sorrow for the dark days of those whom they disappoint. Above all, gather into your soul the sweet friendship of Jesus Christ, and let His words bless your life and fill and enrich your heart.

When Winter Days Come

Then, when the winter days come, the memories of all these precious things will abide, and will shine like soft lamps in the gloom. "The memory of things precious keepeth warm the heart that once did hold them." Such gathering in the summer days of life will make the winter cheerful and bright within, even with storm and darkness outside.

Says Ruskin:

What fairy palaces we may build of beautiful thoughts, proof against all adversity, bright fancies, satisfied memories, noble histories, faithful sayings; treasure-houses of precious and restful thoughts, which care cannot disturb, nor pain make gloomy, nor poverty take away from us—houses, built without hands, for our souls to live in!

27

Fellow-workers with God

For we are laborers together with God (1 Cor. 3:9).

Man May Have No Part in Some Acts of God

There are many things that God does in which we can have no part. A child wished he were a painter, that he might help God paint the clouds and skies and sunsets. God wants no help in this work. He acted unhelped by creature hand in making the worlds. In providence, too, He has no fellow-worker. No one assists Him in keeping the stars in their orbits, in sending rains and dews and summer sunshine. No one helps Him paint the roses and the lilies.

In Some Things We May Be God's Co-Workers

But there are other things in which God permits us to be His co-workers. He calls us up close beside Him, to work with Him, doing a part while He does a part. A story is told of an artist who greatly desired to have a share in the decorating of a famous building. If he could not do it all, he asked that he might be permitted to paint one panel of one of the great doors. If this request could not be granted, he longed to be allowed at least to hold the brushes for the master who should do the work. If it was deemed such an honor to do even the smallest part on a building of only earthly glory, what an honor it is to work with Christ in the building of His great spiritual temple!

Yet this privilege is ours. We may not help God paint His clouds and sunsets, but we can put tints of immortal beauty upon human souls. In a certain sense we are fellow-workers with God in all the affairs of our lives. We often imagine that we are doing certain fine things without God's help. But we are not. A man makes great inventions, constructs wonderful machines, harnesses steam, electricity, the atom, and says, "See what I have done." But who put into nature the mysterious forces and energies which he has made available for us? In their inventions and discoveries men only find the powers God stowed away ages ago. Men are only discoverers and adjusters. They run wires on poles, or lay cables in the sea, but the currents that flash through them, carrying messages of business, commerce, joy, and sorrow, come from God's reserves of energy. Men are working with God, and their part is small.

Mother's As Co-Workers with God

In spiritual life it is also true that we are fellow-workers with God. He calls us to stand beside Him and do a part while He does a part. When a mother with a great joy in her heart takes her baby into her arms and looks into its face, God says to her, "Take this child and nurse it for Me" (Ex. 2:9). It is God's child. He wants it trained, its powers developed, so that when at length the man stands before his tasks, he may not fail, but may do them well. Yet God gives into the mother's hands the duty of nursing the child for Him, teaching it, putting into its heart gentle thoughts, wooing out the sweet love that sleeps there, and thus preparing the life for its work. Yet she alone cannot do anything. God and the mother are fellow-workers.

Sunday School Teachers As Co-Workers with God

The Sunday School teacher sits down with his class. The end of the teaching is to bring the scholars to Christ, to build up in them a Christian character, and to lead them out into ways of usefulness and loving service. What is the teacher's part? He can make plain to his class the Word and will of God, and he can also represent Christ to them, showing them glimpses of the divine compassion, truth, and love in his own life. But he cannot himself do what needs to be done in their young lives; only God can do that. But He works through the teacher. God and he are fellow-workers.

Christian Workers As Co-Workers with God

So it is in all Christian work. We have our part. God has ordained that the heavenly treasure shall be put in earthen vessels. We must never forget, however, that we are not doing the work ourselves. Saddest of all things in Christian workers is the losing out of the heart a sense of dependence upon God, the leaving out of Christ, the feeling that they are doing things alone. God will work through us only when we, in faith and self-renunciation, lay ourselves into His hands, that His life may flow through us to the lives we are seeking to bless.

The Human Worker As God's Chisel

We are the chisel with which God carves His statues. Unquestionably we must do the work. Our hands must touch men's lives and beautify them. The mother, the teacher, the Christian friend must carve and mold the life of the child into the beauty of the Lord. But the human worker is only the chisel. The sculptor needs his chisel, but the chisel can do nothing, produce no beauty, of itself. We must put ourselves into Christ's hand that He may use us.

To Be God's Co-Worker Is a Sacred Responsibility

There is a hallowing influence in this thought, that we are working beside God in what He is doing on immortal lives. Are we worthy to do it? Hawthorne, speaking of a block of marble and the possibilities of beauty that lay in it waiting to be brought out, said that the stone assumed a sacred character, and that no man should dare touch it unless he felt within himself a consecration and priesthood. If this is true when it is only a block of marble that is to be carved upon, how much more is it true of a human soul—a child's life, for example, laid in a mother's arms; any life laid in your hands or mine—that we may free the angel that waits within it! It is a most sacred moment when a life is put before us to be touched by us.

Suppose that the mother—suppose that you or I—should not do the holy work well, and the life should be marred, hurt, stunted, its beauty blurred, its purity stained, its development impaired, its power weakened; think of the sadness of the result. How sweet the mother must keep her own spirit, how gentle, how patient, and pure and true, while she is working with God in nursing her child for Him! How heavenly must the teacher keep her temper, how quiet, how unselfish, how Christlike, when he is sitting beside the Master working with Him on the lives of the scholars! How softly we should all walk continually, with reverent, chastened, uplifted feeling and hallowed spirit, as we remember that we are fellow-workers with God!

God Needs Our Faithfulness

There is here also a strong motivation to faithfulness. The work we do for God and with God we must do well. We are tempted to say, "My part is not important, it is so small. It cannot matter much to God whether I do it well or not. He does not need my work." But that is not true. Our least part is important. God needs our faithfulness. He needs the mother in training the child—needs the most conscientious, most painstaking, most beautiful work she can do, If her hand slackens even for one day, doing its part carelessly, less than faithfully, there may be a defect, a damaging of the child's life, which shall reveal itself in years to come. The completeness of the finished work depends on our doing always our best. We rob God if we are ever less than faithful.

God Can Use Even Those Who Feel Inadequate

There is special encouragement in this truth for those who feel unequal to the duty that the Master assigns to them. They see others who do beautiful things that bless and brighten the world, but it seems to them that all they can do is so commonplace, so dull, so full of error and fault, that it is not worthwhile for them to do it at all. But the clumsiest hands fully surrendered to God may do work that is most beautiful in His sight.

Long ago, in quaint old Nuremberg, lived two boys, Albrecht Dürer and Franz Knigstein. Both wished to be artists, and both studied and worked with great earnestness. Albrecht had genius, but Franz had only love for art, without the power to put on canvas the beautiful visions that haunted him. Years passed, and they each planned to make an etching of the Lord's Passion. When they compared their work, that of Franz was cold and lifeless, while Albrecht's was charged with beauty and pathos. Then Franz saw it all, and knew that he could never be an artist. His heart was almost broken, but he said in a voice choked with tears, yet full of manly courage, "Albrecht, the good Lord gave me no such gift as this of yours, but something, some simply duty, He has waiting somewhere for me to do. Yet now you be the artist of Nuremberg, and I—"

"Wait, Franz, be still one moment," cried Albrecht, seizing his pencil. Franz supposed Albrecht was adding some finishing touches to his exquisite drawing and waited patiently in his attitude of surrender, his hands folded together. With his swift pencil Albrecht drew a few lines and showed the sketch to his friend.

"Why those are only my hands," said Franz. "Why did you sketch them?" "I drew them," said Albrecht, "as you stood there making the sad surrender of your life so bravely. I said to myself, Those hands that may never paint a picture can now most certainly make one. I have faith in those folded hands, my brother, They will go to men's hearts in the days to come."

Albrecht's words were true. Into the world of love and duty has gone the story, so touching has gone the picture—for Albrecht Dürer's famous "Folded Hands" is but a picture of the hands of Franz Knigstein as they were folded that day in lowly, brave resignation, believing that the Lord had some humble duty still worth his doing.

God May Do More with Our Failures Than with Our Successes

This story teaches us that if we cannot do the beautiful things we see others doing for Christ and which we long to do, we can at least do some lowly work for Him. It teaches us, too, that self-surrender to God, though our heart's fondest hope is laid down, is, in God's sight, really the most beautiful thing we can do with our lives. It teaches us, also, that the hands that can do no brilliant thing for God may yet become hands of benediction in the world. If we are truly fellow-workers with God, He can use whatever we have that we really surrender to Him. And many times He can do more with our failures than with our successes.

28

Christ's Reserve in Teaching

Whom shall he teach knowledge? And whom shall he make to understand doctrine? Them that are weaned from the milk, and drawn from the breasts, for precept must be upon precept, precept upon precept; line upon line, line upon line; here a little, and there a little (Is. 28:9, 10).

I have yet many things to say unto you, but ye cannot bear them now (John 16:12).

Teaching Must Be Progressive

Christ never teaches us more rapidly than we can receive His lessons. It was in the midst of His most confidential talk with His disciples that He said He had many things to say to them which they could not yet bear. All wise teaching must be from the simplest rudiments up to the more complex knowledge. The mind is not capable of comprehending the higher elements till it has been developed and trained. Then truth itself is progressive, and the pupil is not prepared to receive the advanced lessons until he has mastered the rudiments.

Diverse Needs Require Different Spiritual Truths

Then spiritual truths can be received only as we come to experiences for which they are adapted. There are many of the divine promises which we can never claim, and whose blessedness we cannot realize until we come to the points in life for which they were specially given. For example: "In the time of trouble He shall hide me in His pavilion" (Ps. 27:5). This word can mean nothing to the child playing with his toys, or to the young man or woman walking in sunny paths, without a care or a trial. It can be understood only by one who is in trouble. Or, take this word: "My grace is sufficient for thee" (2 Cor. 12:9). It was given first in place of an answer to a prayer for the removal of an unrelenting trial. It meant divine strength to offset human weakness, and it cannot be received until there is a sense of need.

Christ stands beside a happy young Christian and says: "I have a precious word to give you, one that shines with the beauty of divine love, but you cannot bear it yet." The disciple moves on along life's sunny path, and by and by comes into the shadows of sorrow or trouble. Again Jesus stands beside him and says: "Now I can give you the word I withheld before: 'My grace is sufficient for thee.' " Then the promise glows with light and love.

Special Promises for Special Needs

There is a very large part of the Bible which can be received by us only when we come into the places for which the words were given. There are promises for weakness which we can never get while we are strong. There are words for times of danger which we can never know while we need no protection, There are consolations for sickness whose comfort we can never get while we are in robust health. There are promises for times of loneliness when men walk in solitary ways, which never can come with real meaning to us while loving companions are by our side. There are words for old age which we never can appropriate for ourselves along the years of youth, when the arm is strong, the blood warm, and the heart brave.

When Night Comes, God Shows Us the Stars

God cannot show us the stars while the sun shines in the heavens; and He cannot make known to us the precious things of love that He has prepared for our nights while it is yet day about us. Christ says to us then, "I have yet many things to say unto you, but ye cannot bear them now." We could not understand them. But by and by, when we come into places of need, of sorrow, of weakness, of human failure, of loneliness, of sickness, of old age, then He will tell us these other things and they will be full of joy for our hearts. When night comes, He will show us the stars.

Older Christians understand this. There are many things in the Bible which had little meaning for them in life's earlier days, but which one by one have shone bright and beautiful along the years, as stars come out in the evening sky when the sun fades from the heavens. Even in childhood the words were said over and over, but they were repeated thoughtlessly because there had been no experience to prepare the heart to receive them. Then one day there crept a shadow over the life, and in the shadow the long familiar words began for the first time to have a meaning. Other experiences of care, trial, and loss followed, and the precious words became more and more real. Now, in old age, as the sacred texts are repeated, they are the very rod and staff to the trembling, trusting spirit.

Thus as life goes on, the meaning of Christ's words comes out clearer and clearer, until the child's heedless repetition of them becomes the utterance of the faithful and trust of the strong man's very soul.

The Master Wisely Withholds Knowledge of the Future

We cannot bear now the revealing of our own future. Christ knows it all. When a young Christian comes to His feet and says, "I will follow Thee withersoever thou leadest" (Matt. 8:19), the Master knows what that promise means. But He does not reveal the knowledge to His happy disciple. People sometimes say they wish they could look on into the years and see all that will come to them. But would this be a blessing? Would it make them happier? Could they shape their course better if they knew all that shall befall them—the struggles, the victories, the defeats, the joys and sorrows, the failures of bright hopes, just how long they will live?

Surely it is better we should not know our future. So the word of the Master is continually: "I have yet many things to say unto you, but ye cannot bear them now." Only as we go on, step by step, does He disclose to us His will and plan for our lives. Thus the joys of life do not dazzle us, for our hearts have been chastened to receive them. The sorrows do not overwhelm us because each one brings its own special comfort with it. But if we had known in advance of the coming joys and prosperities, the exultation might have made us heedless of duty and overly self-confident, thus missing the benediction that comes only to simple, trusting faith. If we had known of the struggles and trials before us, we might have been disheartened, thus failing in courage to endure. In either case we could not have borne the revelation, and it was in tenderness that the Master withheld it.

Much Knowledge of Heaven Would Make Us Useless on Earth

We could not bear the many things Christ has to tell us about heaven, and therefore He does not tell them to us. The blessedness if disclosed now would dazzle and blind our eyes; the light must be let in upon us, little by little, so as not to harm us. Then if heaven were within our sight, as we toil and struggle and suffer here, the bliss would so excite us that we should be unfit for duty.

A traveler tells of returning to France after a long voyage to India. As soon as the sailors saw the shores of their own land they became incapable of attending to their duties on the ship. When they came into port and saw their friends on the dock, the excitement was so intense that another crew had to be found to take their place. Would it not be so with us if heaven were visible from earth? Its blessedness would win us away from our duties. The sight of its splendors would so charm and entrance us that we should weary of earth's painful life. If we could see our loved ones on heaven's shore, we would not be content to stay here to finish our work. Surely it is better that more has not been revealed. The veiled glory does not dazzle us, and yet faith realizes it, and is sustained by the precious hope in its struggles through the night of earthly life until at last the morning breaks.

The Law of Divine Revealing

This is the great law of divine revealing. We learn Christ's teaching as fast as we are able to bear it. So we may wait in patient faith when mysteries confront us, or when shadows lie on our path, confident that He who knows all has in gentle love withheld from us for the time the revelation we crave because we could not yet endure the knowledge.

29

In Time of Loneliness

And, lo I am with you alway, even unto the end of the world (Matt. 28:20).

Companionship Is One of the Deepest Desires

Loneliness is one of the most pathetic of human experiences. The yearning for companionship is one of the deepest of all yearnings. The religion of Christ has something to meet every human need; what is its blessing for loneliness? We may turn to the Master's own life for an answer to our question. He met all the experiences that ever become ours, and He found for Himself the best there is to be found in the divine love to meet His experiences. Thus He showed us what we may find in our times of need and how we may find it.

Christ's Loneliness

Christ's loneliness was one of the most bitter elements of His earthly sorrow. His very greatness of character made it impossible for Him to have any real companionship in this world. Besides, those whom He came to bless and save rejected Him. The only human relief to His loneliness along the years of His public ministry was in the love of His chosen friends, and this was most unsatisfactory. But we know where He ever turned for solace and comfort in His experiences. After a day of pain and suffering He would climb the mountain and spend the night in communion with His Father, returning in the morning renewed and strong for another day of sweet life and service. In His darkest hour He said that though left alone as to human companionship He was not alone because His Father was with Him.

Every Man Has Lonely Experiences

The comfort of our Lord's heart in His loneliness is for us, too, if we are walking in His steps. We, too, have our experiences of loneliness in this world, and we, too, may have the blessed companionship that shall fill the emptiness. In a certain sense all of life is lonely. Even with sympathetic companions all about us, there is an inner life which each one of us lives altogether alone. We must make our own choices and decisions. We must meet our own questions and answer them ourselves. We must fight our own battles, endure our own sorrows, carry our own burdens. Friendship may be very close and tender, but there is a sanctuary of each life into which even the holiest friendship may not enter. Blessed are they who in this aloneness can say, "Yet I am not alone because the Father is with me." God's is the only friendship that can really meet all our soul's deep needs and cravings. Human companionship helps us at a few points; the divine has its blessing for every experience. We never shall be left alone when we have Christ. When other helpers fail and comforts flee, He will ever stand close beside us. When other faces fade out of view, His will shine out with gentle love, pouring its light upon us.

Youth Is a Time of Decision

There are special experiences of loneliness in every life for which Christ is needed. Youth is one of these times. Youth seems happy and light-hearted. Companions swarm all around it. But often a young person feels lonely even amid such scenes and friendships. All of life is new to him. As his soul awakens, a thousand questions arise demanding answers. He is in a world with a thousand paths, and he must choose in which one he will walk. Everything is mysterious. There are perils lurking on all sides. Choices must be made. Lessons must be learned. All is new, and at every step the voice is heard, "You have not passed this way heretofore" (Josh. 3:4). This loneliness of inexperience, when a young soul is taking its earliest steps in life, is one of the most trying and painful feelings of all the years. If Christ is not his companion, then, lonely and perilous indeed is the way. But if He walks beside the young soul in its inexperience, all is well.

The Value of a Christian Home

There are those who are lonely because they are homeless. It is impossible to estimate too highly the value and the helpfulness of a true home of love. Home is a shelter. Young lives nest there and find warmth and protection. There is also guidance in a true Christian home. Many of life's hardest questions are answered by a wise mother or father. Blessed is that young man or young woman who takes every perplexity, every mystery, every doubt or fear and every hunger, home to the sacredness of love's sanctuary, and gets there sympathy, patient counsel, and true guidance. Home has also its blessed companionship. It is the only place where we are absolutely sure of each other and do not need to be on our guard. Youth has its unspeakable longings, its deep hungers, its cravings for tenderness. In the true home these are all met. Those who have such a home do not realize the half of its value to them. It is the very shadow of Christ's wings over their lives, the very cleft of the Rock, the very bosom of divine love. Life's loneliness means far less to them while home shields them and blesses them with its companionship and its patient, wise, helpful, nourishing love.

When the Home Is Broken Up

But sometimes the home is pulled down over youth and its shelter broken up. Few things are sadder than homelessness. Loneliness begins to be really felt when the home is gone, when there is no longer a wise and loving mother to give her counsel in your inexperience, to lay her hand on your head in benediction, to listen to your questions and answer them, to restrain your impetuous spirit, to quiet you when you are perturbed and when your peace is broken, to lead you through perplexing paths, to fill your hungry heart with the comfort of love when you long for sympathy and companionship. Bitter indeed is the sense of loneliness when a young person, used to all that a mother's love means, turns away from a mother's grave to miss thereafter the blessings that have been so much in the past. Nothing earthly will in any full measure compensate for the loss. Other human friendships may be very precious, but they will not give back home with its shelter, its affection, its trust, its guidance, its soothing, its security.

With Christ, Even a Room Can Become a Home

But blessed is that life which in earthly homelessness can say, "Yet I am not alone because Christ is with me." Blessed is that loneliness of homelessness which has Christ to fill the emptiness. With Christ unseen, yet loved and made real to the heart by love and faith, even a room in a boarding house may become a home, a sanctuary of peace, a shelter of divine love.

Old Age Can Be a Time of Great Loneliness

Another time of special loneliness is when sorrow strips off the friendships of life. Old age is an illustration. Old people are often very lonely. Once they were the center of groups of friends and companions who clustered about them. But the years brought their changes. Now the old man stands alone. Still the streets are full, but where are the faces of forty or fifty years ago? There is a memory of vacant chairs, of marriage altars with the unbindings and separation that follow. The old faces are gone. It is the young life that now fills the home, the streets, the church, and the old people are lonely because their old friends are gone.

Old Age Is Near to Glory

Yet in Christ even old age can say, "I am not alone." No changes in life can take Him away. He is the Companion of life's feebleness. He loves the old people. There is a special promise for them: "Even to old age I am He; and even to hoar hairs will I carry you" (Is. 46:4). For the Christian old age is very near to glory. It will not be long till the old people reach home, to stand again amid the circle of loved ones who blessed their youth and early years.

Sorrow Touches All Ages

But not the old people only are left lonely by life's changes. Sorrow touches all ages, and if we have not Christ when other friends are taken, we shall be desolate indeed. Blessed is that life which, when human friends are taken away, finds the friendship of Christ all-filling, all-satisfying, and can say, "Yet I am not alone, for Christ is with me."

Dying Is the Loneliest of All Human Experiences

The loneliest of all human experiences is that of dying. We cannot die in groups, not even two and two; we must die alone. Human hands must unclasp ours as we enter the valley of shadows. Human faces must fade from our vision as we pass into the mists. "I cannot see you," said one who was dying, as the loved ones stood about his bed. So will it be with each one of us in our turn. Human love cannot go beyond the edge of the valley. But we need not be alone even in that deepest of all loneliness; for if we are Christ's we can say, "Yet I am not alone because my Savior is with me." When the human hands unclasp, His hands will clasp ours the more firmly. When beloved human faces fade out, His countenance will shine above us in all its glorious brightness. When we must creep out of the bosom of human affection, it will be only into the clasp of the everlasting arms, into the bosom of Christ. Death's loneliness will thus be filled with divine companionship.

Our Absolute Need of Christ

The inference from all this is our absolute need of the friendship and companionship of Christ, without which we can only sink away in life's loneliness and perish. One reason, no doubt, why our lives are so full of experiences of need is that we may learn to walk with Christ. If earth's human companionships satisfied us, and if we never lost them, we must not care for Christ's. If earth's homes were perfect, and if they never crumbled, we might not grow homesick for heaven.

30

In the Everlasting Arms

> *The eternal God is thy refuge, and underneath are*
> *the everlasting arms (Deut. 33:27).*

The Two Sides of a Religious Life

There are two sides to a religious life. One is the active side. We are urged to faithfulness in all duty, to activity in all service, to victory in all struggle, to work out our own salvation with fear and trembling. But there is another side. We are to trust, to have quietness and confidence, to repose on God. It is well that we sometimes think of the latter aspect of our Christian faith. This is well presented to us in a Bible word which says, "Underneath are the everlasting arms."

God's Arm from Youth to Old Age

The picture suggested is that of a little child, lying in the strong arms of a father who is able to withstand all storms and dangers. We think of John lying upon Christ's bosom. At the two extremes of life, childhood and old age, the promise comes with special assurance. "He shall gather the lambs in His arms, and carry them in His bosom" (Is. 40:11), is a word for the children. "Even to your old age I am He; and even to hoar hairs will I carry you" (Is. 46:4), brings its blessed comfort to the aged. God comes to us first in our infancy, through our mothers, who carried us in

151

their arms. Yet they are only dim revelations of God for a time. They leave us after teaching us a little of God's tenderness, but God Himself remains when they are gone, and His arms never unclasp.

After Dr. Bushnell's death, they found, dimly penciled on a sheet of paper, these words:

> My mother's loving instinct was from God, and God was in her in love to me first therefore; that love was deeper than hers and more protracted. Long years ago she vanished, but God stays by me still, embracing me in my gray hairs as tenderly and carefully as she did in my infancy, and giving to me as my joy the principal glory of my life: that He lets me know Him, and helps me, with real confidence, to call Him my Father.

God Represented in Human Language

The thought of the embracing arms is very suggestive. What does an arm represent? What is the thought suggested by the arm of God enfolded around His child? The language is human. The Scriptures speak continually of God in this way. They tell us of His eyes looking down to behold His people, that He never slumbers nor sleeps—meaning that His watchful care never intermits. They tell us that He listens to earth's cries, and hears the sighing of the oppressed, and the groaning of the prisoner in his dungeon—meaning that He hears our cries of distress. They speak of His wiping away tears, as a mother would dry a child's tears—meaning that He comforts His people in their sorrow. They represent Him as holding us by the right hand, as a father holds his child's hand in his own when it walks over dangerous places—meaning that His guidance is personal and strong.

All these, and like statements in human language of what God does for His people, are efforts to explain to us by means of human acts with which we are familiar, His wonderful care and kindness. Thus the figure of the arm as applied to God is to be interpreted by what it would mean in human friendship.

God's Arm Ensures Protection

One meaning is protection. A father puts his arm about his child when it is in danger. God protects His children, "Thou hast with Thine arm redeemed Thy people" (Ps. 77:15). "Be Thou their arm every morning" (Is. 33:2). "His arm brought salvation" (Is. 59:16). Life is full of peril. There are temptations on every hand. Enemies lurk in every shadow, enemies strong and swift. Many persons think of death with fear, dreading to meet it. But life has far more perils than death. It is easy and safe to die when one has lived well, but it is hard to live. Yet we are assured that "life" cannot separate us from the love of God. "Underneath are the everlasting arms."

God's Arm Tells of Love

Another meaning is affection. The father's arm drawn about a child is a token of love. The child is held in the father's bosom, near his heart. The shepherd carries the lambs in his bosom. John lay on Jesus' breast. The mother holds the child in her bosom because she loves it. This picture of God embracing His children in His arms tells of His love for them. His love is tender, close, intimate. He holds them in the place of affection.

God's Arm in Time of Danger or Suffering

It is especially in the time of danger or suffering that the mother thus embraces her child. She takes him up when he has fallen and has hurt himself, and comforts him by holding him in her arms, and pressing him to her bosom. "As one whom his mother comforteth, so will I comfort you" (Is. 66:13), is a divine word. A mother said that her little sick one had scarcely been out of her arms for three days and nights. Holding in the arms is a peculiar privilege of love for times of pain and suffering. It tells therefore of our heavenly Father's tenderness towards His own when they are in distress.

God's Arm as a Symbol of Strength

Another thought suggested by an arm is strength. The arm is a symbol of strength. A mother's arm may be frail physically, but love makes it strong. When it is folded about a feeble child, all the power of the universe cannot tear the child away. We know what it is in human friendship to have one upon whose arm we can lean with confidence. There are some people whose mere presence seems to give us a sense of security. We believe in them. In their quiet peace there is a strength which imparts itself to all who lean upon them. Every true human friend is more or less a strength to us. Yet the surest, strongest human strength is but a fragment of the divine strength. This is omnipotence. "In the Lord Jehovah is everlasting strength" (Is. 26:4). This is an arm that never can be broken. Out of this clasp we never can be taken.

God's Arm Suggests Endurance

Another suggestion is endurance. The arms of God are "everlasting." Human arms grow weary even in love's embrace; they cannot forever press the child to the bosom. Soon they lie folded in death. A husband stood by the coffin of his beloved wife after only one short year of wedded happiness. It was very sweet the clasp of that love—but how brief a time it lasted, and how desolate was the life that had lost the precious companionship! A little baby two weeks old was left motherless. The mother clasped the child to her bosom and drew her feeble arms about it in one loving embrace; the little one never more will have a mother's arm around it. So pathetic is human life with its broken affections, its little moments of love, its embraces that are torn away in one hour. But these are everlasting arms—these arms of God. They shall never unclasp.

God's Arms Are Always Underneath

There is another important suggestion in the word "underneath." Not only do the arms of God embrace the child, but they are underneath—ever underneath. That means that we can never sink, for these arms will ever be beneath us, wherever we may be found. Sometimes we say the waters of trouble are very deep; like great floods they roll over us. But still and forever underneath the deepest floods are these everlasting arms. We cannot sink below them or out of their clasp. And when death comes, and every earthly thing is gone from beneath us, and we sink away into what seems darkness and the shadow of death—out of all human love, out of warmth and gladness and life, into the gloom and strange mystery of death, still it will be only into the everlasting arms. When Jesus was dying, He said, "Father, into Thy hands I commit My spirit" (Luke 23:46). He found the everlasting arms underneath Him when His spirit left the torn body. Stephen died, praying, "Lord Jesus, receive my spirit" (Acts 7:59). To a believer, dying is simply breathing the life into the embrace of God. We shall find the divine arms underneath us. Death cannot separate us from the love of God.

No Power Can Snatch Us Out of His Hands

This view of the divine care is full of inspiration and comfort. We are not saving ourselves. A strong One, the mighty God, holds us in His clasp. We are not tossed like a leaf on life's wild sea, driven at the mercy of wind and wave. We are in divine keeping. Our security does not depend upon our own feeble, wavering faith, but upon the omnipotence, the love, and the faithfulness of the unchanging, the eternal God. While we trust in Him we never can sink away in any flood. No power in the universe can snatch us out of His hands. Neither death nor life, nor things present, nor things to come, can separate us from His love.

31

Even I Only

And He said, I have been very jealous for the Lord God of hosts: for the children of Israel have forsaken Thy covenant, thrown down thine altars, and slain Thy prophets with the sword; and I, even I only, am left; and they seek my life, to take it away (1 Kgs. 19:10).

Elijah

Elijah at a certain great crisis thought he was the only one left to stand for God. There were others, but he did not know of them. He was indeed the only one in the field for God. He stood alone, one man against king and false priests and people. It was a splendid heroism.

Standing Alone for God at Home

There come times in the lives of all who are Christians when they must stand alone for God, without companionship, perhaps without sympathy or encouragement. Here is a young person, the only one of his family who has confessed Christ. He takes Him as His Savior and then stands up before the world and vows to be His and to follow Him. He goes back to his home. The members of his home circle are very dear to him, but none of them are Christians, and he must stand alone for Christ among them. Perhaps they oppose him in his discipleship—in varying degrees this many times is the experience. Perhaps they are only indifferent, making no opposition, only quietly watching his life to see if he is consistent. In any case, however, he must stand for Christ alone, without the help that comes from companionship.

Standing Alone for God at Work or School

Or it may be in the workshop or in the school that the young Christian must stand alone. He returns from the Lord's table to his weekday duties full of noble impulses, but finds himself the only Christian. His companions are ready to sneer, and they point the finger of scorn at him, with irritating epithets. Or they even persecute him in petty ways. At least they are not Christ's friends, and he as a follower of the Master finds no sympathy among them in his new life. He must stand alone in his discipleship, conscious all the while that unfriendly eyes are upon him. Many a young or older Christian finds it very hard to be the only one to stand for Christ in the place of his daily work.

The Responsibility of Standing Alone for God

This aloneness puts upon one a great responsibility. You are the only Christian in your home. You are the only witness Christ has in your house, the only one through whom He may reveal His love, His grace, His holiness. You are the only one to represent Christ in your family, to show to them the beauty of Christ, the sweetness and gentleness of Christ, to do there the works of Christ, the things He would do if He lived in your home. If you falter in your loyalty, if you fail in your duty, your loved ones may be lost, and the blame will be yours; their blood will be upon you.

In like manner if you are the only Christian in the shop, the store, or the office where you work, a peculiar responsibility rests upon you, a responsibility which no other one shares with you. You are Christ's only witness in your place. If you do not testify there for Him, there is no other one who will do it.

Miss Havergal tells of her experience in a girl's school of Dusseldorf. She went there soon after she had become a Christian and had confessed Christ. Her heart was very warm with love for her Savior, and she was eager to speak for Him. To her amazement, however, she soon learned that among the hundred girls in the school she was the only Christian. Her first feeling was one of dismay—she could not confess Christ in that great company of worldly, unchristian companions. Her gentle, sensitive heart shrank from a duty so hard. Her second thought, however, was that she could not refrain from confessing Christ. "I am the only one He has here," she said. And this thought became a great source of strength and inspiration to her. She realized that she had a mission in that school, that she was Christ's witness there, His only witness, and that she dare not fail.

This same sense of responsibility rests upon every thoughtful Christian who is called to be Christ's only witness in a place—in a home, in a community, in a store, or school, or shop, or social circle. He is Christ's only servant there, and he dare not be unfaithful, else the whole work of Christ in that place may fail. He is the one light set to shine there for his Master, and if his light is hidden the darkness will be unrelieved. So there is special inspiration in this consciousness of being the only one Christ has in a certain place.

Each Christian Has His Own Particular Place of Service

There is a sense in which this is true also of every one of us all the time. We are always the only one Christ has at the particular place at which we stand. There may be thousands of other lives about us. We may be only one of a great company, of a large congregation, of a populous community. Yet each one of us has a life that is alone in its responsibility, in its danger, in its mission and duty. There may be a hundred others close beside me, but not one of them can take my place, or do my duty, or fulfill my mission, or bear my responsibility. Though every one of the other hundred does his work and does it perfectly, my work waits for me and if I do not do it, it will never be done.

We can understand how that if Elijah had failed God that day when he was the only one God had to stand for Him, the consequences would have been disastrous: the cause of God would have suffered irreparably. But are we sure that the calamity to Christ's kingdom would be any less if one of us should fail God in our lowly place any common day?

Stories are told of a child finding a little leak in the dike that shuts off the sea from Holland, and stopping it with his hand till help could come, staying there all night, holding back the floods with his little hand. It was but a tiny, trickling stream that he held back; yet if he had not done it, it would soon have become a torrent, and before morning the sea would have swept over all the land, submerging fields, homes, and cities. Between the sea and all this devastation there was but a boy's hand. Had the child failed, the floods would have rolled in with their remorseless ruin.

We understand how important it was that the boy should be faithful to his duty, since he was the only one God had that night to save Holland.

Your Life May Stem a Flood of Moral Decay

But how do you know that your life may not stand someday, and be all that stands, between a great flood of moral decay and broad, fair fields of beauty? How do you know that your failure in your lowly place and duty may not let in a sea of disaster which shall sweep away human hopes and joys, possibly human souls? The humblest of us dare not fail, for our one life is all God has at the point where we stand.

We Render Our Account to God

This truth of personal responsibility is one of tremendous importance. We do not escape it by being in a crowd, one of a family or of a congregation. No one but ourselves can live our lives, do our work, meet our obligation, bear our burdens. No one but ourselves can stand for us at last before God to render an account of our deeds. In the deepest, most real sense, each one of us lives alone.

We Are Responsible Only for Our Own Life and Duty

There is another phase of this lesson; we are responsible only for our own life and duty. The prophet thought his work had failed because the overthrow of Baalism seemed incomplete. But God comforted him by telling him of three other men who would come, each in his time, and do each his part of the work in destroying Baalism. Elijah's work had not failed, but it was only a fragment of the whole work.

The best work any of us do in this world is but a fragment. We all enter into each other's work, and others in turn shall enter into ours and finish or carry on toward completion what we have begun. Our duty is simply to do well our own little part. If we do that, we need never worry about the part we cannot do. That belongs to some other worker, coming after us, not to us at all.

So while we are alone in our responsibility we need have no concern for anything but our own duty, our own little fragment of the Lord's work. The things we cannot do, some other one is waiting and preparing now to do after the work has passed from our hand. There is comfort in this for any who fail in their efforts and must leave tasks unfinished which they hoped to complete. The finishing is another's mission.

32

In Due Season We Shall Reap

> *Be not deceived; God is not mocked: for whatsoever a man soweth, that shall he also reap. For he that soweth to his flesh shall of the flesh reap corruption; but he that soweth to the spirit shall of the spirit reap life everlasting. And let us not be weary in well doing: for in due season we shall reap, if we faint not (Gal. 6:7–9).*

Discouragement in Christian Life and Work

Sometimes we are inclined to be discouraged in our Christian life and work. We ask, "Is it worthwhile to be holy, to keep God's commandments? What profit is there in godliness? Is it worthwhile to deny ourselves in order to do good to others, to serve them? What comes of it all?" Many of us are apt to have moods in which these questions press upon us with painful stress. It is well that we look into the matter that we may be assured that it is worthwhile to do well, that there is profit in it.

What Is Meant By Well Doing?

There is an inspired word which says, "Let us not be weary in well doing, for in due season we shall reap, if we faint not." What is meant by "well doing"? It is doing right, obeying God's commands, fashioning our lives after the pattern revealed by Him in His word. It is not easy to do right. It costs us many a battle. A life of well doing implies a continual crucifying of self. Inclinations must be restrained. Desires must be curbed. The will must be yielded to God's will. The whole life must be brought into subjection to a law which is spiritual and heavenly.

Is Well Doing Profitable?

"Does it pay?" is the question. There are many people who do not put their lives under this law of God, who go on in the ways of self-indulgence. They put no curb on their inclinations. They let no divine command interfere with the exercise of their own desires. As we look at these people, it seems to us perhaps that they are happier than we are. They appear to get more out of life than we do. It seems to us that we are denying ourselves, sacrificing our comfort, and cutting off our right hands for nothing. Sin seems to have the advantage. Worldliness appears to pay the best. Virtue seems dreary and costly and lonesome. It does not have the good time that self-indulgence has. And sometimes we get weary in well doing because there appears to be no profit in it.

Well Doing Means Doing Good to Others

"Well doing" means also the doing of good to others. We are taught that if we are Christians, we must not live for ourselves. Love is the essence of the new life, and love is doing, giving, sacrificing for the sake of others. Instead of trying to get out of the world all we can for ourselves, we are to give the world all we can possibly give it of blessing and good.

A Life of Well Doing Is Not Natural

It is easy to see that such a life is not natural, is not in harmony with human feelings and tastes. Naturally we care for ourselves and for our own benefit and comfort. We do not incline to put ourselves out, to sacrifice our own convenience, to serve others. We might do it for one we love deeply, but the gospel requires us to love and serve, with all our capacity for serving, those who are not among our congenial friends. An enemy who needs us we must serve. Even the most debased human life that we find in our path we must touch with our healing love and help with the hands that have been given to Christ. We are required to hold our lives and all that we have at the call of love and of human need. We are to bear one another's burdens. We are to have sympathy with all sorrow and need, to be touched ever with a sense of the world's condition. This law of Christian love puts us down among men just as Christ Himself was among men. He kept nothing back. He never thought a thought nor breathed a breath for Himself. He poured out the blessing of His holy life without limit on everyone who came near Him, at last giving His very blood for the saving of man.

Christ, Our Example

That is what "well doing" means. And it is no wonder that some people stop and ask, "Is it worthwhile?" It is very natural for us to raise the question whether the giving of all is the best way to gain all, whether living altogether for others is the way to make the most of our own lives, as we are required to do. We look at Christ, for example, and think of His rich, noble, blessed life. Never in any other human soul were there such treasures of manhood stored as in His. His was the sweetest, gentlest spirit that ever looked out of human eyes. Never in any other mind were there such intellectual powers, and never in any other heart were there such depths and heights and breadths and lengths of love as in His.

What did He do with His rich life? He turned away from the paths in which the world's great men had walked, and devoted Himself to the one work of doing good to others. He gave all He had to this work. He emptied Himself and made Himself poor that others might be made rich. He exhausted His own strength that the weak might be made strong. He poured out His own lifeblood that the dead might live.

Is that the best that Christ could have done with His wondrous life? His own friends thought not. They thought that He had thrown away His life.

Take those who are following in Christ's footsteps. A young American girl, having finished her college courses, came out with high honors. She had a keen intelligence, good social position, influential friends, a beautiful and happy home. Just then there came a call for missionary teachers to go to the South to work among the poor and needy. This young girl heard the call and gave herself to this service. For two or three years she lived among the poor, teaching them, helping them, telling them too of Christ. Then one day she contracted one of the diseases rampant in the ghettos where she served her Lord and soon she died among the impoverished, with no mother's hand to smooth her hair, or cool her fevered brow, or soothe her pain; with no mother's lips to kiss her before her earth's last farewell. They brought her body back and buried it among her friends, but on almost every tongue was the sad complaint, "She had wasted her beautiful life. It ought to have been kept and used for service in more gentle, refined ways. It was too rich a life to be poured out in such costly ministry." So they talked beside her coffin. But was that sweet life wasted? Could she have done anything better with it?

Life's Accounts Are Not Always Settled Immediately

To all these questions there comes as an answer the promise that "in due season we shall reap if we faint not" (Gal. 6:9). It is not in vain that we continue our well doing, that we obey God's commandments, that we devote our lives in self-sacrificing service to men for Christ's sake. What seems to be loss is gain. The good man may seem to have more trouble than his unchristian neighbor. His business may not appear to prosper as well. His ventures may fail. His faithfulness may bring him human enmity and even persecution. But life's accounts are not always settled at once. Harvest does not follow sowing immediately. It is so in nature. There are days and months when the seed seems to have perished. Afterward, however, it yields fruit. It is the same in spiritual life. For a time there may seem to be no blessing in well doing. But in the end righteousness succeeds. "He that soweth to the spirit shall of the Spirit reap life everlasting."

Every Good Deed Is a Good Seed Sown

Every kindness we do to another in the name of Christ is the sowing of a good seed unto the Spirit. Every deed of love, every act of unselfishness, every self-denial—all the things we do to help, to comfort, or to bless others are seeds which we sow unto the Spirit. "In due season we shall reap" (Gal. 6:9). For a time it may not appear that any good or blessing comes from the act of love or the word of kindness spoken. But the seed does not perish; it has in it an immortal germ.

The World Needs Our Help

The world about us is full of needs. One said the other day that everything he was interested in, every piece of good work, every institution, was needing money. We all find it so. On every hand are calls for help.

Either we must shut up our heart or always be giving and doing. We dare not shut up our heart—that would mean moral and spiritual death. So we must always be giving and doing. We can keep nothing long for ourselves. No sooner is it in our hands than we are asked to give it out again because the Lord has need of it in some other life, to meet some need of one of His little ones, or to do some work of love for Him. But we need never fear that anything—the smallest thing we do for another with love for Christ in our heart—can fail of blessing.

We Do Not Know the Full Result of Our Good Deeds

Says Faber: "When men do anything for God—the very least thing—they never know where it will end, nor what amount of good it will do for Him. Love's secret, therefore, is to be always doing things for God, and not to mind because they are only little things." Carlyle says, "Oh, it is great, and there is no other greatness, to make some work of God's creation more fruitful, better, more worthy of good; to make some human heart a little wiser, stronger, happier, more blessed, less accursed." And we never know how little benefactions of ours may bless a life and stay in it as a benediction forever.

A teacher writes this to a friend:

> Once as I came out of the schoolhouse door, after the usual trying day in my first year of teaching, you were passing and waited for me. As you walked with me a short distance you spoke sympathetically about my work. Your manner and voice cheered and comforted me. I have never forgotten it.

Then the writer goes on to say that all the years since, the memory of those simple words had stayed in her heart as a perpetual encouragement, inspiration, and benediction. It had been thirteen years, and she had not seen the friend meanwhile. It was only a bit of wayside ministry—a cheering word to a discouraged primary teacher, as he hurried by on some other errand, but its influence had become immortal.

The incident is full of comfort and incitement. We know not how even a small word may bless a life. We should always keep our heart and hands ready for whatever little ministry we may have an opportunity to render. The least word of good cheer may start a song in a heart which shall sing on forever. The good may drop unconsciously from lip and hand and you may never think of it again, and yet it shall not be lost. It carries in it the life of God and is immortal.

We Should Give Ourselves with Our Gifts

There is a difference in the way different people give, though the gift or favor or act be precisely the same. One gives the help only; the other gives part of himself in the help. There are some very beautiful flowers that have no fragrance, but how much more a flower means that has in it perfume as well as loveliness! We should give ourselves with our gifts. We should let part of our own lives flow out with every deed of kindness we do. Love is the fragrance of the flowers of the heart, and what we do in love—love for Christ and love for man—shall never be lost. The world will be richer and better for even the smallest deeds of Christlike charity. We may not reap the harvest in this world, but beyond the skies we shall gather the sheaves in our bosom. So then, though our lives be imperfect and evil and our work be marred with sin, we know that the Master will accept the humblest thing we do for Him. He will cleanse our work and use it, even though it be only a fragment, in the building up of His kingdom.

Book Two:
Life's Open Door

1

Speak Ye Comfortably

Remember, three things come not back;
The arrow sent upon its track—
It will not swerve, it will not stay
Its speed, it flies to wound or slay;
The spoken word, so soon forgot
By thee, but it has perished not;
In other hearts 'tis living still,
And doing work for good or ill;
And the lost opportunity
That cometh back no more to thee—
In vain thou weepest, in vain dost yearn,
Those three will nevermore return.

From the Arabic

There is need always for comfortable words. Always there is sorrow. Everywhere hearts are breaking. There is no one who is not made happier by gentle speech. Yet there is in the world a dearth of comfortable words. Some people scarcely ever speak them. Their tones are harsh. There seems no kindness in their hearts. They are gruff, severe, querulous. Even in the presence of suffering and sorrow they evince no tenderness.

"Speak ye comfortably" is a divine exhortation. That is the way God wants us to speak to each other. That is the way God Himself ever speaks to His children. The Bible is full of comfortable words. We would say that in view of the wickedness of men, their ingratitude, the base return they make for God's goodness, the way they stain the earth with sin, God would be angry with them every day. But instead of anger, only love is shown. He is ever speaking in words of lovingkindness. He maketh His sun to rise on the evil and the good, and sendeth the rain on the just and the unjust. Every message He sends is love. All His thoughts toward His children are peace. The most wonderful expression of His heart toward the world was in the giving of Christ. He was the Word, the revealer of the heart of God. He never spoke so comfortably to men as when He sent His Son.

Who can measure the comfort that was given to the world in Jesus Christ? Never an unkind word fell from His lips, never a frown was seen on His brow. Think of the comfortable words He spoke in His mother's home. He was a sinless child, never giving way to angry words or violent tempers. His youth and manhood were without a trace of unlovingness. Then we know what He was during His public ministry—having all power, but gentle as a woman; able to call legions of angels to defend Himself, but without resentment, returning only gracious love for cruelty and bitter hate.

Think of the comfortable words He spoke to the sick who were brought to Him for healing, to the mourners sitting beside their dead, to the weary ones who came to Him to find the warmth of love in His presence. The ministry of His gracious words as they were uttered by His lips and fell into sad and discouraged hearts was marvelous in its influence.

In His life Christ set an example for us. He wants us ever to be speaking comfortable words. We shall not meet a man tomorrow in our going about who will not need the comfortable word that we are able to speak. The gift of speech is marvelous in its possibilities. Man is the only one of God's creatures to whom this gift is given. This is one of the qualities that makes him godlike. It is never meant to be perverted—it was intended always to be beautiful and pleasing. Dumbness is very sad—when one cannot speak. But would not one better be dumb than use his divine gift of speech in anger to hurt others? Yet how many are those who never speak to give pain? The hurt that is done any fairest day by words is incalculable. War is terrible. Who can describe the ruin wrought by shot and shell rained upon a city of homes, leaving devastation everywhere? Words may not lacerate, mangle like the missiles of war, but they may be almost as deadly in the cruel work they do. God wants us to use our speech to speak only and ever comfortably.

When this message was first given to the prophets, it had a definite meaning. The people were in sore straits. They were suffering. They were in sorrow because of the judgments visited upon the land and upon the holy city.

> Jerusalem lay in ruins, a city through whose breached walls all the winds of heaven blew mournfully across her forsaken floors. And the heart of Jerusalem, which was with her people in exile, was like the city—broken and defenseless. In that far-off unsympathetic land it lay open to the alien; tyrants forced their idols upon it, the people tortured it with their jests.

It was to these people in sorrow and distress that God bade His heralds go with divine comfort. The words were remarkable for their tenderness. The heralds were to go to carry comfort to these broken-hearted ones.

The words, "Speak ye comfortably," have in them therefore a divine sobbing of love. God cares that men and women and children about us are sad. He knows their distress and pities them. He would have us go out to them in His name, carrying in our hearts and upon our lips the echo of His compassion and yearning. It is our privilege to represent God Himself in our relations with people about us. How can the gentleness of God be passed to those who are being hurt by the world's cruelty and unkindness, if not through us, God's children? Who will carry God's sympathy and impart God's comfort to those who are sorrowing and broken-hearted if we do not? God needs us to be His messengers, His interpreters. If we do not faithfully and truly represent Him, how will people in their suffering and distress know His gracious interest in them and His compassionate feeling toward them? If we fail in showing kindness to those who are in need, if we treat them with coldness, withholding our hands from the ministries of love which we might have performed for them, we are not only robbing them of the blessing which we ought to have given them, but we are also failing to be true to God, are misrepresenting Him, giving men false conceptions of His character and His disposition toward them. Men learn what God is and what His attitude toward them is only when his own friends are faithful to all their duties and responsibilities.

When one in trouble receives no kindness, no help, when one in sorrow receives no sympathy and comfort, it is not because God does not care, but because some child of God neglects his duty. A story is told of a child sitting sadly one day on a doorstep when a kindly man was passing by. "Are you God?" the child asked. The man was struck by the strange question. "No," he answered, "I am not God, but God sent me here, I think." "Weren't you a long time coming?" the boy asked. Then he told the passer-by that when his mother had died a little while ago, she told him that God would care for him. The boy had been watching for God to come. Too often not God, but those He sends are long in coming to speak for God or to bring the relief or comfort God sends by them. People in distress, who have learned to believe that God will provide for them, are oftentimes compelled to wait long, until their hearts grow almost faint before the blessing comes. Sometimes they begin to wonder whether after all God really hears prayers and keeps His promises while the delay is not with God, but with us who are so long coming.

"Speak ye comfortably." We need to train ourselves to remember that we are God's messengers, that it is ours to be attentive to any bidding of our Master and to go quickly with any message of relief or cheer, or comfort He gives us to carry. We must not linger or loiter. The need may be urgent. The person may be near death. Or the distress may be so keen that it cannot be endured a moment longer. What if the sufferer should die before we reach him? We are sent to give comfort to one who is in the anguish of bereavement. We hesitate and shrink from carrying our message. Meanwhile the bereft one has come back from the grave to the desolated home and the emptiness and silence. God's heart is full of compassion and He has blessed comfort for His child, but there is no one to go with the message. There are Bibles in the sad home, but there is no human messenger to speak the comfortable words. It needs a gentle heart to bring in tender and loving words and in warm, throbbing touch the comfort that is needed. We fail God while we do not hasten on His errand to our friend who sits uncomforted in the shadows. We try to excuse ourselves by saying that we ought not to break in on our friends' sorrow, that we should make our condolences formal, that it would be rude and could only add to the pain if we were to try to speak of the sorrow. This may be true of the world of people in general, but there is always one to whom God gives the message, "Go and speak comfortably," one who will fail God if he does not carry the message, leaving the heart to break when God wanted it to be relieved and comforted.

2

The Ministry of Comfort

I am so weak I hardly dare to pray
  That my small light may bless yet further still;
That weary ones, the lone, the far away
  Even I may help to show thy love and will.

And yet I know the weak are strong in thee,
  And knowing this I would, in thy dear name,
The greatest of all blessings that can be,
  This precious gift, this crown of blessings, claim—

To be a blessing in this world of woe.
  "And thou shalt be a blessing"—'twas thy word.
This is the greatest gift thou canst bestow;
  Give it, I pray, to me, even me, O Lord.

A distinguished clergyman said, in reviewing his ministry at its close, that if he were to begin over again, he would preach more comfortingly. There always are in any company of people many who have sorrow, many at least who need uplifting and cheer. There is always a place for the comforter. And there are few who really understand the art of giving comfort. Many who seem to think they do and who are ready on every occasion to seek to console others who are in trouble fail in their efforts. Job said that the friends who came to him in his calamity and spoke to him so volubly concerning his afflictions were only miserable comforters. Those who have passed through experiences of trouble and have had their friends and neighbors come and sit with them and give them what they considered words of consolation have found oftentimes that they gave but small help. The burden of sorrow was not lighter after they had gone. No new light broke through the clouds upon those who sorrowed as they listened to the words of their friends. Their hearts were not quieted. They had learned no new song of joy.

It is worth our while to learn what true comfort is and how we can speak comfortably to others. No ministry is more needed or finds more frequent opportunity for exercise. No men, in any community, become so highly esteemed and loved while the years go by as those who are wise in giving comfort to others. The sad and weary turn to them for cheer and help. They always have a word to give which imparts strength.

Those who would be wise in comforting must be sympathetic. They must be patient with even the smallest griefs of others. It is not easy for the strong to sympathize with the weak. They cannot understand how little sufferings and troubles, such as those which seem so hard for others to bear, should really cause any distress. They are disposed to laugh at the complaints of those who seem to have so little of which to complain. No doubt there are many people who make altogether too much of very small cares and difficulties. They fret over every imaginable inconvenience or discomfort. No matter how well they are, they imagine they have many ills and can never talk to anyone without speaking of their ailments. They magnify the minutest sufferings and sorrows. It seems to be their natural disposition to think themselves particularly unfortunate. They find their chief pleasure apparently in having others commiserate them and sympathize with them.

It is not easy for persons of strong, wholesome spirit, used to looking with contempt on little trials and sufferings in their own lives, to have patience with those who are really weak and unable to endure, or with those who so magnify their little ills and troubles. But if the strong would become real helpers of the weak, they must learn to be patient with every phase of their weakness and to condescend to it. Indeed, weakness of this kind needs comfort that will cure it and transform it into manly strength. Sympathy, to be truly rich and adequate in its helpfulness, must be able to enter into every form of suffering, even the smallest, and to listen to every kind of complaining and discontent, to every fear and anxiety, however needless. It was thus that Christ condescended to all human frailty. He never treated anyone's trouble, however small, or anyone's worry, however groundless, with lightness, as if it were unimportant. He bade to come to Him all who were weary, receiving graciously everyone who came. He was infinitely strong, but His strength was infinitely gentle to the weakest. Nothing in this world is more beautiful than the sight of a strong man giving his strength to one who is weak, that he may help him also to grow strong.

Another class who find it hard to sympathize with sorrow are those who never have any sorrow of their own. They have been reared in sheltered homes, with love and tenderness all about them. They have never had a want unmet. They have never known hardship. They have never watched by the deathbed of a loved one, and there has been no break in their home circle. They have never had a bitter disappointment in their lives. What do they know of the experiences of suffering, of pain, of anguish, of struggle, of want, which comes to such multitudes in some form or other in life? These cannot sympathize with their fellows in their trials, in the things that make their lives so hard. They do not understand what these experiences mean.

An artist has painted a picture which represents the scene of the crucifixion after it was all over. The crowd is gone. The cross is empty. The thorn-crown is lying on a rock, and an angel is looking at it, with his finger touching one of its sharp thorns wonderingly. He is trying to learn what pain is. He had beheld the anguish of the Son of God on the cross, and could not understand the mystery. The angels cannot understand our suffering, for they have never suffered. Nor can men who have never had pain or sorrow understand these experiences in us. They may pity us when they see us enduring our sufferings, but they cannot sympathize with us. Before we can be true comforters of others, we must know in our own lives the meaning of the things that give us pain or distress. If we do not, we cannot help them by any words we may say to them. There is nothing in our experience to interpret to us what they are suffering. If we would help those who are in trouble, we must know what comfort really is. Many people do not. Many think that if they weep with those who weep they have comforted them. There is a measure of help in this. It does us good when we are suffering to know that another feels with us. It brings another life into fellowship with ours. We are not alone—somebody cares. This makes us stronger to endure. We can bear our pain better if a friend holds our hand.

This is the only way some people think of giving comfort. They sit down beside us and listen to our recital of grief. They let us tell it out in all its details. They encourage us to dwell on the painful incidents. They give expression to their pity, entering with us into our suffering as if it were their own. They dwell on the bitterness of our trial, emphasizing its sharpness and poignancy, thus adding to our pain and distress. Then they rise and go their way, leaving us just where they found us when they came in. They have shown their interest in us, their sympathy with us. But they have not given us the best comfort.

The word "comfort" is from a root that means to strengthen. In our modern use of the word we have almost dropped this thought of its original sense. But we would better recall it. To comfort is to strengthen. When we would give comfort to others, we are not merely to let them know we are their friends and are sorry for them. We are not just to try in some way to alleviate their pain. It is not enough that we in some measure relieve their distress. We are to seek to have them grow strong so that they can endure the trouble and rejoice in it.

This should be our aim in our ministry of comfort to others. We have not finished our work with them, therefore, until we have brought them some divine truth which will cast light on their sorrows, which will give a new meaning to it, which will inspire them with hope and courage.

The comforter needs gentleness, for a harsh word would make the sorrow deeper. He needs patience, for grief yields slowly even to most faithful love. He needs tenderness like a mother's. God says to His afflicted ones, "As one whom his mother comforteth, so will I comfort thee." A father's comfort is different from a mother's, and if we would be like God we must learn from mothers how to comfort. He who would give comfort must have faith. He must believe in God, must know Him, must be sure of God's love. Then he will know how to sustain with words him that is weary.

3

How Christ Comforts His Friends

Not so in haste, my heart!
Have faith in God and wait.
Although He lingers long,
He never comes too late.

He never comes too late,
He knoweth what is best;
Vex not thyself in vain;
Until He cometh, rest.

Until He cometh, rest,
Nor grudge the hours that roll;
The feet that wait for God
Are soonest at the goal.

Are soonest at the goal
That is not gained by speed;
Then hold thee still, my heart,
For I shall wait His lead.

BRADFORD TORREY

The little Twenty-third Psalm is the most familiar portion of the Bible and is most often read. It has comforted more sorrow than any other composition the world possesses. Next to it the fourteenth chapter of John is the best known of all the Scriptures. It is a chapter of comfort. How many tears it has dried! To how many sorrowing hearts has it brought peace! Its words were first spoken to a company of broken-hearted friends who thought they never could be comforted. It is well to study how Jesus, the truest comforter the world has ever known, consoled His friends.

Look at the way Jesus comforts His disciples. First of all, in that saddest of all hours, He bade them not to be troubled. Yet they were about to lose their best friend. How could they but be troubled? He comes to His friends today in their bereavement with the same word: "Let not your heart be troubled." This is not mere professional consolation. As Jesus saw it that night, there was no reason why the disciples should be troubled. As Jesus sees it, there is no reason why you should be troubled, even though you are watching your dearest friend pass away in what you call death. It is only the earth side of the event that you see, and it seems terrible to you. The friends of Jesus thought they were losing Him and forever. He had been a wonderful friend. He had a rich nature, a noble personality, power to love deeply, capacity for unselfish friendship, and was able to inspire them to all worthy life. The disciples thought they were about to lose all that.

You think you are losing all friendship's best in the departure of your friend. Yet Jesus, looking upon His disciples and looking upon you, bids you not to be troubled. Death is not an experience which harms the believing one who passes through it. The Christian mother who died this afternoon is not troubled and in sorrow where she is tonight. Dying has not disturbed her happiness—she never was happier than she is now. Leaving her children behind has not broken her heart nor filled her with distress and anxiety concerning them. As she looks upon them from her new point of view, on death's other side, there is no cause for grief or fear. They are in the divine care which is so loving, so wise, so gentle, and so far-reaching, that she has not a shadow of uncertainty regarding them. The children are in distress because they have lost their mother who has been so much to them. They cannot endure the thought of going on without their mother's love and tenderness, her guidance and shelter. Yet the Master says to them: "Do not be troubled." He means that if they understood all that has taken place as He understands it, if they knew what dying has meant to their mother, and what the divine love will mean to them in the days to come, they would not be troubled. What seems to them calamity would appear perfect good if they could see it from the heavenly side.

Jesus told His disciples what they should do. "Believe in God, believe also in me." They could not understand that hour why all was well, why nothing was going wrong, why good would be the outcome of all the things that then seemed so terrible. They could not see how their loss would become gain when it was all wrought out to the end, how what appeared the destruction of their hopes would prove to be the glorious fulfilling of those hopes. Yet they were to believe. That is, they were to commit all the broken things of their hearts that night into God's hands, trust Him, and have no fear, no anxiety, no doubt. They themselves could not bring good out of all this evil, but God could, and faith was committing the whole matter to Him.

"Believe in God." Jesus had taught them a new name for God. He was their Father. A whole world of love-thoughts was in that name. The very hairs of their heads were numbered. Not a sparrow could fall to the ground without their Father, which meant that the divine care took in all the events of their lives, all the smallest incidents of their affairs. We are to believe absolutely in the love of God, and trust Him though we cannot see. We do not need to understand, we do not have to know— the eternal God is caring for us and nothing can ever go wrong in His hands. "Believe in God."

"Believe also in me." They had been believing in Jesus Christ, thinking that He was their Messiah. "Thou art the Christ," Peter had confessed. But they were now in danger of losing faith in Him when they saw Him sent to the cross. He called them to keep their faith through the terrible hours just before them. We are always in danger of losing faith in Christ in time of great sorrow or of trouble that sweeps away our hopes. Again and again Christian people in grief and loss are heard asking, "Why does Christ let me suffer thus? If He loves me, how is it that He allows me to be thus troubled?" The trouble is that our vision is shortsighted. We are impatient and cannot wait. The going away of their Master left the disciples in despair. They thought they were losing Him. They did not know that His going away was part of His love for them, its highest expression, that none of the things about Him they had believed had failed. We need to continue to believe in Christ though everything seems to have gone from us. His way is always right. One comfort comes through abiding trust in Him.

Jesus went further with His disciples. He told them more. He told them where He was going and what His going away would mean to them. "In my Father's house are many mansions. I go to prepare a place for you." On this earth there is no place so sweet, so sacred, so heart-satisfying as home. It is a place of love. It is a place of confidence. We are sure of home's loved ones. We do not have to be on our guard after we enter our home doors. Home is a refuge in which we are safe from all danger, from injustice, from unkindness. Home is the place where hungry hearts are fed on love's bread. Mrs. Craik in one of her books has this fine picture:

> Oh, conceive the happiness to know someone dearer to you than your own self, some one breast into which you can pour every thought, every grief, every joy; one person who, if all the rest of the world were to calumniate or forsake you, would never wrong you by a harsh thought or an unjust word; who would cling to you the closer in sickness, in poverty, in care; who would sacrifice all things to you, and for whom you would sacrifice all; from whom, except by death, night or day, you never can be divided; whose smile is ever at your hearth; who has no tears while you are well and happy, and you love the same. Such is marriage if they who marry have hearts and souls to feel that there is no bond on earth so tender and so sublime.

This is a glimpse of what ideal home love is. We may find the picture partially realized in some earthly homes, but in the Father's house the realization will be perfect. The New Testament paints heaven in colors of dazzling splendor, its gates and walls and streets and gardens, all of the utmost brilliance, but no other description means so much to our hearts as that which the Master gives us in these three words—"My Father's house"—home. One writes:

> *Life changes all our thoughts of heaven:*
> *At first, we think of streets of gold,*
> *Of gates of pearl and dazzling light,*
> *Of shining wings and robes of white,*
> *And things all strange to mortal sight.*
> *But in the afterward of years*
> *It is a more familiar place;*
> *A home unhurt by sighs and tears,*
> *Where waiteth many a well-known face.*

With passing months it comes more near;
It grows more real day by day—
Not strange or cold, but very dear—
The glad home-land, not far away,
Where none are sick, or poor, or lone,
The place where we shall find our own.
And as we think of all we knew
Who there have met to part no more,
Our longing hearts desire home, too,
With all the strife and trouble o'er.

"My Father's house." That is the place where those we have lost awhile from our earthly homes, falling asleep in Jesus, are gathering. That is the place to which the angels have carried the babies and the old people, our mothers and fathers and friends who have passed out of our sight. That is the place where the broken Christian life of earth will find its perfectness, "My Father's house"—home. Is there any comfort sweeter than this in the sorrow of our parting from the dear ones who leave us in the experience which we call dying?

The Master said further in His comforting that He would come and receive His friends to Himself. Dying is no accident, therefore. It is merely Christ coming to receive us to Himself. Do not think something has gone wrong in the ways of God when you hear that a friend is dead. Your friend passed away the other night. You were expecting that he would be with you for many years. Has Christ any comfort? Yes, in all this experience one of God's plans of love is being fulfilled. The end is home, blessedness. One said, "Yes, but my friend was with me such a little while. I could almost wish I had not let my heart fasten its tendrils about the dear life, since so soon it was torn from me." Say it not. It is worthwhile to love and to let the heart pour out all its sweetness in loving, though it be for a day.

Because the rose must fade,
Shall I not love the rose?
Because the summer shade
Passes when winter blows,
Shall I not rest me there
In the cool air?

Because the sunset sky
  Makes music in my soul,
Only to fail and die,
  Shall I not take the whole
Of beauty that it gives
  While yet it lives?

Ah, yes, because the rose
  Doth fade like sunset skies;
Because rude winter blows
  All bare, and music dies—
Therefore, now is to me
Eternity.

4

Be of Good Cheer

Spin cheerfully,
   Not tearfully,
Though wearily you plod;
   Spin carefully,
   Spin prayerfully,
But leave the thread with God

The shuttles of His purpose move
   To carry out His own design;
   Seek not too soon to disapprove
   His work, nor yet assign
Dark motives, when, with silent tread,
   You view each somber fold;
For lo! within each darker thread
   There twines a thread of gold.

   Spin cheerfully,
   Not tearfully,
He knows the way you plod;
   Spin carefully,
   Spin prayerfully,
But leave the thread with God.

Canadian Home Journal

In the story of his voyage and shipwreck, we find Paul not only cheerful himself, but a giver of cheer to others. The storm had grown fiercer and fiercer. It had simply laid hold of the ship, torn it out of the hands of the officers and seamen, and was forcibly bearing along in its teeth. There was nobody in command. The record says, "After no long time there beat down from the shore a tempestuous wind, which is called Euraquilo; and when the ship was caught and could not face the wind, we gave way to it and were driven." No wonder the long hope of being saved was gone. The people on the ship were in despair.

Then came Paul with his inspiring word, "Be of good cheer." That was a splendid message, and it was not a mere idle or empty word. Some people's optimism has no basis. Some people's "Don't worry" is only meaningless talk. But when Paul said, "Be of good cheer," he had reasons for saying it. "I believe God," he said. And it was not an empty faith he cherished. God had sent an angel to him that night, assuring him of deliverance from the storm, both for himself and for all on the ship. So his words had power over the panic-stricken men on the ship. He besought them to take some food. They had been so terrified that they had eaten almost nothing for fourteen days. He urged them now to eat, and said that not a hair should perish from the head of them. Then, to encourage them by example, he himself took bread, and having thanked God before them all, he broke the bread and began to eat. Then they were all of good cheer, and took some food.

Note how the one man lifted up a despairing company of nearly three hundred men, and gave them cheer. There is no mission of faith and love that is more important and Christlike than that of being encouragers, of giving cheer. Everyone needs cheer at some time. Life is hard for many people—for some it is hard at all times. Some are always bending under heavy burdens. Some are in storm and darkness many a night. I am not justifying worry. A child of God never should worry. Paul said, "Be anxious for nothing." Jesus Himself said, "Be not anxious for tomorrow." Discouragement is unbelief, and unbelief is sin. None who love God should ever worry.

Yet there are many who have burdens, cares, sorrows, and trials, who always need encouragement, and to whom we should ever be saying, "Be of good cheer." There is scarcely a person you will meet today or tomorrow who will not be helped on the journey by the hearty word of encouragement which you can so easily give. Jesus told His disciples, when He sent them out to preach, not to stop to salute anyone by the way. Their mission was urgent, and there was no time to lose in mere courtesies. He did not mean, however, to forbid us to show kindness even on our busiest days, or to speak a word to the lowly and suffering ones we meet on the way even when we are most hurried.

The example of Paul on this ship is full of beautiful and inspiring meaning. We cannot know what those two hundred and seventy-six men would have done if it had not been for his earnest and faithful cheer. There was no other person to say a brave word to them. Think how he lifted them up and made their hearts strong. Let us take the lesson. Tomorrow we may be in some panic, may find ourselves in a home of distress, or in the presence of men who are discouraged or cast down. Even if there should be no special trouble, we shall meet people whose hands hang down, whose knees are feeble, to whom no one is giving cheer.

Have you ever noticed how many people were perpetual discouragers? They make life harder for every person they meet. They tell you you do not look well. They remind you of your paleness or sallowness of complexion. If you are sick and they call to see you, they talk ominously of your condition. They seem to think you like that kind of sympathy. When you have had some sorrow or trouble, they appear to think it kind to dwell upon its painful features. They talk pessimistically about your affairs, about religion, about everything. It is hard to speak patiently of this miserable habit of discouraging others, which is so very common. Thousands of people who love you and mean well by you unintentionally become hinderers of your progress, dishearteners, and make life harder for you.

They tell us in mountain regions that avalanches are oftentimes hanging poised so delicately on the crags that even the reverberation of a whisper on the air may cause them to fall with ruinous effect upon the homes and villages in the valleys. The guides caution tourists at certain points not to speak or sing, lest they cause disaster. There are human lives bearing such burdens of sorrow and trouble that one disheartening word may bring them to despair. We should learn never to give discouragement. It is a crime against humanity. Beware that you never speak disheart-eningly to anyone. Only love can save the world. No matter how the person may have sinned, only gentleness can save him.

A writer in *The Spectator* makes the suggestion that for men like himself some kind of league should be formed by which those who join should bind themselves to say some kind word or do some kind act daily. The editor suggests, however, that only one kindness daily is too formal, and altogether too meager. There is need for kindness not once a day to one person, but a thousand times a day to a thousand persons. There is need for cheer continually. If you can truly say, "I believe God," you cannot but be an encourager. God Himself is a God of cheer. Religion is simply love and kindness. Washington Gladden says that "religion is friendship—friendship first with the great Companion, on the Godward side. Then on the manward side the same is true." To be friends with everybody; to fill every human relation with the spirit of friendship; is there anything more than this that the wisest and best of men can hope to do?

So let us seek to make cheer for others wherever we are. You cannot possibly estimate the lifting power of such a life as Paul's, moving among men. You cannot possibly estimate the lifting power of your own life in the community where you dwell. Let us live so that everyone may go away from us heartened and brave. Let our message ever be, "Be of good cheer, for I believe God."

> *Let us be kind;*
> *The way is long and lonely,*
> *And human hearts are asking for this blessing only—*
> > *That we be kind.*
> *We cannot know the grief that men may borrow,*
> *We cannot see the souls storm-swept by sorrow,*
> *But love can shine upon the way today, tomorrow—*
> > *Let us be kind.*
> *Let us be kind;*
> *This is a wealth that has no measure,*
> *This is of heaven and earth the highest treasure—*
> > *Let us be kind.*
> *A tender word, a smile of love in meeting,*
> *A song of hope and victory to those retreating,*
> *A glimpse of God and brotherhood while life is fleeting—*
> > *Let us be kind.*

5

Does God Care?

In the bitter waves of woe,
Beaten and tossed about
By the sullen winds that blow
From the desolate shores of doubt
Where the anchors that faith has cast
Are dragging in the gale,
I am quietly holding fast
To the things that cannot fail.

And fierce though the fiends may fight,
And long though the angels hide,
I know that truth and right
Have the universe on their side;
And that somewhere beyond the stars
Is a love that is better than fate.
When the night unlocks her bars
I shall see Him—and I will wait.

WASHINGTON GLADDEN

About the beginning of this century an unbeliever was reported to have said that the mission of the twentieth century would be to discover God, and when God should be discovered, it would be found that He does not

187

care. It would be a bitter sorrow for the world if this prophecy were to come true. Into countless homes and hearts it would bring the darkness of despair.

The secret of hope in believing souls everywhere is that God does care. This is the one great truth that God has been striving through all the generations to have men believe. This is the whole gospel of redemption. The Bible presents it on its every page. It is the message that Christ came into the world to declare—that God loves all men, every man. The world's condemning unbelief has always been its refusal to believe that God cares.

But does God really care? Is there anywhere an ear that hears the world's cries of pain and gives attention to them? Is there anywhere a heart that is touched by the world's sorrows, that feels with those who suffer, and that desires to give help and comfort, care? The veriest stranger when he is passing along the street and sees one suffering, in pain or distress, cares, pities him. A tender-hearted man feels even with a beast, or a bird that has been hurt. Some great calamity occurs—the destruction of a city by an earthquake, a volcanic eruption pouring its lava streams over homes and villages, an explosion in a colliery burying hundreds of miners, and a wave of pain sweeps over the world. Human hearts are sensitive to every shade of need and experience in others. When we see crape on a door, telling us that there is a death within, that a family is mourning, though they be utter strangers to us, our hearts are touched, we walk softly, laughter is hushed, loud speech is restrained, we speak more quietly. We care. Is God less compassionate than men are?

Someone tells us that God's care is general, not individual. All things in creation and providence are planned for the good of the race. The movements of the earth are so guided as to bring day and night, the seasons in their order, cold and heat, winds and tides and all the changes which bring health, comfort, and fruitfulness. God is good to all. "He maketh His sun to rise on the evil and the good, and sendeth rain on the just and the unjust." Nature is ready with gentle service in all its attributes and forces. But it is the same to all. There is no love in all of this, no care for any individual, no discrimination. The providence of God is kindly, benevolent, helpful, but is no more so to the weak than to the strong, to the sick than to the well, to the distressed and brokenhearted than to the happy and rejoicing. There seems to be no special divine tenderness shown among the homes of a town to a home where there is suffering, or where there is great need or bitter sorrow. Life appears no more kindly to the blind man, to the cripple, to the helpless, to the bedridden, than to those who have the use of all their powers and faculties and are well and strong.

Is there ever in God any discrimination? Does He care for us as we care for each other? Does He give personal thought to any of us—to you, to me—according to our condition? Does pain or trouble in us cause pity in His heart? Does God care? Does He see the individual in the crowd? When you are passing through some great trouble, enduring pain or adversity, does God know it and does He care? Does He have any thought or feeling for you different from that which He has for the person living in the house next to yours who has no trouble, no suffering?

We know how it is with our human friends. Love discriminates. Its interest in us is sympathetic and varies with our condition and our need. When we are happy, without painful condition, our friends love us, but feel no anxiety concerning us. Tomorrow we are sick or are suffering from some painful accident, or enduring some loss. Then they love us no more than before, but their hearts are rent with sympathy. That is what it means to care. Is there any such experience as this in God? When we suffer does He suffer too? Does He know that we are in any particular need, and is His feeling toward us affected by our experience? A mother was speaking to a trusted friend about her daughter. The child had had a bitter sorrow, a sore disappointment. She had not spoken of it to her mother, but was enduring it herself, bravely and quietly, trying to be strong and cheerful. Yet the mother knew just what her daughter was passing through. Her love for her child entered into and shared all the child's experiences. The mother cared.

Is there ever anything like this in the heart of God as He looks upon His children and knows that they are suffering? In one of the psalms the poet says, "I am poor and needy; yet the Lord thinketh upon me." There was wonderful comfort in this assurance. For a man, one man, in the great world of millions—poor, needy, surrounded by enemies and dangers, and with no human friend or helper, to be able to say, "Yet the Lord thinketh upon me," was to find marvelous strength. But was the needy and beleaguered soul justified in its confidence? Was it indeed true that the great God in heaven thought upon His servant on the earth in his loneliness and suffering? Or was it only a fancied assurance, with which to comfort himself? Did God really care for him? And does God care for us and think upon us when we are poor and needy?

When we turn to the Bible, we find on every page the revelation that God does care. The Old Testament is full of luminous illustrations of the truth. A great crime has been committed, a brother slain by a brother, and God cares. A woman is in distress because she has been cast out; heaven cares. "The Lord hath heard affliction," was the message sent to comfort her. The whole Bible story shines with records of like divine care. The Psalms likewise are full of assurances of God's personal interest in men. Christ teaches the same truth. He speaks over and over of the Father's thought and care. He told His disciples that God clothes the grass-blades and the lilies, amid all His care of the worlds finds time to attend to the feeding of the birds, and in all the events of the universe notes the fall of a little sparrow. He assured them further that the very hairs of their heads are all numbered, meaning that God personally cares for the minutest affairs of our lives.

Not only did Christ teach that God cares for His children, but that He cares for them as individuals. His love is not merely a diffused kindly sentiment of interest in the whole human family, but it is personal and individual as the love of a mother for each one of her children. The Shepherd calleth His sheep by name. Paul took the love of Christ to himself as if he were the only one Christ loved. "He loved me, and gave Himself up for me."

God's love is personal. His heart lays hold upon each life. He cares for you, for me. He enters into all our individual experiences. If we suffer, He suffers. In a remarkable passage in the Old Testament, the writer, speaking of the love of God for His people, says, "In all their affliction He was afflicted, and the angel of His presence saved them; in His love and in His pity He redeemed them; and He bare them, and carried them all the days of old." How could the care of God for His children be expressed in a plainer or more positive way? In their afflictions He was afflicted. When they suffered He suffered. In their sorrows He sorrowed. We know how Jesus entered into all the experiences of His disciples. Their lives were His. It is the same today. In heaven He is touched with the feeling of His people's infirmities. If you are weak, the burden of your weakness presses upon Him. If you are hurt, the hurt is felt by Him. If you are wronged, He endures the wrong. There is no experience of your life that He does not share. Whatever your need, your trial, your perplexity, your struggle may be, you may be sure that He knows and cares, and that when you come to Him with it He will take time amid all His infinite affairs to help you as if He had nothing else in all the world to do.

> *"Among so many, can He care?*
> *Can special love be everywhere?"*
> *I asked, My soul bethought itself of this—*
> *"In just that very place of His*
> *Where He hath put and keepeth you,*
> *God hath no other thing to do."*

God cares. His love for each one of us is so deep, so personal, so tender, that He shares our every pain, every distress, every struggle. "Like as a father pitieth his children, so the Lord pitieth them that fear Him." God is our Father, and His care is gentler than a human father's as His love exceeds human love. Much human care has no power to help, but when God cares He helps omnipotently. Jesus said that when His friends would leave Him alone, yet He would not be alone—"because the Father is with me." When human friendship comes not with any relief, then God will come. When no one in all the world cares, then God cares.

6

"You Will Not Mind the Roughness"

Grumble? No. What's the good?
If it availed, I would;
But it doesn't a bit—
Not it.

Laugh? Yes; why not?
'Tis better than crying a lot;
We were made to be glad,
Not sad.

Sing? Why, yes, to be sure.
We shall better endure
If the heart's full of song
All day long.

Love? Yes, unceasingly,
Ever increasingly;
Friends' burdens bearing
Their sorrows sharing;

Their happiness making,
For pattern taking
The One above,
Who is love—Motherhood.

Sometimes there is inscrutable mystery in the hard experiences through which good people are led. A few years ago a happy young couple came from the marriage altar, full of hope and joy. Their home was bright with love. A year later a baby came and was welcomed with great gladness. From the beginning, however, the little one was a sufferer. She was taken to one of the best physicians in the land. After careful examination, his decision was that her condition is absolutely hopeless. Till that moment the mother had still hoped that her child might sometime be cured. Now she understands that how ever long she may live, she will never be any better.

"What shall I do?" was the mother's question when a friend listened to the story of the visit to the great doctor. "What can I do? How can God help me?"

What comfort can we give to such mothers as this? First, we can assure them that their child is quite as dear to God as if she were strong and bright. The weakest and most helpless are nearest to Him. God is like a mother in His tenderness and in His yearning love for those who are suffering. This child has His gentlest sympathy. Then someday, too, she will be well. Her condition is only for earth. Heaven is the place where earth's arrested growths will reach perfection, where earth's blighted things will blossom into full beauty. This child will not be sick, nor blind, nor imperfect there. The hopelessness of her condition is only for the present life. Someday the mother's dreams of beauty for her, not realized here, will all be fulfilled, and her prayer for her child's health will be answered.

But meanwhile? Yes, it is hard to look upon the child's condition, so pathetic, so pitiful, and to remember the great doctor's words, "Absolutely hopeless!" Is there any comfort for this condition? Can this mother say that God is leading her in the path of life? Is this experience of suffering part of that path? Does God know about the long struggle of this mother? Does He know what the doctor said? Yes, He knows all. Has He then no power to do anything? Yes, He has all power. Why, then, does He not cure this child?

We may not try to answer. We do not know God's reasons. Yet we know it is all right. What good can possibly come from this child's condition and from the continuation of this painful condition year after year? We do not know. Perhaps it is that the child may be prepared for a mission in glory which shall surpass in splendor the mission of any child that is well and joyous here. Or perhaps it is for the sake of the mother and father, who are being led through these years of anguish, disappointment, and sorrow. Many people suffer for others' sakes, and we know at least that these parents are receiving a training in unselfishness, in gentleness, in patience, in trust. Perhaps this painful experience in their child is to make them richer-hearted. The disciples asked the Master for whose sin it was, the blind man's or his parents', that the man was born blind. "Neither; no one's sin," Jesus replied, "but that the works of God might be done in this man." May it not be that this child's suffering finds its justification in the ministry of love it has called out in the father and mother? They are being prepared for a blessed service to other suffering ones. Perhaps in the other life they will learn that they owe to their child's suffering much of the beauty of Christ that will then be theirs.

In one of the lace shops of Brussels there are certain rooms devoted to the spinning of the finest and most delicate lace patterns. The rooms are left altogether dark save for the light that comes from one very small window. There is only one spinner in each room, and he sits where a narrow stream of light falls from the window directly upon the threads he is weaving. "Thus," says the guide, "do we secure our choicest products. The lace is always more delicately and beautifully woven when the worker himself sits in the dark and only his pattern is in the light."

May it not be the same with us in our weaving? Sometimes we must work in the dark. We cannot see or understand what we are doing. We cannot discover any possible good in our painful experience. Yet, if only we are faithful and fail not, we shall someday learn that the most exquisite work of our lives was done in those very days. Let us never be afraid, however great our sufferings, however dark life is. Let us go on in faith and love, never doubting, not even asking why, bearing our pain and learning to sing while we suffer. God is watching, and He will bring good and beauty out of all of our suffering.

We must remember that it is "the path of life" that God is showing us. He never leads us in any other path. If we are promoted to go in some evil way, we may be sure it is not God's way for us. He leads us only in paths of life. They may be steep and rough, but the end will be blessed and glorious, and in our joy we will forget the briers and thorns on the way.

> Oh, you will not mind the roughness nor the steepness
>   of the way,
> Nor the chill, unrested morning, nor the searness of
>   the day;
> And you will not take a turning to the left or to
>   the right,
> But go straight ahead, nor tremble at the coming
>   of the night,
>   For the road leads home.

There are days when you do not know what to do. You have perplexities, doubts, uncertainties. You lie awake half the night wondering what you ought to do. Something has gone wrong in your affairs, in your relations with a friend, in your home life. Or one near to you is suffering and you want to help, but you do not know what to do. Your days are full of questions. Instead of vexing yourself, just go to Him who is infinitely wise and say, "Show me the path," and He will.

There is something else. It is told of Saint Wenceslaus, king of Bohemia, that he was one night going to prayer in a distant church, barefoot, over the snow and ice, and his servant, Podavivus, following him, imitating his master's devotion, grew faint. "Follow me," said the king; "set thy feet in the prints of mine." That is what our Master says when we grow weary in the hard way, when the thorns pierce our feet, or when the path grows rough or steep: "Follow me. Put your feet into my shoe-prints. It is but a little way home."

7

"Why Does No One Ever See God?"

Lonely! And what of that?
Some must be lonely; 'tis not given to all
To feel a heart responsive rise and fall—
To blend another life into its own;
Work may be done in loneliness; work on!

Dark! Well, and what of that?
Didst fondly dream the sun would never set?
Dost fear to lose thy way? Take courage yet;
Learn thou to walk by faith and not by sight;
Thy steps will guided be, and guided right.

There are many sincere Christians who are longing for clearer revealings of God. An earnest young Christian wrote to her pastor, "I find myself ever asking, as I read the New Testament, 'These things are very beautiful, but do we know that they are true?'" Several years since a writer told of two girls who were overheard one evening talking as if in perplexity, and one of them said, "Yes, but why has no one ever seen God?" This was all that was heard of the conversation, but that single sentence revealed the

197

questioner's state of mind. Evidently she had been talking about the apparent unreality of spiritual things. Why had nobody ever seen God? She had heard a great deal about God, about His love, His care, His interest in human lives, His kindness. But she had never had a glimpse of Him. How could she know that all she had heard about Him was true? How could she know that the things of Christian faith and hope were real?

Such questions will arise with all who think. Does God indeed love me? If He does, why must I suffer so? If He does, how can I explain all the accidents, calamities, and troubles of life? It is not surprising if sometimes we cannot understand the mysteries of Christian faith. All of life is full of things we cannot comprehend. Can you understand how, on the bushes in your garden, which in March were bare and briery, there are coming masses of glorious roses? In the most common things there is mystery. A great botanist said that there was enough mystery in a handful of moss to give one a lifetime's study. There really are but few things we can understand. How do your eyes see? How do your ears hear? How does your mind think? Shall we refuse to believe these things because we cannot explain them?

We have read how the cry of the wireless went out from the wrecked ship and was heard far and wide over the sea—a prayer of distress—and how help came swiftly. No one doubts this pathetic experience of the sea. Why, then, should we doubt that when a mother sat by her suffering child the other night and pleaded with God, her prayer reached the ears of her Heavenly Father? Why do we question that God loves us, when we believe that our human friends love us? You cannot see the love in your friend's heart anymore than you can see the love in God's heart. You say that your friend is true, is patient, is kind, that he is a tower of strength to you, but you cannot see these qualities in him. Your friend is much out of your sight, and you cannot set spies on him to know that he is always faithful. Yet you never doubt him. How can you not in like manner believe in the love of God, which you cannot see?

A sorrow breaks in upon you. You cannot understand it. We would be far happier sometimes if we did not try to understand things. Sir Robertson Nicoll says:

> There are some very devout people who know far too much. They can explain the whole secret and purpose of pain, evil, and death in the world. They prate about the mystery of things as if they were God's spies. It is far

humbler and more Christian to admit that we do not fully discern a reason and method in this long, slow tragedy of human existence.

But really God does show Himself to us, and we do see Him more often than we think. There is a picture of Augustine and his mother which represents them looking up to heaven with deep earnestness and longing. One is saying, "If God would only speak to us!" The other replies, "Perhaps He is speaking to us, and we do not hear His voice!" Philip said to Jesus, "Lord, show us the Father"; and have you noticed what Jesus said to him in reply? "Have I been so long time with you, and hast thou not known me? He that hath seen me hath seen the Father." What Philip had in mind when he said, "Show us the Father," was some outshining of majesty and splendor, a theophany, a transfiguration. That was the way he thought God must appear. When Jesus said, "He that hath seen me hath seen the Father," He referred to His common daily life with His disciples, not to His miracles. Only a small proportion of the things Jesus did were unusual, supernatural. Ninety-nine hundredths of His acts were simple, common things that did not need deity to perform. He wrought only one recorded miracle in the Bethany home, but in His frequent visits, sitting with the family by the hearth, or at the table, talking with them in the evening, walking with them in the garden, showing them the gentle things of friendship—there were a thousand kindly words and acts which made His name forever sacred to them.

It was so in all Christ's life. There were a few miracles, showing divine power; there were countless revealings of gentleness, sympathy, thoughtfulness, encouragement, which were as full of God as the miracles. It was chiefly to this part of His life that Jesus referred when He said to Philip, "He that hath seen me hath seen the Father." His miracles awed them. Mary could not have sat at His feet and listened calmly if He had appeared transfigured. John could not have leaned on His breast restfully and quietly if supernatural glory had been shining in His face. God is love, and wherever there is love, God is revealing Himself. Jesus showed the disciples the Father in all the sweetness and compassion that they saw in Him continually.

Do we not see Him in like ways? Does He not reveal Himself to us in a thousand familiar things that we do not think of at all as divine revealings? A writer says that most men are religious when they look upon the faces of their dead babies. The materialism which at other times infects them with doubts of God and immortality drops from them in this hushed hour.

> *There's a narrow ridge in the graveyard*
> *Would scarce stay a child in his race;*
> *But to me and my thought it is wider*
> *Than the star-sown vague of Space.*

People see God only in the unusual. "If we could see miracles," they say, "we would believe." But the common things are likewise full of God. Moses saw God in one bush that burned and was not consumed. Yet God is as real in every bush in the woods for those who have eyes to see as He was in a special way in that little acacia at Horeb.

Have you never seen God? If you think of God as only burning majesty, shining glory, you will answer, "No, I never saw God." But splendor, Sinai clouds, and flaming fires are not God. You have seen God a thousand times in love, in peace, in goodness, in comfort. You see Him daily in providential care, in the sweet things of your home, in friendships, in the beauty of little children. You have been receiving blessings all of your life in manifold ways. Do not call it chance, luck, or good fortune. The heart-hungry girl asked, "Why has no one ever seen God?" Yet she had seen God every day, every hour of her life, in the goodness and mercy which had followed her from her infancy.

You have seen God a thousand times. You were in danger, and there came a mysterious protection which sheltered you from harm. You called it chance: it was God. You had a great sorrow which you thought you could not possibly endure, and there came into your heart a strange, sweet comfort. You thought a friend brought it: but God sent the friend. There was a tangle in your affairs which seemed about to wreck everything, and then in an inexplicable way it was all straightened out by invisible hands. The hands were God's. Your years have been full of wonderful providences, strange guidances, gentle comforts, answered prayers, sweet friendships, surprises of goodness, help, and care. All of your life you have been seeing God. Do not question it, but rejoice in the vision, that you may see Him still more.

8

The One Who Stands By

Let nothing disturb thee,
Nothing affright thee;
All things are passing;
God never changeth;
Patient endurance
Attaineth to all things;
Who God possesseth
In nothing is wanting.
Alone God sufficeth.

Jesus spoke to His disciples of the Holy Spirit as the Paraclete. The word used in our translation is "Comforter."

We think of a comforter as one who gives consolation in trouble. There is much sorrow in the world, and there is always need of those who understand the art of comforting. There is constant need for true comforters. Barnabas is called, in the King James Version of the Bible, a "son of consolation." No doubt he was a sunshiny man. No other one can be a consoler. When Barnabas went into a sickroom, we are quite sure his presence was a benediction. It is a great thing to be a son or daughter of consolation. Christ Himself was a wonderful comforter. The Holy Spirit is a comforter. He brings the gentleness and healing of divine love to hurt hearts.

But the best scholars agree that "comforter" is not the word which most adequately gives the sense of the original word which our Lord used. It is "Paraclete." It is used only a few times and only by John. In the Fourth Gospel it is translated "Comforter." Then, in John's First Epistle, it is translated "Advocate." "Advocate" is perhaps the more accurate translation—not merely a comforter who consoles us in trouble and makes us stronger to endure sorrow, but one who stands for us. The word "advocate" means one who stands by; strictly, one called to the side of another.

The thought "stands by" is very suggestive. This is one of the best definitions of a friends. He must be one who always stands by. He may not always be close to you, always manifesting affection in some practical way, always speaking words of cheer. He may be miles away in space, but you know that he is always true to you, your real friend, wherever he may be. He always stands by you. He may not be able to do many things for you. Indeed, it is but little that a friend, even your best friend, really can do at any time for you. He cannot lift away your load. Each one must bear his own burden, meet his own life's questions, make his own decisions, endure his own troubles, fight his own battles, accept his own responsibilities. The office of a friend is not to make life easy for you.

But he always stands by you. If ever you need him in any way and turn to him, he will not fail you nor disappoint you. If you do not see him for years, nor even hear from him, and if you then should go to him with some appeal, you will find him unchanged, the same staunch, strong, faithful friend as always. Though your circumstances have changed, from wealth to poverty, from popular favor to obscurity, from strength to weakness, still your friend is the same, stands by you as he did before, meets you with the old cordiality, the old kindness, the old helpfulness. Your friend is one who stands by you through everything. Such a friend is the Holy Spirit.

Jesus said the Father would give "another Comforter," that is, one like Himself. He was an advocate for His disciples, who always stood by them, their comrade, their defender, their shelter in danger. His friendship was unchanged through the years. His disciples failed Him, grieved Him, disappointed Him, but when they came back to Him they found Him the same, waiting to receive them.

Jesus said they would receive another comforter when He was gone. He was not really going away from them. They would not see any face, would not feel any hand, but He would be there, as He always had been—ever standing by. They would lose nothing by His going away. In the Paraclete He would still be with them and would still be their comforter, their comrade. Think what it was to them to have Jesus for a personal friend. There never was such another friend. Think of His gentleness, His tenderness, His sympathy, His kindness, the inspiration of His love. Think of the shelter He was to them, the strength, the encouragement. Then remember what He said—that the Holy Spirit would be "another Comforter," one like Himself, and that it would be more to them to have the Spirit for their friend than if Jesus had stayed with them. He is everything to us which Jesus was to His personal friends. He is our Advocate. He always stands by, and for us.

We speak of the love of the Father. We are His children. He comforts us with His wonderful tenderness. We talk and sing of the love of Christ. We do not speak or sing so much of the love of the Spirit. Yet the Spirit's love is just as wonderful as the Father's or the Son's. For one thing, He loves us enough to come and live in our hearts. Does that seem a little thing? We speak a great deal, especially at Christmas time, of the condescension of the eternal Son of God in coming to earth, to be born in a stable and cradled in a manger. Is it a less wonderful condescension for the Holy Spirit to make your heart His home, to be born there, to live there as your Guest? Think what a place a human heart is. Think of the unholy thoughts and desires, the impure things, the unlovingness, the jealousy, the bitterness, the hate, all the sin of our hearts. Then think of the love of the Spirit that makes Him willing to live in such a place in order to cleanse us and make us good and holy.

The love of the Spirit is shown in His wondrous patience with us in all our sinfulness, while He lives in us and deals with us in the culturing of our Christian lives. We speak of the patient love of Christ with His disciples the three years He was with them, having them in His family, at His table, enduring their ignorance, their dullness, their narrowness, their petty strife, their unfaithfulness. It was a marvelous love that never grew weary of them, that loved on in spite of all that so tried His love, and endured the hate of men, their plottings, their treacheries. We never can understand the depth of the love of the Holy Spirit in what He suffers in His work with us.

A young Christian had a friend whom she had long loved deeply. She had regarded this friend as like an angel in the truth and beauty of her life. She never had had a shadow of doubt concerning her. Then she learned that this girl had been leading a double life for years. The discovery appalled her. At first she refused to believe it, but the evidence was so unmistakable that she could not but believe it, and it almost killed her. She wrote: "I understand now a little of the bitter sorrow of my Savior in Gethsemane, as He drank the cup of His people's sins." If a human friend can be broken-hearted over the sin of a friend, how the Holy Spirit must suffer in His cherishing of us, in His wondrous brooding over us! How He must grieve when we fall into sin!

After Bereavement—What?

*I lift my head and walk my ways
  Before the world without a tear,
And bravely unto those I meet
  I smile a message of good cheer;
I give my lips to laugh and song,
  And somehow get me through each day;
But oh, the tremble in my heart
  Since she has gone away!*

*Her feet had known the stinging thorns,
  Her eyes the blistering tears;
Bent were her shoulders with the weight
  And sorrow of the years;
The lines were deep upon her brow,
  Her hair was thin and gray;
And oh, the tremble in my heart
  Since she has gone away!*

*I am not sorry; I am glad;
  I would not have her here again;
God gave her strength life's bitter cup
  Unto the bitterest dreg to drain;*

I will not have less strength than she,
I proudly tread my stony way;
But oh, the tremble in my heart
Since she has gone away!

There is something in bereavement which makes it mean a great deal in a woman's life. It is a sore disappointment. Dreams of love's happiness are shattered. The beauty which had only begun to be realized in her home, in her wedded joy, in her social life, in the development of her plans and hopes is suddenly left to wither. Very great is the sorrow when one of two lovers is taken and the other left. Widowhood is very desolate and lonely. When she has been a wife only a brief time, there is special loneliness in her case.

The experience is particularly perplexing and trying. For one thing, she has probably had no training in the affairs of life. She has never learned self-reliance. Her husband, in the gentleness of his manly love, has sought to spare her from everything hard and rough. He has never permitted her even to know of the struggles and perplexities of his daily business life. He has sought to carry home in the evening only the bright things, the cheerful things, with not a breath of anything that would give pain. He has not permitted his wife to know the smallest things of business. She had no bank account. She did not know how to write a check. She never knew how much money she might properly spend in a month. She had no more idea of business than a child. The day after her husband's funeral she saw herself utterly unprepared for the duties and responsibilities which she found suddenly devolved upon her.

Just how shall she meet her perplexities? She is a Christian. She knows that her husband was God's child, and she is comforted by the thought that he is not dead, but has only passed into the immortal life. She is comforted also in her own grief by the truth of the divine love, that her sorrow was no accident, that her bereavement was not the plan of God to break up the goodness and beauty of her life, that nothing has really gone wrong in the plan of Christ for her. But the question presses itself upon her mind—I am sure it has done so a thousand times—"How am I to go on in this broken life of mine? What am I to do in my shattering and bereavement?" Her life is not finished. She is only a girl in years.

She may live—she probably will live—forty years or more. What does Christ want her to do with her life? What does He want her to do with the broken dreams that lie shattered about her feet?

These questions and questions like these are coming to her every day and every night. This is the deeper meaning of her sorrow. Sometimes women in her position see no brightness, find no hope, think the story all written out to the finish, their dream only shattered, and sink away into despair. But that is not the way to meet a sorrow like this. The story of her life is not finished. God's plan for her was not spoiled when her sorrow came and interrupted everything, leaving her in darkness. The sorrow was only an accident in the plan. It was not a surprise to God, and His plan for her life runs on to the end of her years. What the remainder of the plan is she does not know for the present. She must not know. It is not best that she should know. Her faith must not fail, she must not despair. She must go on in trust and confidence.

What then is her part? First, faith in Christ. Believe that all these broken things are in His hands. Let her remember what He said after the miracle of the loaves—"Gather up the broken pieces that remain, that nothing be lost." That is what He is saying to her today. Let her gather up the broken pieces from this miracle of love and happiness. Let nothing she has had these days of joy, of blessing, of experience, be lost. Let her keep all the fragments.

The next thing is for her to recommit her life, with its grief, its disappointments, its desolation, its broken things, all to Christ. She must not herself undertake to rebuild it. She must not make plans of her own for the years to come. She never needed Christ more than she needs Him now, and will need Him in the days and the months before her. She must let Him lead her, let Him plan for her, mark out the way. He must build the life for her. He must have much of the love she has to give.

Bereavement is common. No family long misses a break in its circle. Let the break be met with courage! Courage and unselfishness are developed by great sorrow or suffering. In times of overwhelming danger and disaster people rise to unusual heroism. George Kennan tells of the remarkable exhibition of courage and generous characteristics shown by the people of San Francisco during the great earthquake and fire. The behavior of the population after the disaster impressed those who witnessed it. One thoughtful and undemonstrative man said he was glad he had lived to see the things that happened the first ten days after the great catastrophe. Those days were the best and most inspiring, he said, of all his life. Religious people talked about the kingdom of heaven.

> Cowardice, selfishness, greed, and all the baser emotions and impulses of human character practically disappeared in the tremendous strain of that experience, and courage, fortitude, sympathy, generosity, and unbounded self-sacrifice took their places. Men became and for a short time continued to be all that we may suppose the Creator intended them to be, and it was a splendid and inspiring thing to witness.

A like display of the finer and nobler qualities of human nature was witnessed that terrible night on the sea when the Titanic went down. The majority of the passengers and crew behaved with the most remarkable courage and the most noble unselfishness.

Let God—through your bereavement—bring out the finer and nobler qualities in you.

10

Comfort through Personal Helpfulness

*"When I have time so many things I'll do
To make life happier and more fair
For those whose lives are crowded now with care;
I'll help to lift them from their low despair—
        When I have time!*

*"When I have time the friend I love so well
Shall know no more these weary toiling days;
I'll lead her feet in pleasant paths always,
And cheer her heart with words of sweetest praise—
        When I have time!"*

*When you have time the friend you hold so dear
May be beyond the reach of all your sweet intent;
May never know that you so kindly meant
To fill her life with sweet content—
        When you have time!*

*Now is the time! Ah, friend, no longer wait
To scatter loving smiles and words of cheer*

209

To those around whose lives are now so dear;
They may not need you in the coming year—
Now is the time!

Every true Christian desires to be helpful. He longs to make his life a blessing to as many people as possible. He wishes to make the world better, his neighborhood brighter and sweeter, every life he touches, in even casual associations, somewhat more beautiful. Just how we must live if our lives would reach this ideal is worthy of our thought.

We cannot come upon this kind of a life accidentally. We do not drift into a place and condition of great usefulness. Every man has his secret, something that is the keynote of his life. The secret of personal helpfulness is love in the heart. No one can be a blessing to others if he does not love. Nothing but love will make another happier, will comfort sorrow, will relieve loneliness, will give cheer. You never can be of any real use to a man if you do not care for him, and you care for him only so far as you are willing to make sacrifices to help him, to go out of your way to do a favor.

It is never by chance therefore that one finds oneself living a life that is full of helpfulness. Such a life comes only through a regeneration that makes it new. That is what it means to become a Christian. The secret of Christ was abounding personal helpfulness. We say He gave His life for the world, and we think of the cross. But the cross was in His life from the beginning. He never had a thought or a wish for Himself. He never pleased Himself. Ever He was ready to give up His own comfort, His own ease, His own preferment, that another might be pleased or helped. With this thought in mind, it will be a most profitable piece of Bible-reading to go through the Gospels just to find how Christ treated the people He met. He was always kind, not only polite and courteous, but doing kindly, thoughtful, obliging things. His inquiry concerning every person was, "Can I do anything for you? Can I share your burden? Can I relieve you of your suffering?" The Good Samaritan was Christ's illustration of love, and it was a picture of His own life.

Always that is the one answer to our question. There is no other way of personal helpfulness but this way, and there is no other secret of attaining it but His secret. You cannot learn it from a book of rules. It is not a system of etiquette. It is a new life—it is Christ living in the heart.

It is personal helpfulness of which we are thinking. A man may be useful in his community, may even be a public benefactor, may do much for the race, and yet may fail altogether to be a real helper of individual lives he touches in his daily associations. A man may do much good with his money, relieving distress, founding institutions, establishing schools, and may not be a helper of men in personal ways. People do not turn to him with their needs. The sorrowing know nothing of comfort ministered by him. The baffled and perplexed do not look to him for guidance, the tempted for deliverance, the despairing for cheer and encouragement. It is this personal helpfulness that means the most in the close contacts of human lives.

Jesus never gave money to anyone in need, so far as we are told. He did not pay rents for the poor, nor buy them food or clothes, but He was always doing good in ways that meant far more for them than if He had helped with money. There are needs that only love and kindness can meet. Countless people move about among us these days starving for love, dying for loneliness. You can help them immeasurably by becoming their friend, not in any marked or unusual way, but by doing them a simple kindness, by showing a little human interest in them, by turning aside to do a little favor, by manifesting sympathy if they are in sorrow. A little note of a few lines sent to a neighbor in grief has been known to start an influence of comfort and strength that could not be measured.

It is the little things of love that count in such ministry—the little nameless acts, the small words of gentleness, the looks that tell of interest and care and sympathy. Life is hard for many people, and nothing is more needed continually than encouragement and cheer. There are men who never do anything great in their lives, and yet they make it sunnier all about them, and make all who know them happier, braver, stronger. There are women, overburdened themselves, perhaps, but so thoughtful, so sympathetic, so obliging, so full of little kindnesses, that they make the spot of the world in which they live more like heaven.

How can we learn this lesson of personal helpfulness? It is not merely a matter of geniality of disposition, a matter of natural temperament. A selfish man can learn it if he takes Christ for his teacher. Then self must be displaced in the thought and purpose and affection by "the other man." If love fills the heart every expression of the life gives out helpfulness. A young woman, speaking of the way different people had been a comfort to her in a great sorrow, said, "I wish some persons knew just how much their faces can comfort others." Then she told of an old gentleman she sometimes sat beside in the street car. He did not know her, but she was always helped by just being near to him and seeing his face.

There is a great deal of this unconscious helpfulness in the world. Indeed, many of the best things we do we do without knowing we are doing them. If we are full of love, we will be helping others wherever we go, and the things we do not plan to do when we go out in the morning will be the divinest things of the whole day.

Not only is the life of personal helpfulness most worthwhile in the measure of good it does, in its influence upon others, but no other life brings back to itself such rewards of peace, of strength, of comfort, of joy. What of love you give to another you have not really given away—you have it still in yourself in larger measure than before. No gain one gets in this world is equal to the love of hearts that one receives from those one serves in unselfish love.

> *My dear, the little things I did for you*
>   *Today have brought me comfort, one by one,*
>   *As through the purple dark a shaft of sun*
> *Strikes far as dawn, and changes dusk to blue;*
> *The little things it cost me naught to do,*
>   *Remembering how slow life's sands may run,*
>   *Today a web of purest gold have spun*
> *Across the gulf that lies between us two.*

11

Christ and I Are Friends

Shut in. Shut in from the ceaseless din
Of the restless world and its heat and sin;
Shut in from its turmoil, care and strife,
And all the wearisome round of life.

Shut in with tears that are spent in vain
With the dull companionship of pain:
Shut in with changeless days and hours,
And the bitter knowledge of failing powers.

Shut in with dreams of days gone by,
With buried hopes that were born to die;
Shut in with the hopes that have lost their zest
And leave but a longing after rest.

Shut in with a trio of angels sweet,
Patience and grace all pain to meet,
With Faith that can suffer and stand and wait
And lean on the promises strong and great.

Shut in with Christ—O glorious thought!
Shut in with the peace His sufferings brought;
Shut in with the love that wields the rod;
O company blest—shut in with God.

213

If we ask what was the beloved disciple's religion, we may put the answer into the phrase Christ and John were friends. It was a great, all-absorbing, overmastering friendship that transformed John. This friendship began that day when the Baptist said to two young men, as Jesus passed near, "Behold the Lamb of God." The two young men followed Jesus and were invited to His lodgings, spending the afternoon with Him. What took place during those hours we do not know, but we do know that a friendship began between one of the two—then scarcely more than a boy—and Jesus whose bonds have never slackened since. For three years this friendship grew in sweetness and tenderness, and during those years it was that the wonderful transformation took place in the disciple.

We know a little about the power of a strong, rich, noble human friendship in shaping, inspiring, uplifting lives.

> *O friend, my bosom said,*
> *Through thee alone the sky is arched,*
> *Through thee the rose is red;*
> *All things through thee take nobler form,*
> *And look beyond the earth;*
> *The mill-round of our fate appears*
> *A sun-path in thy worth.*
> *Me too thy nobleness has taught*
> *To master my despair;*
> *The fountains of my hidden life*
> *Are through thy friendship fair.*

There are many lives that are being saved, refined, sweetened, enriched by a human friendship. Here is one of the best of the younger Christian men of today who has been lifted up from a life of ordinary ability and education into refinement, power, and large usefulness by a gentle friendship. The girl he loved was rich-hearted, inspiring, showing in her own life the best ideals and attainments, and her love for him and his love for her lifted him up to love's nobility. She stayed with him only a few years and then went home, but he walks among men today with a strength, an energy, and a force of character born of the holy friendship which meant so much to him.

George Eliot's Silas Marner was a miser who hoarded his money. Someone took away his hoard, and his heart grew bitter over the wrong to him. Then a little child was left at his door. His poor, starved heart took in the little one, and love for her redeemed him from sordidness, bitterness, and anguish of spirit. God has saved many a life by sending to it a sweet human friendship. A church visitor climbed the rickety stairs to the miserable room where a woman lay in rags on a pile of straw. She bent over the poor woman, all vile with sin, said a loving word and kissed her. That kiss saved her. Christ comes to sinners and saves them with love. That is the way He saved the prodigals of his time. He came to them and became their friend.

It is to a personal friendship with Himself that Christ is always inviting men. He does not come merely to make reforms, to start beneficent movements, to give people better houses, and to make the conditions of life better. He does not try to save the world by giving it better laws, by founding schools, by securing wholesome literature. Christ saves men by becoming their friend. John surrendered his heart and life to this friendship with Jesus. He opened every window and door to his new Master.

The basis of John's friendship with Christ was his trust. He never doubted. Thomas doubted and was slow to believe. This hindered the growth of his friendship with Jesus. We cannot enter into the joy and gladness of friendship unless we believe heartily. Peter was one of Christ's closest friends, but he was always saying rash words and doing rash things which interrupted his fellowship with Christ. Such a spirit as Peter's, however loyal and courageous, cannot realize the sweet and gentle things of the holiest friendship. But John loved on in silence and trusted, and his friendship was deep and strong. At the Last Supper he leaned on the Master's breast. That is the place of confidence—the bosom is only for those who have a right to the closest intimacy. It is the place of love, near the heart. It is the place of safety—in the secret place of the Most High. The bosom is the place of comfort too. It was the darkest night the world ever saw that John lay on the bosom of Jesus. But he found comfort there. Then trust is the secret of peace. "Thou wilt keep him in perfect peace whose mind is stayed on thee."

That is what leaning on Christ's breast means. Do not think that that place of innermost love was for John only and has never been filled since that night. It is like heaven's gates—it is never closed, and whosoever will may come and lie down there. It is a place for those who sorrow—oh, that all who have known grief knew that they may creep in where John lay and nestle there!

John's transformation is the model for all of us. No matter how many imperfections mar the beauty of our lives, we should not be discouraged. But we should never consent to let the faults remain. That is the way too many of us do. We condone our weakness and imperfections, pity them and keep them. We should give ourselves no rest till they are all cured. But how can we get these evil things out of our lives? How did John get rid of his faults? By letting the love of Christ possess him. Lying upon Christ's bosom, John let Christ's sweet, pure, wholesome life permeated his own and make it sweet, pure, and wholesome as well.

So it is the friendship of Christ alone that can transform us. You are a Christian, not because you belong to a church, not because you have a good creed, not merely because you are living a fair moral life—you are a Christian because you and Christ are friends. What can a friend be to a friend? Let us think of the best that earth's richest-hearted friend can be to us and do for us. Then lift up this conception, multiplying it a thousand times. If it were possible to gather out of all history and from all the world the best and holiest things of pure, true friendship and combine them all in one great friendship, Christ's friendship would surpass the sum of them all.

Even our human friendships we prize as the dearest things on earth. They are more precious than rarest gems. We would lose everything else we have rather than give them up. Life without friendships would be empty and lonely. Yet the best earthly friendships are but little fragments of the friendship of Christ. It is perfect. Its touch is always gentle and full of healing. Its help is always wise. Its tenderness is like the warmth of a heavenly summer. If we have the friendship of Christ we cannot be utterly bereft, though all human friends be taken away. To be Christ's friend is to be God's child, with all a child's privileges. This is one essential in being a Christian.

> *Behold Him now when He comes!*
> *Not the Christ of our subtle creeds,*
> *But the light of our hearts, of our homes,*
> *Of our hopes, our prayers, our needs*
> *The Brother of want and blame,*
> *The Lover of women and men.*

We could not say Paul is our friend, or John, but Jesus is living, and is with us evermore. He is our Friend as really as He was Mary's or John's.

We may not climb the heavenly steeps
To bring the Lord Christ down;
In vain we search the lowest deeps,
For Him no depths can drown;

But warm, sweet, tender, even yet
A present help is He;
And faith has still its Olivet,
And love its Galilee.

The healing of His seamless dress
Is by our beds of pain;
We touch Him in life's throng and press,
And we are whole again.

Christ is our friend. That means everything we need. No want can be unsupplied. No sorrow can be uncomforted. No evil can overmaster us. For time and eternity we are safe. It will not be the streets of gold, and the gates of pearl, and the river and the trees, that will make heaven for us—it will be the companionship, the friendship of Christ.

But we must not forget the other part of this friendship. We are to be Christ's friends too. It is not much we can give to Him, or do for Him. But He would have us loyal and true. One writes of the influence of a human friend's life:

Each soul whispers to itself: 'twere like a breach
Of reverence in a temple, could I dare
Here speak untruth, here wrong my inmost thought.
Here I grow strong and pure; here I may yield
Without shamefacedness the little brought
From out my poorer life, and stand revealed
And glad, and trusting, in the sweet and rare
And tender presence which hath filled the air.

If a sacred human friendship exerts such influence over a true life, surely the consciousness that Christ is our friend and we are His should check every evil thought, quell every bitter feeling, sweeten every emotion, and make all of our lives holy, true, and heavenly.

12

More Than Conquerors

O Lord, I pray
That for this day
I may not swerve
By foot or hand
From thy command,
Not to be served but to serve.

This, too, I pray
That for this day
No love of ease
Nor pride prevent
My good intent,
Not to be pleased, but to please.

And if I may
I'd have this day
Strength from above
To set my heart
In heavenly art
Not to be loved, but to love.

MALTBIE D. BABCOCK

It is better that we should not sing of sadness. There are sad notes enough already in the world's air. We should sing of cheer, of joy, of hope. This is what Paul did when he said: "We are more than conquerors through Him that loved us." We do not need to be defeated in our battles, to sink under our loads, to be crushed beneath our sorrows. We may be victorious.

We all have our struggles. Life is not easy for any of us; or if it is, we are not making much of it. Good life is never easy. It must be from first to last in the face of opposition. Jacob saw life visioned as a ladder, its foot resting in the earth, its top reaching up to heaven, into God's very glory. That meant that man could go up from his earthliness, his sinfulness, into nobleness and holiness of character, gaining at last likeness to God and home with God. But it meant also that the ascent never could be easy. A ladder bids us to climb, and climbing is always toilsome. It is slow, too, step by step. It never becomes easy, for heaven is ever above us and the climbing cannot cease till we enter the pearly gate.

Paul constantly pictured life as a battle, a warfare. We are soldiers with enemies to fight. The enemies are strong, not flesh and blood, but evil angels, spiritual foes, wicked spirits. They are invisible. They lurk in the darkness. They hide in ambush. Too often they nest in our own hearts. They take forms of good angels to deceive us. The battle is terrific and it never ends until we overcome the last enemy and pass within the gates of blessedness.

Every life has its cares, its duties, its responsibilities. There are sicknesses and sorrows and pains and losses and a thousand things that make it hard to live victoriously.

It is possible for us, if we are Christians, to overcome in all these struggles and trials. "In all these things we are more than conquerors." To be more than conquerors is to be triumphant conquerors, not merely getting through the battle or the trouble, but coming out of it with rejoicing, with song and gladness. Some people bear trial and are not overcome by it, but bear it without any glad sense of victory. Others endure their sorrow, and all through it you hear, as it were, the notes of triumph. Paul himself was this sort of a conqueror. His life was one unbroken series of struggles. It never became easy for him to live nobly. He gives us glimpses sometimes of his experiences. He was beaten with rods. He was stoned. He was shipwrecked. He was in perils of robbers, in perils in the wilderness, in the sea, among false brethren, in watchings, in fastings, in cold and nakedness. He spent years in prison. Then he had enemies in his own heart—read the seventh chapter of Romans to find what it cost him to live right. But in all these things he was "more than conqueror." Someone compares Paul's life to one who goes along the street in a dark stormy night singing sweet songs; or to a whole band of music moving through the rain and darkness, playing marches of victory. That is the way we should all try to live as Christians, not merely enduring our trials and coming through our struggles, but doing so enthusiastically—"more than conquerors."

Not only may we be conquerors, but if we are Christians we must be conquerors. We believe that we should be conquerors in temptation, that we should not sin. We know that the evil in us and the evil around us should not be allowed to overcome us; that appetites and base passions and bad tempers should not be permitted to rule us. But this is not the only phase of life in which we meet resistance and opposition, and must be conquerors, if we would live nobly. This is true in physical life. Health is simply victory over disease and weakness. It is true in mental life. It is never easy to have a trained mind. It can be gotten only through long and patient study and severe discipline. It is so in all experiences in life. We should never yield to discouragement or depression, for there is no reason that we should. In the description of the good man, in Psalm 1, where he is compared to tree planted by streams of water, we read: "And whatsoever he doeth shall prosper." There is no real failure possible in a true Christian life. There may be seeming failure; indeed, oftentimes there is. Christ's life failed, as it appeared to men. Paul's life failed. Henry Martyn's life failed. Harriet Newell's life failed. But you know what glorious successes all these lives were in the end. If we are truly Christians, in Jesus Christ, it is impossible for us to fail. Hence in all adversity, in all loss, in all feebleness of health, in all persecution, injustice, wrong, we have but to remain true to Christ, and we cannot fail. "Whatsoever he doeth shall prosper." Hence we should never yield to discouragement. We should be more than conquerors.

The same is true in sorrow. Sorrow comes into every life. We cannot shut it away. But we can be conquerors in it. When the snows melt away in the springtime, I have often seen under them sweet flowers in bloom. The very drifts were like warm blankets to keep them safe. So it is in sorrow. Under the cold snows of grief the flowers of the Christian graces grow unhurt. We can overcome in sorrow; we ought to overcome. This does not mean that we should not shed tears in our sorrows. The love of Christ does not harden the heart; it really makes it more sensitive. The grace of Christ does not save us from suffering in bereavement. Yet we are to be conquerors. Our sorrow must not crush us. We must go through it victoriously, with sweet submission and joyous confidence.

In the same way must we meet worldly losses and adversities, the failures in our human plans and hopes, the fading of our human joys. "More than conquerors" is the motto that is written upon our crown.

But do not forget the closing words of Paul's statement: "In all these things we are more than conquerors *through Him that loved us.*" The text would not be true if these last five words were left off. We cannot leave Christ out of life and ever in anything be true overcomers. The Roman Emperor saw the symbol of the cross blazing in the sky and over it the legend: "By this shalt thou conquer." Before every young soldier of the cross, as he goes out to begin life's battles, shines the same symbol, with the same legend: "By this shalt thou conquer." "We are more than conquerors through Him that loved us." It is only through Christ that any of us can overcome sin or sorrow or trial.

Some of you may be asking, with deep eagerness, in what way Christ helps us in our battles and struggles. How can we overcome through Him?

One part of the answer is that He has overcome all things Himself. He came in the flesh for us. He was the captain of our salvation. He entered into life for us. He met every enemy that we have ever met. And He was more than conqueror in every struggle. He was tempted in all points like as we are, yet without sin. That is, He conquered all sin. Then He met poverty, and was victorious in that, living sweetly, patiently, trustingly in it, without discontent, without envy, without repinings. He labored as a carpenter, but He never chafed at the hardness of the work or the smallness of the pay. Later, He had not where to lay His head—even the foxes and the birds being better homed than He, but He never complained. When the people scattered off to their homes in the gathering shadows, leaving Him alone, He quietly climbed the mountain and spent the night under the stars in peace. Thus He was more than conqueror in poverty.

So He was victorious in all the wrongs He had to endure. From enemies and from friends He suffered wrongs. His enemies pursued Him with hate and persecution, which at last nailed Him on the cross. His own chosen friends did many things to pain and try Him; one of them at last betraying Him for money, another denying Him in His darkest hour. Enmity and hate and wrongs cannot hurt us unless they rouse us to resentments, to anger, to bitter feelings, to acts of revenge. But Jesus was victorious in all His endurance of injury. His love never once failed in any of its sore testings.

Then He was conqueror in His struggle with the last enemy. It did not seem so at first. Death overcame Him on the cross, and bore Him captive into its dark prison. But it could not hold Him. He burst the bars of death and triumphed over the grave. He came forth a glorious conqueror, out forever from death's power, with all the radiance of life.

Thus Christ is universal conqueror. There is no enemy we shall ever have to meet that He has not met and vanquished. If we are in His train, He will lead us also to victory. We cannot overcome ourselves, but He will fight the battles for us. "We are more than conquerors through Him that loved us."

But again, He does not merely fight our battles for us; He helps us to become victorious. "We are more than conquerors *through* Him." We must not get the impression that Christ merely wraps us up in the folds of His mighty love and carries us over the hard place in life. When we are in the presence of temptation, He does not with His divine hand smite down the adversary; we must fight the battle, and He will strengthen us. There is a verse which says, "The Lord will bruise Satan shortly," but that is not all of it. "The Lord will bruise Satan under your feet shortly." You must tread down the enemy beneath your feet, but the Lord will bruise him. We must become the conquerors through Him. He wants to make us strong; and therefore, He does not do all things for us and fight all of our battles. He sends us out to meet the enemies, the trials, the oppositions, and then He goes with us to help us. He does not take the burdens off of us, but He sustains us in bearing them.

What then is our part? It is implicit, unquestioning obedience. Do you remember those cases in the Gospels when persons were healed as they obeyed? The man with the withered arm was bidden to stretch it out—an impossible thing, in a human sense, but as he sought to obey he was enabled to do it. Health came into his shriveled arm. The ten lepers were bidden to go away and show themselves to the priest. "And as they went they were cleansed." Obedience made them overcomers. So it is always in the receiving of divine help. We stand in the presence of some opposition, some hindrance, some trial. We say we cannot go through it. But we hear the voice of God commanding: "Go: and lo I am with you."

If we quietly and believingly go forward, the difficulties will melt before us; the sea will open and make a path for our feet; the mountain will remove and be cast into the sea; the enemy will flee as we advance. Christ never gives a duty but He will give also the strength we require to obey.

There is a blessed secret in this very simple teaching. If we do God's will we are invincible, and shall always be more than conquerors. You stand face to face with a sorrow or a discouragement or some adversity. The problem of Christian faith now is to overcome in this experience—not to get rid of the experience, but to meet it and pass through it victoriously, so that it shall not hurt you, but that you shall get blessing out of it. Now, how can you do this? Never by resisting and rebelling. You cannot by doing this repel the trial or evade it. You might as well try to fight a cyclone, and by resisting it turn it back. Your resisting can only hurt and bruise your own life. But if you sweetly and quietly yield to the trial or the sorrow and bow before it, it will pass over you, and you will rise again unhurt.

Such meeting of trial changes the curse in the cup to blessing. He who overcomes in temptation gets new strength out of his conquest. He who is patient and submissive in the sickroom gets a benediction out of the pain. He who overcomes in adversity and keeps faith and love bright has changed its loss into gain. So it is in all things. To be conqueror in the battles and struggles of life is to climb ever upward toward glory and blessedness.

God so shapes all of our life's events and experiences that in every one of them there is a blessing for us. We miss it if we resist and rebel and thus fail of victoriousness. But if we let God's will be done in us, some good will come out of every cup He puts into our hand.

So we shall go on conquering and to conquer, overcoming in all of life's sorrows and getting blessing out of them; victorious over sins and rising into sainthood out of them, as lilies spring up out of black bogs; putting the old nature under our feet more and more as the new nature grows in us into strength and beauty; triumphing over all the ills of life over all adversities, until at last, rising out of death, we shall stand before God, without spot or blemish, wearing the image of Christ.

13

Reaching for the Mountain Splendors

It is well to live in the valley sweet,
Where the work of the world is done,
Where the reapers sing in the fields of wheat,
As they toil till the set of sun.
But beyond the meadows, the hills I see
Where the noises of traffic cease,
And I follow a voice that calleth to me
From the hilltop regions of peace.

Aye, to live is sweet in the valley fair,
And to toil till the set of sun;
But my spirit yearns for the hilltop's air
When the day and its work are done.
For a Presence breathes o'er the silent hills,
And its sweetness is living yet;
The same deep calm all the hillside fills,
As breathed over Olivet.

Christ clearly stated the purpose of His mission to the world when He said, "I came that they may have life, and may have it abundantly." We do not begin to understand the possibilities of our lives in the hands of Christ, what He will make of us if we truly submit ourselves to Him. There are enemies about us. The thief comes to kill, to destroy. Christ comes to give life and to give it in fullness. When the English laureate was asked what Christ was to him, he replied by pointing to a rose bush, full of glorious roses, and said, "What the sun is to this rose bush, Christ is to me." Think what Christ was to John, the disciple, whom He found resentful, ungentle, whom He made into a disciple of love, and whose influence fills the world today like a holy fragrance. Think what Christ has been to believers in all the Christian centuries, what He is to the saints who today are living in the world.

> *He that hath the Son, hath life.*
> *The life of the Son is love, is goodness,*
> *is spirit of kindness and gentleness.*

Think what it is to have the life of Christ in you. One of Paul's re-markable words is, "Christ liveth in me," and the words mean a literal indwelling of Christ. That is what it is to be a Christian. Think what they are missing who are not letting Christ live in them.

Christ wants us to live richly, abundantly. He is ever calling us to something larger and better. Looking back over our lives at the close of a year, we see how often we have failed. But failures, if we are faithfully following Christ, are not final. They are but beginnings which are left for completion in the future. Browning's lines are suggestive:

> *The high that proved too high,*
> *The heroic for earth too hard,*
> * The passion that left the ground to lose itself in the sky,*
> * Are music sent up to God by the lover and the bard;*
> *Enough that he heard it once;*
> *We shall hear it by and by.*

We say that we find these high things unattainable, and that we never can reach them. No; we shall reach them if we continue to strive. We are at school, only learning, and learning is always slow. We try to get the les-son and we fail, but that is not defeat. We will try again and again, and at last we shall master the hard lessons. Nothing we can think of is beyond ultimate possible attaining. Last year's failures were not final; they were only things we tried to do and did not quite master. Someday we shall finish them. We are immortal. Our failures now are only immaturities; someday they will reach maturity.

Paul gives us a good lesson for progress when he counsels us to leave the things that are behind and to stretch toward the things that are before. Some things, of course, we are not to forget. It would be a sin to forget our mercies—the kindnesses we receive, the self-denials and sacrifices others have made for us. We should cherish with most sacred regard and gratitude the memory of friendships that have meant so much to us.

But there are some things which we should resolutely and determinedly forget and leave behind. We should forget our worries. We see afterward how foolish they were, and how useless. Some of the things we fretted about a year ago, and allowed to vex and harry us, we now thank God for. They were among the best things of the whole year. We should forget our sorrows. "No," we say, "we never can. They were too bitter." Yes, but they brought blessing in their bitterness. It may be too soon yet for us to give thanks for them, but someday we shall. At last we shall see that the greatest good to our lives has come out of the things which at the time seemed disastrous.

We should forget the sins of our past. Should we indeed? Should we ever forget our sins? Not until we have confessed them and given them up. But when they have been forgiven, we shall forget them in the love and praise of our hearts. We must not make light of sin—it is an exceedingly bitter thing. Sin has filled the world with ruin. It blots and stains and spoils everything it touches. We need to make very sure that we have repented of our sins and that they have been forgiven. It will never do merely to forget them, to cover them up and leave them uncancelled and pass them by. Only God can safely cover sins. Sins which only men themselves cover will plague them afterward. But the sins which God has blotted out and ceased to remember we may forget while we go on in the joy of our new lives.

We should not drag our old habits with us. There are habits which marred last year which we should leave behind amid the rubbish. There are companionships which we should give up positively today. Only at our souls' peril can we continue them. Our friendships, if they are pure and good and uplifting, we should cherish—they are making our lives rich, strong, true, beautiful. But if they are unholy, if they are corrupt in their influence, if they are hurting us in our character, drawing us toward evil, the only true thing to do is to break them off, not to carry them with us into the new, bright, clean life of the new days.

One is grieving over a lost friendship. Once it was everything to you. It was in all your thoughts. You built no dream fabric, but this friendship was in it. You made no plans for the future, but this friend and you were close, side by side. How can you go on with this friendship out of your life? How can you begin the new year and know that it has forever passed away? Let Christ answer your questions. Let Him take your life, and He will give you a joy that will fill your heart. He will be better to you than all the earth. You ask, "How?" I do not know. Trust the way with Him. He came to give you life abundantly.

Another class of things we should not carry forward into a new life is our quarrels, if we have any: our angers, our resentments, our grudges. "Let not the sun go down upon your wrath" (Eph. 4:26) ran the old teaching. We may not live overnight, and we may never have a chance to ask forgiveness, if we do not do it before we sleep. Most positive is the Master's teaching that we must forgive if we would be forgiven.

"When you stand praying, forgive." Then the prayer the Master taught us is, "Forgive us our debts as we forgive our debtors." If it was wrong to carry the unforgiveness for one day, and through the night, it must be still worse to carry the resentments, the quarrels, the angers, over into the new year. We should carry nothing but love with us into any tomorrow. Bitterness is most undivine; only love is divine. If anyone has wronged you, and a bitter feeling has lingered in your heart toward him, forgive the wrong and let love wipe out the bitterness. If you remember before God that you have done an injury to another, spoken some angry word, spoken anything unloving, hurt a life by anything you have done, do not enter the new year without seeking forgiveness.

> *If fault of mine, or pride, or fear,*
> *Has cost one soul, or far or near,*
> *May the hurt die with thee, Old Year.*

These are suggestions of what Christ means by life. He came that we may have life and that we may have it abundantly. Have you noticed that to live and to love seem to be parts of the same verb? To live is to love. Love is the perfect of live. Christ is love. Abundant life is abundant love.

A new year calls us to better life, that is, to love better. When Jesus bids us to be perfect, He means perfect in living. "For if ye love them that love you, what reward have ye?" Even the publicans loved that way. "And if ye salute your brethren only, what do ye more than others?" The Gentiles go that far. "Ye therefore shall be perfect, even as your heavenly Father is perfect."

You say, "I never can be perfect." True, the lesson is hard, and it will take you a long time to learn it. It is hard to learn to love unreasonable people. It is hard to love your enemies. It is a long lesson to become perfect in loving; nevertheless, there the lesson stands—"Be ye perfect." And it must be learned—not in a day, or in a year, but like all great lessons, slowly, today a little, and tomorrow a little. Someone writes among New Year's lessons:

> *Speak a shade more kindly than the year before;*
> *Pray a little oftener; love a little more;*
> *Cling a little closer to the Father's love;*
> *Thus life below shall liker grow to life above.*

This is the way in all our learning and growing. It is thread by thread that makes the web. It is note by note that makes the thrilling music of the great oratorio. It is block by block that builds the majestic temple. It is touch by touch of the brush that paints a marvelous picture. It is line by line that makes the beautiful life. "Speak a shade more kindly," until you have learned always to speak more kindly. "Pray a little oftener," till your whole life becomes a prayer. "Love a little more," until you have learned to love every sort of person, and can give your life in loving, serving the worst.

We must remember that it is not in any easy or self-indulgent life that Christ will lead us to greatness. The easy life leads not upward, but downward. Heaven always is above us and must be reached up toward, and we must ever be reaching up toward it. There are some people who always avoid things that are costly, that require self-denial or self-restraint and sacrifice, but toil and hardship show us the only way to nobleness. Not by having a mossy path made for you through the meadows, but to be sent to hew out a roadway by your own hands. Are you going to reach the mountain splendors?

14

Life's Open Doors

Cast out all envy, bitterness, and hate;
And keep the mind's fair tabernacle pure.
Shake hands with Pain, give greeting unto Grief,
Those angels in disguise, and thy glad soul
From height to height, from star to shining star,
Shall climb and claim blest immortality.

Life is full of doors. A door is a very simple thing. It may be only a plain, unadorned piece of board. It's significance is not in the material of which it is made or in its costliness or its artistic beauty, but in the fact that it is a door which opens to something. One may open to a noble gallery of pictures; enter, and you stand amid the finest works of art. Another opens into a great library; enter, and you find about you the words of the wise men of the ages. Another opens to a school, a great university; enter, and you are listening to distinguished teachers whose learned teachings will enrich your mind. It is not the door itself that matters, but that to which the door is the entrance.

Life's doors are not shut and locked. They may not be gilded, and they may not invite to ease and pleasure, but they open to the truest and best things, to the finest possibilities of character and attainment, and to the noblest ultimate achievements.

There are doors that open to good. They may not invite us to easy things. The best things do not offer themselves to us as self-indulgences. Someone says:

> I fought something out myself, once, and I won. It was hard, but I did it, and I'd do it again—I wouldn't be coward enough to run away. When things hurt you, you don't have to let anybody know. You can shut your lips tight, and if you bit your tongue hard enough it keeps back the tears. I always pretend I'm a rock, with the waves beating against me. Let it hurt inside, if it wants to—you don't have to let anybody see.

The doors may not be attractive that we ought to enter, but they open to the truest and best life, to the finest possibilities of character and attainment, and to the noblest ultimate achievement.

There is the door of education. All of life is a school. Young people are graduated by and by from college and university, but their education is not finished. This should go on in the occupations and struggles that follow. It is there we learn the real lessons of life.

There is the door of hardship and pain. One of the papers pays tribute to one unnamed man who died recently after years of intense suffering. He never asked pity or any concessions because of his suffering, but grew more and more devoted to his work. There are many people who permit their pain and misfortune to make constant appeal to human sympathy instead of bearing these burdens quietly and heroically, as a soldier wears the marks of his profession. Suffering properly endured develops power and adds to usefulness. The school of hardship and pain is where we learn many of the finest things.

> The man who wins its real successes is not he who has the most perfect health, but he who bears disease and misfortune with silent courage and gains from them a more daring spirit; who meets failure as if it were veiled victory; who challenges death by ignoring its fearful aspect, tearing off its mask, and meeting it with a smile.

Another of the doors which opens to us in life is the door to kindness. Many people think of kindness as only a kindergarten lesson, but one who accepts the task finds it very long. Kindness begins in unselfishness, the crucifying of self. It is sacrificial in its every feeling and act. Wherever self stays in the heart there will be unkindness in the life, in some form. To be kind is to be gentle. Kindness will not break a bruised reed nor quench the smoking wick. Kindness is thoughtful, so sensitive in the consciousness of others' condition that it refrains from every act, word, or look that would give pain. Kindness is sympathetic, touched with the suffering of others and quick to give comfort. It is a great door this, that opens into the school of kindness.

Another of life's doors opens into the school of helpfulness. When we begin to be like God we begin to be helpful. We think we love each other, but the love is only a mere sentiment until it has been wrought into sacrificial act, into service which costs. Personal helpfulness is the test as well as the measure of the quality of the mind of Christ that is in us. Evermore people need to be helped. This does not mean that we are to carry their burdens, pay their debts, do their work, fight their battles. Such helpfulness does evil rather than good. We help others truly when we make them strong and brave, that they may carry their own burdens and meet their own struggles. Helpfulness should cheer, encourage, inspire, impart larger visions and greater hope and confidence. There are men everywhere who are pressed, beleaguered, ready to sink down and perish, whom strong brotherly sympathy would save. They are in sorrow, disappointment has staggered them, or they have been defeated in their purposes. To be able to help these is the highest service we can render to the world. "To be a strong hand in the dark to another in the time of need," says Hugh Black, "to be a cup of strength to a human soul in a crisis of weakness, is to know the glory of life." There would seem to be no limit to the possibilities of this higher helpfulness. The true Christian life is reached by the emptying of self and the filling of the emptiness with Christ. When Christ is in us, we are able to help others with His strength.

It is a wonderful door which opens into a noble Christian life. Men are trying to make us believe that there is nothing in Christianity, that taking Christ into one's life does nothing for one. But what has Christ done for the lives of His friends along the centuries? What did He do for John and Peter? What did He do for Paul? What is He doing continually for those who follow Him in faith and consecration? Dr. Robertson Nicoll, in a recent address, referred to John G. Paton's work in the New Hebrides.

His wife died when he and she were laboring in a savage island and had made practically no converts. The missionary had to dig her grave himself and to lay her there with the dark, hostile faces round him. "If it had not been for Jesus," Dr. Paton says, "and the presence He vouchsafed me there, I should have gone mad and died beside that lonely grave."

If it had not been for Jesus the world would never have seen the glorious ministry of Dr. Paton. Nor is that splendid life singular in its story. Say what we may about the failures of Christians which so sadly mar the beauty of the Christian life, we know that thousands of believers have realized wonderful things and accomplished marvelous results, which if it had not been for Jesus they never could have done.

By and by in even the best life we come to a door which opens into old age. Many are disposed to feel that this door can lead to nothing beautiful. We cannot go on with our former tireless energy, our crowded days, our great achievements. But there is altogether too much letting go, too much dropping of tasks, too much falling out of the pilgrim march, when old age comes on. We may not be able to run swiftly as before. We tire more easily. We forget some things. But old age may be made very beautiful and full of fruit. This door opens into a period of great possibilities of usefulness, a true crowning of the life. Old age is not a blot, if it is what it should be. It is not a withering of the life, but a ripening. It is not something to dread, but is the completion of God's plan.

> *Grow old along with me!*
> *The best is yet to be*
> *The last of life, for which the first was made;*
> *Our times are in His hand*
> *Who saith, "A whole I planned."*
> *Youth shows but half; trust God: see all, nor be*
> *afraid.*

Last of all we come to the door of death. Into what does this door lead? Is there anything beyond—anything beautiful, anything glorious? Our Christian faith tells us that death is not a wall, but a door. We do not in dying come to the end of anything beautiful and good, but only pass through into blessedness and glory. We are immortal and shall never die. All the lessons we have been learning in earth's schools we shall go on practicing forever. We shall enter into the joy of Christ when we pass through this last door of earth.

15

Some Lessons on Spiritual Growth

Lead me, yea lead me, deeper into life—
This suffering, human life wherein Thou liv'st
And breathest still and holdst Thy way divine.
Tis here, O pitying Christ, where Thee I seek—
Here where the strife is fiercest, where the sun
Beats down upon the highway thronged with men,
And in the raging heart. O! deeper lead
My soul into the living world of souls
Where Thou dost move.

Jesus loved nature. He saw in it the tokens and expressions of His Father's love and care. What could be more exquisite, for example, than the thoughts a little flower started in His mind, as we find them expressed in the Sermon on the Mount? He was urging people never to be anxious. Just then His eye fell on a lily growing in its marvelous beauty by the wayside, and He used it to teach a lesson about the care of God. He cares even for the smallest flower, and His hand weaves for it its exquisite raiment. "And why are ye anxious concerning raiment?" Thus our Lord saw in every flower that blooms something His Father had made and beautified, something He cared for with all gentleness. And of whatever other use the flowers are, He at least wants us to learn from them this truth of trust so that we shall never be anxious. The flowers never are.

One of the most suggestive of our Lord's parables of growth is given by Mark only. The kingdom of God is likened to a sower's seed cast upon the earth and growing the sower knows not how. In our modern agriculture we are losing much of the picturesqueness of the farmer's life as it was in our Lord's day. Still the lesson of the seed is the same whatsoever way it may be planted. It is a very little thing, but Jesus notes in it and in its mode of growing a picture of something very wonderful, a picture of the kingdom of God. The same laws prevail in things natural and things spiritual. "So is the kingdom of God, as if a man should cast seed upon the earth." We are all sowers. We may not be farmers or gardeners, yet everywhere we go we are sowing seeds. We talk to a friend an hour, and then go our way, never giving thought again to what we said, but years afterwards something will grow up in the friend's life and character from the seeds we dropped so unconsciously, or without purpose, that day. We lend a friend a book, and he reads it. We never think of the book again; our friend never tells us whether he liked it or not. But many years later there is a life moving about among other lives, and leaving upon them its impress, which was inspired by the book we lent, something in it which influenced the course and career of the life.

Seeds are wonderful things. There is mystery in the secret of life they carry in them. Diamonds or pearls have no such secret in them. Men do not plant them. They never grow. We do not know what marvelous results will come from some slightest word of ours spoken any day. It may not always be good—it may be evil; all depends upon the seed. The farmer sowed good seed, expecting a rich and beautiful harvest. An enemy came one night, while the farmer was sleeping, and sowed tares, and the tare seeds grew and spoiled the harvest. We need to watch what we are sowing lest a trail of evil and unbeauty shall follow us. We need to watch what we say in our little talks with the people we meet through the days, or in our influence over them, lest we leave stain or hurt behind.

But it is of the growth of the seed that our Lord speaks in His parable. "As if a man should cast seed upon the earth; and should sleep and rise night and day, and the seed should spring up and grow, he knoweth not how" (Mark 4:26, 27). He does not stay out in the fields and watch his seed growing. He only casts it into the ground and lets it grow as it will. When the seed is once in the soil, it is out of the sower's hands forever. Good or bad, it is gone now beyond his reach. You may write a letter full of bitter words. You were angry when you wrote it. Your conscience told you you ought not to send it, for it would only cause bitterness. You went out to mail it. All along the way as you went toward the post-box the voice within you kept saying, "Don't mail it." You came to the box and hesitated, for still there was a clamorous voice beseeching you, "Do not send it." But the anger was yet flaming, and you put the letter in the box. Then you began to wish you had not done it. You began to think of the unlovingness in the bitter words. It was too late now, however, for the cruel letter was forever beyond your reach. No energy in the world could get it back.

So it is when one drops a seed into the ground, whether it be good or evil. The die is cast. The seed is in the ground. There is no use to watch it. So it is when one has dropped an evil influence into a life. Until the word was spoken or the thing was done, it was in your own power and you could have withheld it. Till then you could have kept the word unspoken or the deed undone. But now it is out of your power. No swiftest messenger can pursue it and take it back. The seed is sown, and you can only let it stay and grow. A man goes on with his work, busy in a thousand ways, and the seed he dropped is growing continually, he knows not how, into what form; the word he spoke, the thing he did, is in people's hearts and lives, and its influence is at work, he knows not how. And no power in the universe can arrest it or get it back. You may pray, but prayer cannot get back the regretted word or deed.

There is something startling in this thought of how what we have once done passes then forever out of our hand, beyond recall, and how it goes on in its growth and influence in the silence, while we wake and while we sleep. The time to check evil things, to keep them from forever growing into more and more baleful evil, is before we cast the seed into the ground. We need to think seriously of this truth, that there is a line beyond which our power over our words and deeds and influence ceases forever.

There is a marvelous power, too, in the earth, which, when it receives the seed, begins to deal with it so as to bring out its mystery of life. If the seed is not cast into the ground, it will not grow. Its life can be brought out and it can grow only through being cast into the ground. "The earth beareth fruit of herself." We cannot help the soil take care of the seed, and we do not have to help God take care of the good words we speak to others. The seed is divine, and the influences that act upon it are divine. So all we have to do is to get the truth into the hearts of those we would save and build up; God will do the rest. We are not responsible for the growth of the seed, for the work of grace in a human heart. Great is the mysterious power in the earth which touches the seed, enfolds it, quickens it, and causes it to grow. But this only illustrates the power that works in human hearts and lives, the power of the divine Spirit. This holy life receives the heavenly truth that is put into the heart, and brings out its blessed possibilities, till we see a new life like unto God's own life, a Christlike life, blessing the world with its beauty and its love.

16

The Thanksgiving Lesson

It's O my heart, my heart,
  To be out in the sun and sing!
To sing and shout in the fields about,
  In the balm and the blossoming.

Sing loud, O bird in the tree!
  O bird, sing loud in the sky!
And honeybees blacken the clover seas;
  There are none of you glad as I.

The leaves laugh low in the wind,
  Laugh low with the winds at play;
And the odorous call of the flowers all
  Entices my soul away.

For O but the world is fair, is fair!
  And O but the world is sweet!
I will out in the gold of the blossoming mold,
  And sit at the Master's feet.

And the love of my heart would speak
  I would fold in the lily's rim,
That the lips of the blossom more pure and meek
  May offer it up to Him.

Then sing in the hedgerow green, O thrush!
  O skylark, sing in the blue!
Sing loud, sing clear, that the King may hear,
  And my soul shall sing with you.

British Weekly

Gladness may not be thanksgiving. It certainly is not all of thanksgiving. One may have a heart bubbling with joy without a note of thanksgiving. The task of happiness is one to which we should all firmly set ourselves. To be miserable in this glorious world is most unfit. We should cultivate a joyousness. But our present lesson is a larger and deeper one.

Thanksgiving implies thought of God. One may be glad all the day and never think of God. Thanksgiving looks up with every breath and sees God as Father from whom all blessings come. Thanksgiving is praise. The heart is full of gratitude. Every moment has something in it to inspire love. The lilies made Jesus think of His Father, for it was He who clothed them in beauty. The providence of our lives, if we think rightly of it, is simply God caring for us.

Our circumstances may sometimes be hard, our experiences painful, and we may see nothing in them to make us glad. But faith teaches us that God is always good and always kind, whatever the present events may be. We may be thankful, therefore, even when we cannot be glad. Our hearts may be grateful, knowing that good will come to us even out of pain and loss. This is the secret of true thanksgiving. It thinks always of God and praises Him for everything. The song never dies out in the heart, however little there may be in the circumstances of life to make us glad.

Thanksgiving is a quality of all noble and unselfish life. No man is so unworthy as he who never cherishes the sentiment of gratitude, who receives life's gifts and favors and never gives back anything in return for all he gets.

There is one thing I fear—
  Not death, nor sharp disease,
Nor loss of friends I hold most dear,
  Nor pain, nor want—not these,

> *But the life of which men say:*
>   *"The world has given him bread;*
> *And what gives he to the world as pay*
>   *For the crust on which he fed?"*

Until we think seriously of it we do not begin to realize what we are receiving continually from those about us. None may give us money or do for us things which the world counts gifts or favors, but these are not the best things. Our teachers are ever enriching us by the lessons they give us. Those who require hard tasks of us and severely demand of us the best we can do are our truest benefactors.

> The man who gives me a new thought, enriches me. The man who puts iron into my blood, puts health into my blood. The man who in this world of snow and sleet keeps me moving, saves my life; and if the movement be an upward and onward movement, every step is so much nearer the kingdom of heaven.

Sometimes we complain of the hardness of our lives, that we have had so little of ease and luxury, that we have had to work so hard, bear so many burdens, and sometimes we let ourselves grow bitter and unthankful as we think of the severity of our experience. But oftentimes it has been in these very severities that we have got the richest qualities in our character. If we are living truly, serving God and following Christ, there is no event or experience for which we may not be thankful. Every voice of our lips should be praise. Every day of our years should be a thanksgiving day.

He who has learned the Thanksgiving lesson well has found the secret of a beautiful life. "Praise is comely," says the Hebrew poet. Comely means fit, graceful, pleasing, attractive. Ingratitude is never comely. The life that is always thankful is winsome, ever a joy to all who know it. The influence of an ever-praising life on those it touches is almost divine. The way to make others good is to be good yourself. The way to diffuse a spirit of thanksgiving is to be thankful yourself. A complaining spirit makes unhappiness everywhere.

How may we learn the Thanksgiving lesson? It comes not merely through a glad natural disposition. There are some favored people who were born cheerful. They have in them a spirit of happiness which nothing ever quenches. They always see the bright side of things. They are naturally optimistic. But the true thanksgiving spirit is more than this. It is something which can take even an unhappy and an ungrateful spirit and make it new in its sweetness and beauty. It is something which can change discontent and complaining into praise, ingratitude into grateful, joyful trust. Christian thanksgiving is the life of Christ in the heart, transforming the disposition and the whole character.

Thanksgiving must be wrought into the life as a habit before it can become a fixed and permanent quality. An occasional burst of praise in years of complaining is not all that is required. Songs on rare, sunshiny days and no songs when skies are cloudy will not make a life of gratitude. The heart must learn to sing always. This lesson is learned only when it becomes a habit that nothing can weaken. We must persist in being thankful. When we can see no reason for praise, we must believe in the divine love and goodness and sing in the darkness.

Thanksgiving has attained its rightful place in us only when it is part of all our days and dominates all our experiences. We may call one day in the year Thanksgiving Day, and fill it with song and gladness, remembering all the happy things we have enjoyed, all the pleasant events, all the blessings of our friendships, all our prosperities. But we cannot gather all our year's thanksgivings into any brightest day. We cannot leave today without thanks, and then thank God tomorrow for today and tomorrow both. Today's sunshine will not light tomorrow's skies. Every day must be a thanksgiving day for itself.

17

The Indispensable Christ

To stretch my hand and touch Him,
Though He be far away;
To raise my eyes and see Him
Through darkness as through day;
To lift my voice and call Him—
This is to pray!

To feel a hand extended
By One who standeth near;
To view the love that shineth
In eyes serene and clear;
To know that He is calling—
This is to hear!

The closest of all relationships is that of Christ and the believer in Him. Our Lord Himself used the vine and the branches to illustrate this relation. The branch actually grows out of the vine. It cannot exist apart from it. There are some friends whom we might lose and be a little poorer. But to lose Christ out of our lives is the greatest of all losses.

There is a story by Henry van Dyke called "The Lost Word," which in a most striking way illustrates the irreparable loss of one who parts with

Christ. It is a story of one of the early centuries. Hermas had given himself to Christ. He belonged to a wealthy pagan family. His father disin-
herited him and drove him out of his home when he accepted Christianity.

In the Grove of Daphne one day Hermas sat down by a gushing
spring, and there came to him a priest of Apollo, who saw his unhappy
mood and began to talk to him. In the end the old man had made this
bargain with Hermas. He was to assure him of wealth, happiness, and
success, and Hermas was to give him only a word; he was to part with
the name of Him whom he had learned to worship. "Let me take that
word, and all that belongs to it, entirely out of your life. I promise you
everything," said the old man, "and this is all I ask of you in return. Do
you consent?" "Yes, I consent," said Hermas. So he lost the word.

Hermas went back to Antioch to his old home. He found his father
dying. The old man received his son eagerly. Then he asked Hermas to
tell him the secret of the Christian faith he had chosen. "You found something in that faith that made you willing to give up your life for it. Tell
me what it is!" Hermas began, "Father, you must believe with all your
heart and soul and strength in——" Where was the word? He had lost
it.

Happiness came. Sitting one day with his wife beside him and his
baby on his knee he thought of his old faith, and longed to thank Christ
and seek His blessing. Going to an old shrine in the garden he tried to
pray, but could not. He had lost the Name in which alone prayer could
be offered. One day his boy was terribly hurt and he wanted to pray for
his life, but again the Name was gone.

Thus in three great hours of need Hermas, forgetting that he had
given up the blessed name, turned to seek the help that could be got only
through that name, and found nothing but blankness and emptiness.

This is only a little story, but it is one that has become true in actual
life thousands of times. People have given up the name of Christ, sold
it for money, pleasure, power, fame, or sin. Then, when times of need
came and they turned to find help, they received no answer to their cries.

"Without me ye can do nothing." Of course, there are certain
things that men can do who are without Christ. There are people who
are very useful, benefactors to others, yet who never pray, who do not love
Christ, One may be an artist and may paint lovely pictures which the
world will admire and yet not believe in Christ. One may be a writer and
may prepare books which will interest others and enlighten, cheer, and

inspire lives to noble deeds, and yet utterly disregard Christ. A man may be a good father, kind to his family, making his home beautiful with the loveliest adornments, providing for his children, and not know Christ. When Jesus says, "Without me ye can do nothing," He does not mean that we cannot live a moral life, cannot be good merchants, good lawyers, good physicians, good teachers, good fathers and mothers—what He means is that we cannot bear spiritual fruit.

No friend can say to any other friend, "Without me ye can do nothing." A mother cannot say it to her child. It is a sore loss when a mother is taken away from her little child—how sore a loss cannot be explained. Even God cannot twice give a mother. No other woman, however loving in spirit, however wise in guiding the young life, can be to it all its own mother would have been. Yet even the best and holiest mother cannot say to her child, "Without me ye can do nothing." The child may live, and live nobly, without its mother.

There are other human friendships that seem to be really indispensable. The trusting, clinging wife may say to her husband, who is being taken from her: "I cannot live without you. If you leave me, I will die. I cannot face the cold winds without your shelter. I cannot go on with the duties, the burdens, the struggles, the responsibilities without your comradeship, your love, your cheer, your strong support, your wise guidance." So it seems to her as she stands amid the wrecks of her hopes, but when he is gone, the strong man on whom she had leaned, and the sorrowing woman takes up the tasks, the duties, the burdens, the battles and walks alone, courage comes into her heart and she grows in heroic qualities. "I never dreamed that I could possibly get along as I have," said a woman the other day after a year's widowhood. Then she told of her utter faintness when she realized that he was gone. He had been everything to her. She had wanted for nothing, had never known a care. But as she turned away from his grave it seemed to her that everything was lost. What could she do? But Christ was with her. Peace came into her heart, calmness came, then courage began to revive. She grew self-reliant and strong. She was a marvel to her friends as she took up the work of her life. She showed resources which none ever imagined she had. The problem of life in such cases as hers is not to be hurt by the sorrow, but to grow strong in it. This woman's bereavement made her. She lived, and lived grandly, without the one who had seemed absolutely indispensable.

We learn at least that no human life, however close it has been, whatever its strength, however much it was depended upon, is actually essential to any other life. To no one can we say, "I cannot live without you." The frailest prove oftentimes the hardiest. The broken are often the strongest. Someone says, "The soul is never more magnificently strong and safe than when tribulation, shutting it up to simple love and trust, causes it to behave itself like a weaned child." Sorrow, if it be received as it should be, wakes up our lives to their best. After the bitterest blows have fallen, and apparently have left you nothing but frailty, you can still go on. No other human life is actually necessary to your continued existence. The taking away of the human reveals God. That perhaps is sometimes why God takes our earthly trust—that we may find Him and learn to trust Him.

"Without me ye can do nothing." But we do not have to do without Christ. We have Him. We are not severed from Him. We live because He lives in us.

18

In That Which Is Least

The work of our hands—establish Thou it,
How often with thoughtless lips we pray,
But He who sits in the heavens shall say,
"Is the work of your hands so fair and fit
    That ye dare thus pray?"
Safely we answer, "Lord, make it fit—
The work of our hands, that so we may
Lift up our eyes and dare to pray.
The work of our hands—establish Thou it."

One of the secrets of a full and rich life is in being always watchful of the little things. We could accomplish marvels in the quarter-hours we are wasting. We hear of men who have learned a language at their dressing bureaus, or have read volumes in the minutes they have had to wait in reception rooms of friends they were calling upon, of others who have memorized poems in walking about the country. Notable achievements in the way of study and research have been made by men with only minutes of leisure, little interstices of time between their absorbing occupation in great tasks. There have been men with feeble health, who could work only in little quarter-hours, who have achieved amazing results in a short lifetime, or men with poor eyes who could read only a few minutes at a time, but who have amassed great stores of knowledge and attained distinction, even eminence, in years of masterful diligence.

The way we use the fragments of our time, what we do with the moments, determine largely what we will make of ourselves in the end. Hurry is a dreadful waste of time. A great surgeon said to his assistants when he was beginning a serious operation, "Do not be in a hurry, gentlemen; we have no time to lose." We never can do our work with celerity, and we never can do it well, if we hurry. We must have full possession of all our powers if we would do our best. "He that believeth," wrote the great prophet, "shall not be in haste," and one rendering by scholars is, "He that believeth shall not fuss." Someone says: "Energy is not mere fuss. It is often a high achievement of energy to say 'Peace, be still!' "

In recent years few words have been so much in use and few have come to mean so much as the word conservation. It means stopping the waste, utilizing every particle, whether of material or energy. In certain lines of industry a great deal is made of by-products. A by-product is something produced in addition to the principal product. In making gas, for instance, there is a large waste in what is called coal-tar. Coal-tar is now used in the process of dyeing and is very valuable. Thus the waste is turned to profit. In the refining of oil the by-products, such as benzine, naptha, and paraffin, are captured from the waste and are very important.

The same conservation should be practiced in life itself. Most people employ but a fragment of the capacity of their lives and then allow great measures of capacity to lie undeveloped, and in the end to atrophy. A volume could be filled with a description of a human hand, its wonderful structure, and the things it can be trained to do. Yet how many hands ever reach the limit of their possible achievements? Think of the powers folded up in a human brain and of the little of all these powers most of us ever bring out in life. Now and then a man starts in ignorance and poverty and reaches a greatness in ability and in achievement which amazes the world. Doubtless thousands and thousands who never attain anything beyond mediocrity have just as great natural capacity, but the splendid powers of their lives are allowed to run to waste. They are lacking in energy and do only a little of what they might do.

In Christian life and character the same is true. Jesus came to give His disciples not life merely, but abundant life. We know what He did with His first disciples, what wonderful men He made of them, and what they did with their lives. Is there any reason to think that these men were capable of greater things than the men whom the Master is calling in these days? They were not beings of a different order from the mass of men: the difference was in the way they used their gifts. Not a particle of power in them was allowed to waste. There is capacity enough in every little company of Christian people to transform the community in which they live into a garden of the Lord. It is to such consecration that we are called. We are letting our powers and abilities run to waste instead of training them and using them to bless the world. We are not making the most of ourselves.

There is a great waste of power also in our failure to appreciate our opportunities. "If I only had the gifts that this man has, I would do the large and beautiful things that he does. But I never have the chance of doing such things. Nothing ever comes to my hand but opportunities for little commonplace things." Now, the truth is that nothing is commonplace. The giving of a cup of cold water is one of the smallest kindnesses anyone can show to another, yet Jesus said that God takes notice of this little act amid all the events of the whole world, any busy day, and rewards it. It may not be cabled half round the world and announced with great headlines in the newspapers, but it is noticed in heaven.

We do not begin to understand what great waste we are allowing when we fail to put the true value on our little opportunities of serving others. Somehow we get the feeling that any cross-bearing worthwhile must be a costly sacrifice, something that puts nails through our hands, something that hurts till we bleed. If we had an opportunity to do something heroic, we say we would do it. But when it is only a chance to be kind to a neighbor, to call at his house when he is in trouble, to sit up with him at night when he is sick, or to do something for a child, we never think for a moment that such little things are the Christ-like deeds God wants us to do, and so we pass them by, and there is a great blank in our lives where holy service ought to be.

When the great miracle of the loaves had been wrought, Jesus sent His disciples to gather up the broken pieces, "that nothing be lost." The Master is continually giving us the same command. Every hour's talk we have with a friend leaves fragments that we ought to gather up and keep to feed our own heart's hunger or the hunger of other hearts, as we go on. When we hear good words spoken, or read a good book, we should gather up the fragments of knowledge, the suggestions of helpful thoughts, the broken pieces, and fix them in our hearts for use in our lives. We allow large values of the good things we hear or read to turn to waste continually because we are poor listeners or do not try to keep what we hear. We let the broken pieces be lost, and thereby are great losers. If only we would gather up and keep all the good things that come to us through conversations and through reading, we would soon have great treasures of knowledge and wisdom.

19

The Master and the Children

In the House of Too Much Trouble
    Lived a lonely little boy;
He was eager for a playmate,
    He was hungry for a toy.
But 'twas always too much bother,
    Too much dirt and too much noise,
For the House of Too Much Trouble
    Wasn't meant for little boys.

And sometimes the little fellow
    Left a book upon the floor,
Or forgot and laughed too loudly,
    Or he failed to close the door.
In the House of Too Much Trouble
    Things must be precise and trim—
In the House of Too Much Trouble
    There was little room for him.

He must never scatter playthings,
    He must never romp and play;

Every room must be in order
            And kept quiet all the day.
He had never had companions,
            He had never owned a pet—
In the House of Too Much Trouble
            It is trim and quiet yet.

Every room is set in order—
            Every book is in its place,
And the lonely little fellow
            Wears a smile upon his face.
In the House of Too Much Trouble
            He is silent and at rest—
In the House of Too Much Trouble,
            With a lily on his breast.

We who are working for the children cannot too often remind ourselves of our Lord's words to Peter about the lambs. He speaks of them as "my lambs." So the little children belong to Christ. Then He makes definite provision in His church for their care. He bade His apostle to feed His lambs. Feeding is a large word, however. The care must cover the whole life—the body, the mind, the spirit.

This is mother's work, first of all. No teacher can be substituted for a mother. It is God's ordinance that the mother comes first in shepherding the child. If she does her part faithfully, according to her ability, her hand never slacking, nothing will go wrong with the keeping of her child. There is no miracle of beautiful result in the bringing up of children who turn out well. That is the divine way when the home care has been what it was ordained to be, and it cannot fail.

Next to the mother comes the teacher. The mother cannot do all. Her part is large and essential. God and the mother do the first work in the training of the child. Not God only—God and the mother. You cannot leave the mother out. God does not make men without mothers. You cannot substitute prayer for a mother—someone praying for the child instead of being a living mother to it. The human link may not be left out. It must be God and the mother.

Then the teacher. Here another heresy sometimes creeps in. Too much is left to God. The teacher depreciates his own work. He thinks he can do nothing. This is true of the teacher alone. "Apart from me ye can do nothing." But this does not mean that all the work is done by Christ and nothing by the teacher. God's plan is that we shall be co-workers with Him. It is God and you. The weakness of a great deal that is called Christian work is that it has in it an abundance of dependence upon the divine power, but the human part is lacking. If the teacher does indifferent work instead of his best, there will be a blank instead of splendid, Christ-made men and women. Christ still calls Peter to feed His lambs, and if Peter's hand slacks, the lambs will go unfed.

The teacher's work is essential. It is like the mother's, yet different. A great deal has been done in recent years to exalt the importance and widen the scope of the teacher's work. We have thousands of training classes in which students are drilled in the knowledge of the Bible, in child study, and in matters which make them more skillful in teaching. There cannot be too much preparation and we must do our best. What Jesus had in mind and laid on Peter's heart was feeding His lambs. We know quite well the outcome our Lord desires to have from the work done by the church for the children. He wants them shepherded until they are full-grown.

It is enough to say here a little in general of the way the teachers should do their work. It must be more than intellectually educational; it must result in character building. We are to bring the young people to Christ and then train them for Christian life and service. Christ Himself is their Shepherd. He knows them by name. He leads them out. He shelters them from dangers. He gives His life for them. It is our part as teachers to make the love and ministry of Christ real to those we teach. As nearly as we can, we must be Christ to them.

No name of Christ means more to us in the interpretation of His life and love than Friend. We are not only to tell those we teach of the beauty of the friendship of Christ, we must interpret that friendship in ourselves. What Christ was to those to whom He became a personal friend we must be to those we make our friends. He did not seem to do many things for them. He did not greatly change their condition; He did not make life easier for them. It was in a different way that His friendship helped them. He gave them sympathy. They knew He cared for them, and then the hard things meant less to them. It is a great thing for a boy to know that a good man is his friend, is interested in him. To many a lad it is the beginning of a new life for him. "If you will be my friend, I can be a man," said a pupil in a mission school to his teacher who had spoken to him the first really kind word he ever had heard. The greatest moment in anyone's life is when he first realizes that Christ is his Friend.

One of the most winning and impressive pictures one sees is a Christian teacher in the midst of a company of young girls, who gather about her to hear her words. They open their hearts and her words enter their lives and have lasting impressions there. No doubt it is the woman herself who is the vital element in the problem. The same result will not be attained without regard to the personality of the teacher.

But there is also the problem of the lesson. The woman must have the good and the beauty in her or her friendship will build up nothing in the lives that wait on her words. It is a great thing for a worthy woman to be the friend of a group of girls, but the question is, What is there in her friendship for these girls that will help them? What has she to give them that will make them better? There are trivial women who can fascinate a group of girls and do nothing for them. What had Jesus to give to Mary when she sat down at His feet and heard His words? We may be sure He did not talk of trivialities—He spoke of God and life and things that are above.

The teacher must be in living contact with Christ—there is no life but His that will give her the power she needs, and will make her work really effective. Then her influence upon her class will be Christ-inspired. Her love for her girls will glow with Christ's love burning in it. Then all her teachings will be divine teachings, whether given as set lessons from the Scriptures or in pleasant social conversation without any formal religious teaching. It is first the woman's personality, with her genius for friendship, with her gift for impressing, interesting, and helping. Then, it is the woman filled with the word of Christ and with His Spirit. One writer puts it thus: "Given the right person in vital union with the living God, and we shall get conversions, and build up Christlike character, through the instrumentality of the Word, selected and applied by religious instinct and experience."

20

Portions for Those Who Lack

Our lives are full of odds and ends,
   First one and then another—
And though we know not how or when,
   They're deftly woven together.

The Weaver has a master's skill,
   And proves it by this token—
No loop is dropped, no strand is missed,
   And not a thread is broken.

Not e'en a shred is thrown aside,
   So careful is the Weaver,
Who, joining all with wondrous skill,
   Weaves odds and ends together.

AUBREY DE VERE

After eating the fat and drinking the sweet of the feast in their own homes the returned captives were bidden by Nehemiah to send portions to those for whom nothing had been prepared. "For this day is holy" was added to the exhortation. Part of the holiness of worship is loving service. We are never to eat our bread alone; we are to share it. "It is better to be lost than to be saved all alone," says Amiel. In Job's self-justification, when his friends had spoken bitterly against him, he says among other things:

> *If I have withheld the poor from their desires,*
> *Or have caused the eyes of the widow to fail,*
> *Or have eaten my morsel alone,*
> *And the fatherless hath not eaten thereof,*
>
> ....
>
> *Then let my shoulder fall from the shoulder-blade,*
> *And mine arm be broken from the bone.*

We may never eat our morsel alone while others are hungry. This lesson was taught thus emphatically in the Old Testament and still more earnestly in the New. In the Lord's Prayer we are bidden to pray not for our own bread alone, but for bread for others as well. "Give us this day our daily bread." While we are feasting at our own table we must remember those who are hungry outside, and send portions to them. The days are holy—all the days are holy, and no day set apart for God must be stained by selfishness.

The direction that the people, after eating the fat and drinking the sweet of their feast, should send portions to those for whom nothing had been prepared was in keeping with the teaching of the Bible throughout. The poor were always to be remembered. The stranger was never to be forgotten. He who let the needy go hungry when he had plenty on his own table was severely condemned. In the New Testament the lesson was taught with marked emphasis. Generosity is a quality of all true Christian character. To think only of ourselves and give no thought to others is contrary to the Spirit of Christ, which teaches us to share our plenty with those who lack. Meanness is always condemned. Generosity is always praised. It is a large word. It has a root which means excellence, goodness. It is a word of rank. Its first definition in the dictionary is "nobility: the order of the nobles." A Prussian order of distinction, founded 1665, bears the name, The Order of Generosity, later changed to The Order of Merit. The word was applied only to the good, the brave, the noble. Christ was generous. He had largeness of heart, magnanimity. He taught His followers to be generous. The lack of generosity in one who calls himself a Christian is a blot on his name. It marks him as unworthy. It dishonors him as cowardice dishonors the name of him who calls himself a man.

The brightest deeds that shine in the story of humanity are the deeds of generosity. History records that when Nero was dead someone came secretly and spread flowers on his grave. Dr. David Smith, in *The British Weekly*, tells of the strange devotion:

> *Nero, the bloody emperor, was dead;*
> *And Rome, like one who waketh suddenly*
> *Out of an evil dream, lifted her head*
> *And wondered. Presently one strong, fierce cry*
> *Burst from unnumber'd throats, and swelling high,*
> *Rang to the hilltops—the wild jubilance*
> *Of bondsmen who had gained their liberty*
> *After much wrong and bitter sufferance.*
> *No voice lamented: had no heart a thought*
> *Of ruth? Ay, as each season came and went,*
> *An unknown hand, belike a woman's, brought*
> *Sweet flowers and strewed them on his monument:*
> *Fond tribute of a clinging love that yearned*
> *For the dead tyrant whom an empire spurned.*

It was a splendid generosity that strewed the flowers on that grave. Once, perhaps, amid all his cruelties and tyrannies the emperor had done a kindness, and thus it was remembered. Generosity does not merely return good for good, does not merely measure its giving by what it has received. Like Christly love, it blesses the hand that has smitten, it repays cruelty with gentleness, it serves most unselfishly those who have done the sorest wrong.

Generosity is the perfect flower of love. It does not think who it is that needs, but gives and serves the unworthiest. It thinks only of the fact that there is one for whom nothing has been prepared and sends a portion to him that he may share love's fat and sweet.

It is this spirit that glorifies true Christmas keeping. Christmas is a wonderful day. It works miracles of love all over the world. Its feast is kept with joy and song in countless Christian homes. But the true glory of Christmas is seen in what it is doing among the poor, in prisons, hospitals, orphanages, and refuges of all kinds, where it brings its portion for those for whom nothing has been prepared. Love is very sweet when it pours out its gifts for those who love us, but it teaches its sweetest and divinest when it brings its blessing to those who do not love us, perhaps who will never thank us, nor remember what we have done, nor return gratitude for our kindness.

Let us cultivate the spirit of generosity, thinking ever in our enjoyment of God's goodness of those who lack the blessings we enjoy, and sending to them love's portion. Thus shall we continue the work which our Lord began in this world. Thus shall we enlarge our own hearts and the ministry of love we have been sent here to perform. Thus shall we come nearer and nearer to those who need us, more and more able to be a blessing to them.

This is a lesson we cannot learn too well, nor fix too deeply in our hearts. We sometimes forget that nothing is given to us for ourselves alone. When abundance of blessing or prosperity in any form comes to us, we may not shut ourselves in with it and use it only for ourselves. We are only God's almoners, and the good we have received we are to dispense to others who need. Peter's mistake on the Transfiguration Mount was in wanting to build tabernacles and stay there with the Lord and the heavenly visitors, keeping the glorious vision to themselves. The duty was rather to go down from the splendor of the mountaintop to carry the holy light into the darkness of the world below.

Ever this is our duty when we have eaten the fat and drunk the sweet of any blessing at our own table. We are to think of those outside who have no such blessing or favor as we are enjoying and are to send portions to them.

> *Bow thy head and pray*
> *That while thy brother starves today*
> *Thou mayest not eat thy bread at ease;*
> *Pray that no health or wealth or peace*
> *May hold thy soul while the world lies*
> *Suffering, and claims thy sacrifice.*

21

Slow and Steady Advance the Best

"How wrought I yesterday?" Small moment how,
　　To question with vain tears, or bitter moan,
Since every word you wrote upon the sands
　　Of yesterday hath hardened into stone.

"How work tomorrow?" 'Tis a day unborn,
　　To scan whose formless features is not granted.
Ere the new morning dawns, soul, thou mayest wing
　　Thy flight beyond tomorrow, disenchanted.

"How shall I work today?" O soul of mine!
　　Today stands on her threshold, girt to lead
Thy feet to life immortal; strive with fear;
　　Deep pitfalls strew the way, take heed! take heed!

Many young men are impatient of slow success. In their enthusiasm they expect to advance rapidly and without hindrance in their chosen career. The young physician is eager to find at once a large and remunerative practice. The young aspirant for literary honors is disappointed if immediately his work is not accepted and his name written high in the light

259

of popular writers. The young businessman expects to have success from the day he begins. The artist thinks that the excellence of his work should win fame for him the day his pictures are shown to the public. The same is true in all professions and callings.

The fact is, however, that, with very few exceptions, beginners in every occupation must be satisfied for a time with but meager recognition and slow results. Many young men who know that this is true in general have the feeling that their own case will be an exception. We like to think ourselves a little different from other people. We may as well make up our minds, however, to the fact that there are no exceptions to this rule. The only genius that counts is the capacity for hard work. The men who have achieved the greatest success in the various callings have had to struggle for it most intensely.

Robert Louis Stevenson, for example, is thought of as a genius. We would probably think, from reading his masterpieces, that literary work was always easy for him. But he has told us what it cost him to attain success as an author. He says: "I imagine nobody ever had such pains to learn a trade as I had; but I slogged at it day in and day out, and I frankly believe (thanks to my dire industry) I have done more with smaller gifts than almost any man of letters in the world." He writes further

> All through my boyhood and youth I was known and pointed out for the pattern of an idler; and yet I was always busy on my own private end, which was to learn to write. I kept always two books in my pocket—one to read, one to write in. As I walked my mind was busy fitting what I saw with appropriate words; when I sat by the roadside, I would either read, or a pencil and a penny version book would be in my hand, to note down the features of the scene or commemorate some halting stanzas. Thus I lived with words. What I thus wrote was for no ulterior use; it was written consciously for practice. It was not so much that I wished to be an author (though I wished that too) as that I had vowed that I would learn to write.

There are reasons why it is better that young men should not get on too rapidly or too easily at the beginning. No matter how gifted they may be or how well prepared, they are not ready at once for full responsibility. At the best, their preparation is theoretical, not practical. They need to learn by experience, and it is better that they should do so leisurely, without too great pressure. A young physician who should have the responsibilities of a large practice thrust upon him at once could only fail.

A young businessman who, immediately after leaving college, should take sole charge of a large establishment would find himself unable for its management. It is better that every young man should begin in a quiet way and grow up with his growing practice or business.

It is also better for a young man's personal development that his progress should not be too rapid. Easy success is the bane of many a life. It is struggle with difficulty and hardship that brings out the best that is in a man. Those who rise quickly, without much effort, too often fail to grow into noble character meanwhile. The object of living in this world is not to make a brilliant career, but to build up a worthy manhood. To have large worldly success and not to grow into strength of character is a great misfortune.

In putting up tall buildings a great deal of work is done on the foundations. The workmen dig down deep until they find rock or solid ground. They will spend weeks in work below the surface of the ground, and all of this is covered up and hid out of sight. It is necessary to have a strong and secure foundation if an imposing and durable superstructure is to be reared upon it. In the building of character it is the same. The foundations must be strong and secure. There may be a mushroom success, without any really worthy character, but the end can be only failure. A one- or two-storied man may be built on a cheap and flimsy foundation. But a twenty-story man, who is to face the storms and stand

foursquare
To all the winds that blow.

must have strength of character, principles from which nothing ever can swerve him, and almost infinite power of endurance; and these qualities can be got only in life's common experiences. While a young man is struggling to get a foothold in his profession or occupation he is meanwhile building up in himself the qualities of a noble manhood which will endure the severest tests.

22

What To Do with Our Unequal Chance

Never in a costly palace did I rest on golden bed,
Never in a hermit's cavern have I eaten idle bread.
Born within a lowly stable, where the cattle round me stood,
Trained a carpenter in Nazareth, I have toiled and found it good.
They who tread the path of labor follow where my feet have trod;
They who work without complaining do the holy will of God.
Where the many toil together, there am I among my own;
Where the tired workman sleepeth, there am I with him alone.
I, the peace that passeth knowledge, dwell amid the daily strife,
I, the bread of heaven, am broken in the sacrament of life.

Henry Van Dyke

Some people feel that they do not have a fair chance in the world. They look at others who seem to have more advantages and fewer hindrances, and they conclude that the allotments of providence are not just and equal. Some young people let their minds run in this unwholesome channel. They have to work hard and live in the plainest way, without luxury, not enjoying opportunities for pleasure and for education that they long for.

They see other young people in easy circumstances, wanting nothing, with no hardships to endure, called to no self-denial, living in ease, with every opportunity for study, travel, and recreation. It is not easy for them to avoid a feeling of envy in such circumstances. Nor is it easy to accept the limitations of condition complacently, without any feeling of being unfairly treated.

Yet the problem to be worked out by those who appear not to have an equal chance is to accept their place with its disadvantages and its in-equalities, and to live just as sweetly and cheerfully as if they were in the most luxurious circumstances. The danger always is that we may be hurt by life in some way. Yet nothing can really hurt us so long as we keep love and peace in our hearts. No hardship of any kind can do us actual harm if we meet it victoriously. But when we allow ourselves to chafe and fret because things are hard, or to complain because things seem unfair, or to grow bitter because we do not have a fair chance, that moment life is hurt-ing us.

The worst mistake anyone can make, in such a case, is to brood over what seems to be unfairness in his lot in life, indulging the feeling that he has not been justly dealt with. The result is that his heart grows bit-ter and hard, that he begins to pity himself and to look upon others more highly favored with envy, which soon grows into hatred. Nothing but harm can come out of such a feeling. It does not reduce the inequalities in any degree. It does not make it easier to get on. On the other hand, it spoils the life, turning its sweetness into bitterness. It also lessens the heart's enthusiasm and diminishes its power to live nobly.

The only worthy way to meet such a condition is with courage and purpose to master disadvantages. One who does this disarms life of all its power to do him harm and makes even the hardships and disadvan-tages elements in his success. A hindrance conquered makes us stronger. When one accepts his place in life and makes it a school, he is going to get out of it lessons which will fit him for worthy and noble living. Hand-icaps become uplifts and occasions for fine attainment and achievement when they are faced with courage and determination.

There is a good philosophy here for him who is wise enough to carry it out in his life. It is well known that the men who have risen to the lofti-est heights of excellence and have done the most for their race have not come as a rule from the ranks of those who have been reared in luxury, but from among those who began in lowly ways, with few advantages and many hindrances. The very struggles they had to make to overcome the obstacles lifted their feet higher on the stair. The efforts it cost them to get an education made men of them. Thus they easily found compensation for the hard things in their lot in their early days.

The least worthy thing any young fellow can do with an unequal chance is to allow himself to be disheartened by it and give up. Nothing really noble or valuable is ever got easily. One does not find gold lying about on the streets. One does not get any place of honor in the world as a luxury. We have to dig our way through rocks to get to earth's treasure-houses. We always have to work hard to achieve anything worth achieving.

An unequal chance, as it seems to human eyes, oftentimes proves to be the very pearl of chances. It wakes up in men's souls sleeping possibilities of energy which never would have been awakened in the experiences of ease. We are not put in this world merely to have a good time, to enjoy ourselves, to eat and drink and dress well, and move about in paths of pleasantness. We are here to grow into the nobleness and strength of the best manhood we can attain. He who misses this, though he live in luxury all his days, has missed all that is really worthwhile in life.

Young people should always remember, too, that in their school of life they must do their own toiling; nobody can do it for them. There are some who like to dream of fortunate surprises by which they shall find themselves lifted to positions of ease and prosperity without struggle or effort of their own. It is not often that such surprises come, nor is it always really "fortunate" when they do come. A few years since a young man struggling with peculiarly hard conditions became suddenly the possessor of a large sum of money. Instead, however, of being a good thing for him, the money proved the end of whatever hope there was of the young man's making anything of his life. He dropped the work which was in a fair way to train him into manliness and usefulness, and entered upon a course of ease and extravagance which in a brief time left him penniless and with all the high ideals of his early days of struggle shattered.

The best thing one can do with hard conditions is to depend upon himself, to take up his own burdens courageously and bear them. Then in carrying them he will grow into noble manhood.

23

If Two of You Shall Agree

Twas long ago,
When I was young. Alas! I did not know
A better way. I said, "It must be so,
Or God cannot be good."
Alas! alas! weak human pride;
How differently would I have quickly cried
If I had understood.

And now I bear
A thankful heart for that unanswered prayer.
And so I think it will be when, up there
Where all is known,
We look upon the things we longed for so,
And see how little were they worth and know
How soon they were outgrown.

Unidentified

Why two? Would it not be the same for one? Is not the gate of prayer
open to everyone? May not a lonely soul anywhere call upon God and be
sure of answer? Why, then, does the Master say two—"If two of you shall

267

agree the prayer will be granted"? Certainly He did not mean that God does not hear one who prays alone. Jesus oftentimes prayed by Himself. He went apart from His disciples up the mountain, into the depths of the Garden. Yet there is a special promise when two agree.

For one thing, when two pray together each is drawn out of self to think of something besides his own needs. We are naturally selfish. We easily form the habit of thinking only of our own things, of seeking only our own good, of looking only after our own interests. One of the tendencies of praying alone is to seek only things we need or desire for ourselves. "Forgive my sins, prosper my affairs, heal my sickness, bless my daily bread, make me holy, give me joy," our prayer is apt to run. To pray only thus is to allow ourselves to narrow our lives into sheerest selfishness. We may pray alone and yet train ourselves to think of others, to reach out to the needs and experiences of others. Only thus will we make our secret prayers spiritually wholesome.

When we pray together the selfish tendency is corrected. We think of the other and his condition. We are trained to sympathize with him in his trouble, to reach out our hand to strengthen him when he is weak. We forget our own danger in thinking of his. His needs seem so much greater and more pressing than ours that we plead for his deliverance and altogether forget our own; we beseech God to lift away his crushing burden and cease to think at all of our own lesser load. Our own sorrow, which, if there were no other one suffering by our side, would seem immeasurably great, seems too small even to mention in the presence of our friend's overpowering grief, so we pray for his comforting and only thank God that our affliction is so light.

Another good that comes from two praying together is in the influence of life upon life. We need the impact of others. We cannot reach our best alone. It is a happy thing for one child in a home when another child comes to be its companion. A child living alone is in danger of growing into selfishness and all undiscipline. It never learns to share its possessions, its happiness. When two children are brought up together they are trained to think of each other, to give up for the other, to seek to make the other happy. One of the blessings of marriage is that the two learn to live for each other. Then they inspire each other. The woman who thinks only of what she can get from her marriage has not begun to learn the real secret of love. Wedded love reaches its true splendor only when it thinks of what it can do for the other.

When we pray together the one quickens the other and both become better Christians. When two love God and then talk about Him, the love of both grows warmer. One stimulates the other. We need companionship in our Christian lives. It is not good for us to be alone. Jesus had a wise purpose in sending out His disciples two and two. They would have been lonely if they had gone out singly and would not have done their best work. Thus the one supplemented the other. Two together did more than two apart. They had their limitations of capacity and one supplied the other's lack. But perhaps the chief advantage in going out two and two was that each kindled and inspired the other. We do not know how much we owe to each other. Our unconscious influence on the lives and actions of those close to us is immeasurable. Dr. Bushnell has shown us how Peter's rugged force acted on John's sensitive nature at the empty tomb. John hesitated to enter until Peter came up and went in boldly. "Then entered in therefore the other disciple also." We do not know how often or in how many ways the older disciple quickened the younger. Soldiers say that the hardest of all experiences in battle is to stand or fight alone. Two together make each other brave. We do better work and live our lives better in every way, two and two, than we would do separately.

> *A log will not burn alone!*
> *The flame grows less, the hearth is dark,*
> *Low sings the sap in crooning tone;*
> *The room grows chill, and cold, and stark,*
> *One's heart holds back, as if to hark*
> *For ghostly sobs and eerie moan—*
> *A log will not burn alone.*
>
> *A life will not glow alone!*
> *The smile seems sad, the senses start,*
> *The will lies useless, limp and prone;*
> *Unchallenged and uncheered the heart;*
> *And one by one the stars depart*
> *From all one's sky, to darkness grown—*
> *A life is death alone!*

Again, when two pray together they will be more likely to widen their intercessions. We may not appreciate the value of prayer for others. Jesus prayed much for Himself. He lived with His Father in unbroken communion, but we are sure that the burden of His prayer was for others, for His disciples, for the need and suffering ever about Him.

The best work we can do for those we love usually is prayer. Of course, there are things love should do—acts of kindness, ministries of good; we must never withhold help that is needed. But oftentimes we cannot tell what really is kindness to another. Perhaps the effort we make to help only harms. The taking away of a friend's burden may only interfere with the plan of God for making the friend strong. Much of our helping is over-helping. We would do better to let our friends struggle through themselves without relieving them. When we see people with their loads, their cares, their difficulties, their hard tasks, we really do not know what we ought to do for them, or whether we ought to do anything but cheer them.

But we may always pray for them, and perhaps this in most cases is all we can wisely do. At least, prayer is always a safe way of helping. We need never be afraid that it will do them harm, for we only ask God to give the help that is wise and that will make them better, nobler, stronger, and truer. We may not ask God to make all hard things easy for them— we may ask only that He will watch that the burden is never too heavy for them, the temptation too sore, the sorrow too great, and that they never faint or fail. Always, prayer is love's great duty. "Pray for whom thou lovest." Not to pray is to sin against one's friend and against God. People always need our prayers. Those need them most who seem to have least need. We pray readily for those in trouble—but those in no apparent trouble are in greatest peril.

24

When We Are Laid Aside

"They also serve who only stand and wait."
  Yea, Lord, and many such perchance there be,
  Who, unawares, in patience serving thee,
Stand all day long before some fast-barred gate.

Beyond, there lie sweet dreams yet unfulfilled,
  Or hope deferred that sickens the stout heart
  And makes it far from gladness dwell apart,
While faith yet keeps its clamorous outcry stilled.

Some wait with wistful faces ever set
  With eager longing toward the distant prize;
  And some, whose hope is dead, yet lift their eyes,
Waiting and praying still with lashes wet.

So few that wait with smiling, hopeful cheer!
  Yet these serve best, for that they seem to say:
  "Waiting is blessing; those who wait must pray,
And praying brings the kingdom even here."

We do well when we let God shape our lives. He "writes straight on crooked lines." He has a plan for every life, and His plan goes on without interruption through all the ambitions, the mistakes, the failures, of our aims and strivings. The problem of faith is to accept God's will when it breaks into our will, and believe that always it is right, and that there can be no mistake and no failure when it is His way we take.

It is here too often that our faith fails. A Christian man was telling how hard it is for him to maintain the peace and joy of his life in the experiences through which he is passing. For long years he has been in Christian work of great importance. He has devoted his best energies to the development of this work, and seemed about to see all his hopes realized. Then his health gave way, and for months he has been compelled to lie on his bed unable to do anything. It is by no means certain that he can ever again resume his work and carry to completion the plans and schemes upon which he has been so long engaged. He was speaking to a friend of his condition. It is very hard, he said, to remain quiet and be at peace in all this uncertainty. It is hard to be still and do nothing while there is so much yet to be done. It is hard, after having wrought so long in the work, to lie still in a sickroom, inactive, not taking any part in the work to which he has given his strength all his years, letting others carry it own.

In varying forms this is a problem of faith which very many people are meeting all the while. We are in the midst of pressing activities which fill our hands and require our best energies every hour. What we are doing seems essential. If our hands should willingly slack, there would be a blank in the work we are doing, and this would be disloyalty to God. Besides, it requires the full wages of all the days to provide for our family. Then suddenly one morning we cannot leave our bed to go to our work. The doctor says it will be weeks before we can leave our bed. We are in consternation. We were happy in our trust before this interruption. All things were going well. We thanked God every day that He was providing for us so abundantly. But how shall we meet this new problem?

The first thing to remember is that this is our Father's world, and that all its events are in His hand. He is not dependent, in His care of us, upon what we can do for ourselves. He indeed needs us; and, while we are able to do our part, His providing for us depends on our doing our part. If we fail to do our part, and, growing indolent, drop our tasks while we have strength to do them, we are proving unfaithful, marring God's plan of providence, and must suffer. But if we are stricken down and can no longer go on with our task, God is not at the end of His power to care for us. We may trust His love to provide for us when we cannot do it.

The sick man thinks he is losing time when he must stay on his bed and do nothing, day after day, for weeks. But really he is not losing. He is no longer essential. Nothing will suffer because his hands are not doing his accustomed tasks. Work in stone or wood is not all that the builder is in the world for. There is building to go on in his own life and character which is far more important than what he does in the house on which he is working. Some time he will know that his days of illness were his best building days. As to his family, God has a way to provide for them while the natural breadwinner is not able to do it.

While he was busiest in material things, accomplishing most in earthly labors, he was leaving untouched the work in his own life and character which was absolutely essential to the spiritual completeness of his life according to God's purpose. One of the busiest men of the generation now closing, busiest too in the best things, who has devoted his life to others with self-forgetful ability, said the other day to a friend that he was discovering he had left a whole section of his life-work undone. While he was caring so diligently for the comfort, the good and the spiritual culture of others, he had not been giving due attention to his own inner life. When he was shut in, and the work for others could not be done as heretofore, he found quite enough to do in the things that were waiting for his hands. The months when he was laid aside from active duty he had found serious work to do in getting right within, in the cultivation of the graces, of humility and love and patience and unselfishness. If he had come to the end of his life when he had finished his active tasks, he would have stood before God most incomplete in spiritual readiness. He needed the period when his hands must be still and he must suffer in order to make his life complete. This was not lost time.

The principle thus stated applies in all relations of life, whatever the circumstances may be. While we are able to work we may never slacken our diligence. Our own hands must earn our daily bread. But when we cannot longer work, work is not our duty; God does not require it of us. It is some other one's duty then, not ours. If you are a teacher, you cannot evade the responsibility of meeting your class regularly, if you are well enough to do so. But if really ill and cannot be in your place, you have no duty there and no responsibility. If you are a minister, and for years have never missed a service, and then are sick and unable to get to

your pulpit for a certain appointment, your Master does not expect you
to be there; He has no message for you to deliver to the people that day,
and nothing will go wrong with your work because you are not there.

A pastor who had wrought long and had hardly ever been absent
from his church was broken down, and for months could not come to
his accustomed place. During his long absence he wrote to his people
words like these:

> I understand that when I am physically unable to do the work I would be
> doing gladly if I could, it is not my work at all. It would have been mine
> if I were well, but now my only duty is to be quiet and still. Duty is not all
> activity; sometimes it is to wait and sing. Nothing is going wrong in my life,
> because I am not in what would be my place if I were well. My ministry
> is not broken or even interrupted by this experience. My work for my Mas-
> ter has not been stopped, its form only has been changed.

No doubt this pastor was doing as much for his people those quiet days
away from them as he had ever done in his active days in their midst.

We dare not take comfort from this teaching if we are not called
from our duty in some providential way. Some of us are too easily taken
from our work. Small excuses are allowed to draw us away. Obstacles are
not always meant to interrupt our efforts, oftentimes they are meant to
be overcome, making us more earnest and persistent. There is altogether too much resignation in some Christians—resignation may be only
indolence. We must be sure that the Good Shepherd calls us to "lie down
in the green pastures" before we stop in our service. But if lying down is
our duty, then we must do it as joyfully as ever we listened to a call to
move strenuously forward.

This lesson is not easily learned. For many it is very hard to accept
interruptions in happy activities without chafing and fretting It is hard
for a man to break down in the midst of some great task, and be as trustful and songful in his disappointment as if he had been allowed to go on
in his busy way. Some people find it very hard to grow old, to let go the
work of years, and see others do it.

The lesson is that our faith shall not fail when interruptions of any
kind break in, but shall keep our hearts brave and sweet and strong in all
human weakness and disappointment. We must take care that our religion does not fail in these testings. We say that Christ will suffice us in
every experience; we must show that He does. If He does not, the trou-

ble is with us. There is marvelous power in a witnessing life. A young Christian woman wrote to a teacher, who through years had taught her to love Christ and trust Him, and who was now broken in health and a sufferer, but joyous as ever: "I want to thank you for teaching me this beautiful lesson of all your life, this peaceful and joyous acceptance of all trouble. You are living out now all you have taught me. I am glad you let Christ speak so plainly through you." Suppose this teacher, having taught the lesson of faith and trust and peace for years, had then in pain and loss and trouble chafed, complained, and fretted, how different would the effect have been upon the pupil!

We may be laid aside from our active work, but God never lays us aside from Himself. So we need never lay aside our joyous witnessing for Him, His love, and His keeping power. If that witness had counted for much when we were active, it can count for more in our inactivity. If we wasted the days of our activity by failure to witness for Him, we may yet in Christ's strength start today, in our new helplessness, upon a showing forth of God's presence in a life that shall gladden Him and change His world.

25

Face to Face With One's Own Life

It was only a helping hand,
And it seemed of little availing,
But its clasp was warm
And it saved from harm
A sister whose strength was failing.
It's touch was tender as angel's wings,
But it rolled the stone from the hidden springs,
And pointed the way to higher things,
Though it seemed of little availing.

A smile, a word or a touch,
And each is easily given,
That one may win
A soul from sin
Or smooth the way to heaven.
A smile may lighten the failing heart,
A word may soften pain's keenest smart,
A touch may lead us from sin apart,
How easily each is given.

A writer in one of the magazines said recently that if he were a preacher he would raise his voice in behalf of the individual life. He thinks the individual is lost sight of by too many preachers in considering the needs of society in general. The personal human soul is starving while men are discussing the problems of mankind. "If I were a preacher," he says, "I would talk usually just to one person."

Everyone who has received any good thing ought straightway to begin giving it out that others may have it too. But one must receive before one can give. So the personal life must come first. You must feed your own soul or you cannot feed another's soul.

This is universally true. There is the duty of helping others—the strong are bidden to help the weak—but one must have in himself the ability and the resources of helpfulness before he can do for others what they need. If you are to teach others, you must be taught yourself. Before you can lead men, you must know the paths yourself. No one about to climb mountains would accept a guide who had never acquired skill in mountain-climbing in experiences of his own.

You must face life's problems yourself and master them. No one can do it for you. "Each man shall bear his own burden," says the Scripture. Another scripture says, "Bear ye one another's burdens." There is no conflict in these teachings that seem contradictory. It is everyone's duty, always, to put his shoulder under his brother's load, but always it is true that everyone must bear his own burden, and that no one can bear it for him. God's promise in all the work of the world is the making of men. Here what is done must be done by the individual himself. Each man must build his own house. The process is going on continually. All experience contributes to it. Tennyson says:

I am a part of all that I have met.

Every life we touch leaves something of itself in us. Every book we read puts some mark on our character. Every temptation makes us either stronger if we resist it, or wounds and hurts us if we yield to it. Every sorrow that befalls us makes us better or spoils our beauty. The effect of these experiences upon us is not accidental, but depends upon the way we receive them.

God's purpose in all our lives is our edification, to use one of Paul's suggestive words. This upbuilding is not all wrought out in church services, in acts of worship. Christ is building men all the while—in love-filled homes, in places of labor, in daily companionships and associations, as well as at communion tables or prayer meetings. We say that the business of the carpenter is to make the things that a carpenter usually makes. But God's purpose for the carpenter is the making of a man. The work of a farmer, we say, is to till the soil and reap harvests. But the thought of God in the farmer's work, what He looks for as the real outcome, is a beautiful life. If this result is not reached, the farmer's life is not successful, however prosperous he may be as a farmer. We say that a man's circumstances make him, but at the center of all the circumstances the real, determining factor is the man himself. Whether the hard knocks you experience through the years make a man of you or wreck your life depends upon the way you meet them. It is you, not your circumstances, that will determine the outcome in your life.

There is need, therefore, for personal preaching at this point. It will not do to tell men merely that their lives are plans of God, that God thought about them before He made them, and then made them to fill a certain place and to do a certain work. This is not the whole truth. The other part of the truth is that we have now to fulfill this divine purpose and live out this divine plan. We can spoil God's beautiful plan for our lives if we will—every man does who lives in sin, rejecting the will of God for him and taking his own way instead. We can fall far below God's perfect plan for us by living indolently, self-indulgently. Every man is required to do his best if he would measure up to the divine plan. An English writer says the three words, "That will do," have done more harm than any other three words in the language. Men get easily into the habit of looking at something they have made or done, and, though knowing it is not what it ought to be, or what they could make it, indolently let it pass, saying, "That will do." Thus they suffer their work to deteriorate in quality and fall far below God's plan, which requires the best.

It is said that the great violin maker, Stradivarius, would never allow any violin to leave his hands which was not as nearly perfect as he could make it. George Eliot makes Stradivarius say:

> *If my hand slacked,*
> *I should rob God—since He is fullest good—*
> *Leaving a blank instead of violins.*
> *He could not make Antonio Stradivarius' violins*
> *Without Antonio.*

It is true we rob God when we do any of our work less well than we could do it. God will help us to do our best, but we must work with Him. He will not do our work without us. He will not do our best for us if we work indolently. "He could not make Antonio Stradivarius' violins without Antonio."

Thus at every point we need this lesson of individuality. We must meet life as individuals. We are responsible in a certain way for the good of all men. We owe a duty to "the other man" which we dare not fail to pay. But we must not forget that our first duty is to let God have His full way with us. Keeping other people's vineyard will not be enough if meanwhile we have neglected our own. Doing a great work for others is not enough if we have not let God care for our own lives.

26

The Meaning of Immortality

Out of myself, Lord!
　　　　　From the narrowing prison,
The grave-clothes bound on hand and foot and knee,
Up to that life and light where Thou art risen,
Call me, and set me free.

Out of myself, Lord!
　　　　　From the reckless seeking,
The babel of earth's care and fret and loss,
Into the hush where love alone is speaking—
The silence of the cross.

Out of myself, Lord!
　　　　　From life's tangled story,
The doubts unsolved, the fears unanswered still,
Into the clear white morning of Thy glory,
The peace which is Thy will.

Out of myself, Lord!
　　　　　What shall yet befall me,
I ask no more; enough that Thou art mine.

Turn but Thy face, O Son of God! and call me
To lose my life in Thine.

MABEL EARLE, *in The S.S. Times*

It is intensely interesting to try to tell ourselves the meaning of immortality. Not to think of existence projecting beyond the clods of the grave is to miss the glory of life. To think of it, however, as extending into the future indefinitely, to think of ourselves as born to live, not seventy years, but seventy thousand years, and this deathlessness gives to our lives a meaning whose grandeur is overwhelming. We talk about the brevity of life, only a span, the flying of a shuttle, a breath—it seems too short for doing anything worthwhile, but immortality will give us time to finish the most stupendous tasks. There will be time enough then to correct the mistakes and the misunderstanding of our ignorance and willfulness in our immature earthly years. One was grieving that he would never have an opportunity to unsay certain unkind words he had spoken to his mother, or undo certain acts of his which had broken her heart. She was gone now, and he could not see her to ask her pardon or atone by love and worthy living for all that had so wronged her. Immortality will give opportunity to make such things right. A poem quoted in *The British Weekly* tells of "The Land of Beginning Again":

> *I wish that there were some wonderful place*
> *Called the Land of Beginning Again,*
> *Where all our mistakes and all our heartaches*
> *And all of our poor, selfish grief*
> *Could be dropped, like a shabby old coat at the door,*
> *And never put on again.*
>
> *I wish we could come on it all unaware,*
> *Like the hunter who finds a lost trail;*
> *And I wish that the one whom our blindness has done*
> *The greatest injustice of all*
> *Could be at the gates, like an old friend that waits*
> *For the comrade he's gladdest to hail.*
>
> *We would find all the things we intended to do*
> *But forgot and remembered—too late,*

Little praises unspoken, little promises broken,
And all of the thousand and one
Little duties neglected that might have perfected
The day for one less fortunate.

There is something extremely fascinating in the thought expressed in these lines. Nor is it a mere fancy. If we believe in immortality, we shall begin again the morning after we have died, if we have given ourselves to Christ and have His life in us. At the best we are imperfect here. We live far below our ideals. We are continually making mistakes, mistakes of ignorance and mistakes of weakness. Then death will come. Men think it the end, but it is only a new beginning. For the Christian it will be a beginning of life in new conditions. The old will be left behind; all will be new. The light will be clearer. We shall not repeat the old blunders again. We shall be beyond jealousy and envy and all the narrow things that so marred the life here.

It wouldn't be possible not to be kind
In the Land of Beginning Again;
And the ones we misjudged and the ones whom we grudged
Their moments of victory here
Would find in the grasp of our loving hand-clasp
More than penitent lips could explain.

Easter starts in our minds many thoughts and questions about immortality. Good Friday shows us Christ dying and laid away in the grave. Easter morning we see Him risen and living again. Is that always the story of death? We know that all die. Shall we all live again? Are we immortal?

People have always thought so. But does that prove that death is not the end? Has anybody ever come back after dying to tell us? A few have been raised, three by Christ Himself, but these were brought back not to immortality, but only to a little more of the old life, and they had to die again. None were ever raised to immortality—none but Christ Himself. He rose to die no more.

What proofs have we then that we shall live again and go on living forever? The greatest proof of all is that Christ rose again. He said, "Because I live ye shall live also." He said, too, "I am the resurrection, and the life: he that believeth on me, though he die, yet shall he live; and whosoever liveth and believeth on me shall never die." Thus all who believe in

Christ have the assurance that they will live forever. Death is not the end of life for them. It seems to put a stop to their living and doing. It does to bodily life. Physical activity ceases. Our unfinished tasks will drop out of our hands. The house the builder was erecting will stand uncompleted. The letter the father was writing to his boy will never be finished. But five minutes afterward the person we say is gone will be going on with life somewhere, in some form. Death is not a period in the sentence of life—it is only a comma, a little breathing place, with more to come after.

What should this mean to us? Should it make any difference in the way that we live the years we stay here? Should it make any difference in the way young people improve their schooldays and their opportunities? Should it have any influence on the principles of conduct by which we live, on the kind of personal character we build up? Should it affect our choice of friends or of things we do in this world?

There is a phrase in one of the Epistles that speaks of the power of an endless life. We may apply the thought in many ways. It is an endless life that we are living any moment. It makes a vast difference whether the word you say to another will be forgotten as its sound dies, or whether its influence will last for ages. It matters infinitely whether the choice or decision you make today is only for an hour, or whether it is the fixing of the course of your life for a career and the settling of your immortal destiny.

If you are immortal, you are dealing now and always with the things of an endless life. Everything you let another do to you is for an immortal impression, whether it be for beauty or for stain. The fabric you build up in yourself through the years will be endless. No prayers will change it or make it beautiful, if you find, near the end, that it has all been wrong. The work you are doing on the lives of others cannot be torn out and something else altogether different put in its place, if you should discover by and by that it has been false and ruinous. Pilate did not know the full meaning of his words when he said, "What I have written I have written." The law of an endless life gives a stupendous meaning to every moral act of our lives, and ought to make us thoughtful and careful in all that we do.

Many of those who read these words are young people. But they are not too young to think about the matter of immortality. It may not be wholesome for youth to think about death. But immortality is not death.

It is something which annihilates death. It throws a plank across the grave. It shows us a life that goes on forever.

It is a glorious conception of living, therefore, which enables us to think of it as endless, beginning with infancy's first breath and going on without break forever. It gives us a splendid reach for effort. The years of earth are too short to make much of our lives. We have some vast dream and begin to work it out, then what we call death breaks in with its interruption when we seem to be only beginning. But if our conception of life is endless, the interruption is only for a moment, and we can plan for things that will take ages.

Just how the sentences after the comma will read we cannot know. Just in what form we shall continue to live we may not even guess. We know that we shall be the same persons. Individuality will never be lost. I shall be I through all changes and transformations. The being that shall be serving God a million years hence will be the same person that played about the home early in childhood, wrought in the hard tasks of mature days, and suffered and sorrowed. I will always be I—there never can be any confusion of individuality. This is perhaps all we can assert positively about the immortal life. But this is a great deal. We shall lose nothing in our efforts. This makes it immensely worthwhile to live.

One lesson we may take from all this is that we should begin now to live the immortal life, to practice immortality. We should think and plan and choose, these common days, for immortality. We should do nothing we should ever wish we had not done. We should say no word we shall ever want unsaid. We should build only fabrics we shall be glad to look upon in endless years. Immortality has begun already in the youngest life. It is not something we shall enter upon when we get to heaven. It is going on now in the schoolroom, on the playground, in the friendships and amusements of the young people, and in all their hours, however spent. We must practice immortality all of our days if we would realize its fullest meaning.

27

The Christian View of Death

All around, man's acres lie,
Under this same brooding sky.
There, the plowman blithely sings;
Broadcast, there, the sower flings
Golden grain, to die in gloom,
Making every clod its tomb.
Lo! a miracle is seen—
Acres clothed in living green.

In their midst, God's acre lies,
Under these same yearning skies.
Here, men move with dirges slow;
Here, their tears unbidden flow;
Loved forms, here, in earth they lay;
Leave to darkness and decay.
Autumns wane, and springs return;
Still they sleep 'neath shaft and urn.

Side by side, those acres lie,
Under this expectant sky.
What? On God's lies death's dark spell,

While in man's comes miracle?
No! for love's eyes pierce the gloom!
No! for Christ hath burst the tomb!
God will give, by power unknown,
Each a body of its own!

Somehow most people never get beyond the heathen idea of death. They think of it as darkness and terror. They talk of it as floods of waters through which they must pass. The fear of death is almost universal. Dying is surrounded in the minds of the great majority of men and women with all that is gloomy and dreadful. We shudder to think of our loved ones passing out of our homes of comfort, out of the gentle care of our love, into the strange mystery of dying. We tremble to think of ourselves sinking away into the shadow of death. There are many Christian people who do not have in their conception of the final departure a single gleam of the beauty and the blessedness with which the New Testament invests the death of the believer. If we could bring the Christian conception of dying into our everyday thought of it, it would change all the terror and darkness which we are accustomed to associate with the great event into brightness and glory.

The New Testament does not employ a single alarming word in all its allusions to the subject. In the ruler's house when they said "Thy daughter is dead," Jesus said, "Weep not; for she is not dead, but sleepeth." It was a priceless blessing that Jesus gave to the world when He gave the name sleep to what men had always called death.

It is interesting to notice how Jesus Himself spoke of dying as He came toward it. We must not think of the darkness and mystery which were so terrible to Jesus before He came to the end as part of His experience of dying. The anguish of the Garden was most bitter. "He began to be sorrowful and sore troubled." Then on the cross when the darkness spread over all the land, there was heard from the holy Sufferer a cry, the saddest cry earth ever heard, "My God, my God, why hast thou forsaken me?" But these were not part of our Lord's experience of dying. This anguish, this feeling of forsakenness, He endured as He was bearing the sin of the world. We may not try to understand the sufferings of those hours.

But turn to His real experience of death. The six hours of agony were ended. The darkness was past. Jesus, crying with a loud voice, said, "Father, into thy hands I commend my spirit." There was no darkness now, no feeling of forsakenness. The Father's face was not hidden now, but instead it beamed its love upon the Sufferer on the cross, and the words Jesus spoke were full of joy and confidence. "Father, into thy hands I commend my spirit." That was the way Jesus died. There was no fear. There was no blackness. He was not confused nor bewildered. He was face to face with His Father. He was calm and quiet, not startled as if some fearful experience were before Him. Dying—what was it for Him? Simply breathing out His spirit into the hands of His Father. His body was to stay on the cross until gentle hands would take it down and lay it away in the grave. But His spirit, the deathless part, was breathed into the hands of His Father.

Was there anything dreadful about that? The spirit had not been pierced by nails, nor hurt by thorns, nor touched in any way by the anguish or pain of the terrible hours on the cross. The spirit now was breathed out and commended into the Father's hands. Those were gentle hands, safe hands, hands out of which no one could ever snatch that spirit.

Note well that this is death, this and nothing else, as Jesus found it. There never was a simpler, gentler, quieter, gladder experience in all of our Lord's life.

And this is a true picture of death as it will be in the story of every believer. There will not be anything to make it hard or terrifying. It will mark the end of all darkness, pain, and trouble. We think of death as full of mystery. We cannot understand it. We cannot see anything. But this picture of Jesus dying ought to show us that to us, too, dying is only joy, life, blessedness. "Into thy hands!" One moment dazed and confused as we leave the body, but next moment in the Father's hands. When we have been dead only a minute or two the terror will be past, if there is terror at all in the experience, and we shall find ourselves in joy in the presence of God. There is not a word in the New Testament to suggest that there it has horrors for the believer in Christ. Dying is only a phase of life.

The only death scene we have in the New Testament besides our Lord's is that of Stephen. It was a death of violence. He had a wonderful vision. Looking up steadfastly into heaven, he saw the glory of God and Jesus standing at the right hand of God. His enemies in rage rushed upon him, cast him out of the city, and stoned him. The martyr prayed as the stones smote him: "Lord Jesus, receive my spirit." The simple narrative says: "He fell asleep." It is a scene of peace, so far as the dying of Stephen is concerned. He saw Jesus standing up at the right hand of God to receive His servant who was being driven out of the earth. When he died he was only received by the living Savior in glory. His broken body lay dead on the ground, but his spirit was safe, unhurt, in the keeping of his Lord.

But little is said in the New Testament about death. We have very clear and definite assertions of the fact of immortality, but mere hints only of the form of the life into which the earthly life emerges, through dying. One of the most vivid of the expressions used by Paul in speaking of what occurs in dying is in two phrases—"absent from the body" and "at home with the Lord." In dying we leave the body which has been "the earthly house of our tabernacle" during our stay. The old house is empty—the tenant has gone out of it. But we are not homeless now because of our eviction from the earthly house; we are "at home with the Lord." That is, we have a far more glorious dwelling-place than the one we were in before. "We know that if the earthly house of our tabernacle be dissolved, we have a building from God, a house not made with hands, eternal, in the heavens." Instead of a tent, which is frail and temporary, liable to decay and dissolution, our new habitation is a building from God, not made with hands, eternal. Instead of an earthly house, our new home is in the heavens. Instead of a place of pain and suffering in which we groan, being burdened, when we leave it we shall find ourselves at once at home with Christ. There is no time for wandering, unclothed, as disembodied spirits, seeking for a new habitation in which to dwell, but a minute after the earthly tabernacle is dissolved and we are absent from it, we shall find ourselves at home—not in another frail tent, but in a home in heaven. This is what Jesus promised His disciples in His words of comfort spoken to them at the Last Supper.

> Let not your heart be troubled; believe in God: believe also in me. In my Father's house are many mansions. . . . I go to prepare a place for you. And if I go and prepare a place for you, I will come again, and will receive you unto myself; that where I am, there ye may be also.

Our new habitation will be a home, with all the blessed meaning of that word; it will be eternal; it will be with Christ.

We see how simple and beautiful Christian death is as we read these descriptions of it. We ought to find richest comfort in these glimpses. There is nothing in dying to give us fear or terror. It will not interrupt our living for a moment. Five minutes after watching friends say "He is gone!"

we will be through the experience and will be living as we have never lived before. Dying is but leaving the old tent to be received into the heavenly home. It is but changing mortality to the glory of immortality. We shall love on, only our love will be purged from all its imperfections, its selfishness, its envy, its grudging, its resentment, its earthliness, and made perfect. We shall not lose interest in our friends, but shall think of them, speak to God for them, save them in some way, as helpfully and far more wisely than when we were living. Moses and Elijah, after they had been hundreds of years in heaven, were sent back to earth to cheer and strengthen the weary Son of God as He was bearing the cross of His love. The mother will not forget her children, nor the faithful pastor his people after death.

Death will not break any sacred tie of friendship. It will not separate us from Christ. "Whether we live or whether we die, we are the Lord's." It will not rob us of any real treasure. It will empty our hands of money and property we have invested in our name, but have never made ours by proper use for Christ, but not one penny we have used in honoring God and blessing our fellowmen shall we lose in dying. Millionaires who have truly consecrated their money will be millionaires still after dying. Death will leave no blot, no scar, no wounding on us, but will only strip off every blemish, purge from us every spot, bring out all hidden beauty and transform us, for when we see Him, we shall be like Him, for we shall see Him as He is.

We need not dread to see our Christian friends die, for they have come to the most blessed and glorious moment of their existence, and are only departing from us to be forever with the Lord.